THE GRANDEUR THAT WAS ROME:

OUTLINES OF ROMAN HISTORY

WRITTEN BY

WILLIAM C. MOREY, PH.D., D.C.L.

EDITED BY

JEFFREY C. KALB, JR.

HONORS HISTORY SERIES, VOLUME 4

ISBN: 9781073606931

TABLE OF CONTENTS

TABLE OF CONTENTS
(CONTINUED)

INTRODUCTION TO THE *HONORS HISTORY SERIES*

To the Parent, Teacher, and Student:

The value of historical instruction is threefold: First, it allows the student to locate himself within the broader story of humanity. Second, it instructs him through concrete examples of virtue and vice, wisdom and foolishness. Third, it transmits to the student whatever elements of previous cultures are worthy of adoption or imitation.

The *Honors History Series* is a projected five-course study in which the flowers of the historical record are examined for their cultural value and moral lessons. In the first course, students are immersed in the aesthetic and investigative spirit of the ancient Greeks. In the second, they observe the Roman political, military, and legal genius. In the third course, they study the rise and flourishing of Christendom. In the fourth, students follow the political, intellectual, and cultural development of Europe from the Age of Exploration to modern times. Finally they explore the distinctive history, character, and government of their own American nation. In discovering their ancient and modern origins, students arrive at deeper self-knowledge and a better appreciation of their cultural patrimony. What is here called the Florilegium approach to history is no educational novelty, but rather the methodical application and intensification of what many excellent instructors have always practiced. It is best understood by contrasting it to the "textbook" and "great book" methods. These are the extremes of secondary education to which the Florilegium method is a mean. Consider first the strengths and weakness of these other two methods.

The "textbook" (or "lecture") method conveys the primary facts of history, as best as these have been ascertained, together with a coherent and temporally progressive interpretation of the whole subject. This method has the virtue of simplifying and clearly organizing the material for consumption by students. If done well, it can provide a framework for the student to meaningfully locate himself, the current culture, and his nation within the larger course of human events. The deficiencies of this system are also manifest to anyone who has examined a contemporary history textbook. Textbook authors naturally project into the past our present attitudes and biases, thereby unconsciously making ourselves the term, purpose, and meaning of all history. The consequent familiarity bores the student and vitiates genuine learning. Only a single perspective is presented, and quite often not the traditional one. In the worst case, the textbook becomes a mere platform for the authors to preach their own idiosyncratic values. By no means are these texts able carry the student beyond the horizon of our debased modern culture.

In response not only to the inherent weakness of such a method, but also its present abuse, the "great book" (or "tutorial") method is favored by many who attach signal importance to literary excellence and active rational inquiry. Great teachers of the past, it is said, have left behind for us profound works that even today inform and educate. Our education should therefore consist principally in reading and studying these texts. With rhetorical flourish, the image is presented of Thucydides and Plutarch, Livy and Tacitus, Hamilton and De Tocqueville, eagerly attending to the devouring intellects of our students. The real teachers, it is said, and with some truth, are these great minds. Practice, however, is unequal to the theory. Students are left without a common framework or timeline to unify these histories. Visual aids are discounted, making imaginative synthesis all the more difficult. Art and architecture are generally passed over in silence. Moreover, excepting perhaps one in a thousand, the minds of adolescents are unprepared to absorb lofty genius unaided. Common sense tells us that too little learning takes place, and experience confirms it. Ideas and aphorisms, poorly comprehended, are merely parroted. Minds obtain a veneer of learning which, when scratched, discloses a lack of depth, integration, and coordination. Indeed, early exposure to "great books" without adequate guidance can produce an allergy to all such reading or, worse yet, the presumption of having mastered what is still above one's understanding.

The excellence of the writing notwithstanding, much that is compassed by these authors is irrelevant to the student and tedious in its detail. Let it be granted than an author is insightful and elegant; nevertheless, his intent in writing will not likely conform to our intentions in educating. Much of the narration may have served well the original audience, but has little value today to anyone but the professional historian. The funeral oration of Pericles, the death of Cæsar, the battle of Agincourt, and Edmund Burke's observations on the character of the American colonies can make indelible marks upon young minds. But endless parades of Athenian military skirmishes, Roman consuls, French dynastic squabbles, or New Deal legislation produce no improvement in the student. He would be wholly justified in asking, "Why am I studying this?" Finally, the moral standards of many significant authors depart radically from those we would impart to our students. We cannot surrender children to perverse and dangerous authors simply because the latter have been inscribed into a canon of *historically* important writers.

An effective answer to these difficulties is the Florilegium method. The ideal remains to read the best that has been written: the most significant, the most beautiful, the most edifying. Yet even the greatest of authors cannot maintain himself perpetually on that high plane of wisdom; for lesser authors, brilliance is the exception rather than the rule. Given the limited time of the student and the mountain of cultural material available to the instructor, a selection process is inevitable. To demand that historical records be read in their entirety is to guarantee that much of serious value is kept entirely out of view. The *Florilegium* excerpts and collates what is worthy of the student's time, thereby increasing his cultural exposure. With proper help and encouragement as an adolescent, he will acquire a taste for such reading, in which case he may, as an adult already proficient in the necessary intellectual tools, read these same works in their entirety.

To address the remaining weaknesses of the "great book" method, the readings are indexed to concise *Outlines*, thereby supplying a framework in which they may hang together coherently. The *Outlines* also supply the visual helps that are necessary to better appreciate the history of a bygone era or the culture of a foreign people. A pronunciation guide is appended as an aid to mastery. The student will typically read each chapter of the *Outlines*, mastering names, dates, and facts to be tested by the instructor. He will then read the corresponding passages of the *Florilegium* to perfect and deepen his understanding. The *Florilegium* serves as a starting point for discussion and written essays. It is not intended to convey easily tested historical fact of the sort presented in the *Outlines*, but rather the historical, cultural, and simply human perspective that students should obtain before becoming adults. All the while, students are steeped in fine English. For the student preparing for higher learning and an intellectually engaged life, this is a method of study more fruitful than either the "textbook" or "great book" method.

Beatae Mariae Semper Virgini
Mediatrici, Coredemptrici, et Advocatae

Jeffrey C. Kalb, Jr.
Honors History Series Editor

EDITOR'S PREFACE

If Greece has supplied the world with so many of its rational and aesthetic standards, Rome has given us its law, its architecture and organization, and its many examples of natural virtue. Morey's *Outlines of Roman History* and the *Florilegium* seek to communicate these accomplishments. The *Florilegium* aims to communicate more than mere political history by including excerpts of philosophers, orators, poets, and other bearers of culture. These figures are treated in their historical and human significance. This is no course in philosophy, rhetoric, or poetry; representative passages from these disciplines are included in order to gauge the temper of their times and the real influence these individuals have had upon our culture. For the *Florilegium*, which is integrated with the *Outlines* and indexed to its chapters, I have selected the most edifying readings in order the convey to the student the substance of the Roman achievement. For this reason, I have stripped Morey's *Outlines* of all appendices and indices, as well as suggestions for further reading.

I have improved the cultural inclusion and aesthetic appeal of Morey's text has improved by replacing the rude black-and-white sketches of artifacts with public domain or freely licensed color photographs. I have likewise replaced the original maps of Morey's text with newly drawn maps that sometimes lack the detail of the originals, but exceed them in clarity and legibility. Some follow Morey's; some follow Westpoint military maps; some follow still other sources. Whereas Morey introduced new Roman names with an accent following the accented syllable, thus dividing the word, I have used an accent over the principal vowel in the accented syllable. Moreover, I have done this for all instances of foreign or unfamiliar words in the *Outlines*, not only the first occurrence. Additionally, a pronunciation guide for each of these has been appended to the text, together with general information about Roman names. It is my hope that all of these changes have preserved the conciseness and clarity of the original *Outlines*, while improving its accessibility and visual impression for today's student.

Jeffrey C. Kalb, Jr.
Honors History Series Editor

AUTHOR'S PREFACE TO THE 1901 EDITION

This book is intended to be a guide and a help to the study and teaching of Róman history. Its purpose is to assist the teacher to do what Dr. Arnold regarded as the great work of every instructor of Róman history, namely, "to lodge in the mind of the pupil the concept of Rome." To this end, care has been taken to select and emphasize those facts and events which illustrate the real character of the Róman people, which show the progressive development of Rome as a world power, and which explain the influence that Rome has exercised upon modern civilization.

The history of Rome has, in many respects, the unity of a great epic; and the interest in its study grows and becomes intensified to the extent that this unity is perceived. The attempt has been made, therefore, to keep before the mind of the pupil the real sequence of events, to show the relation between successive periods, to place facts in their logical order, and to omit whatever might draw the mind away from the main lines of historical progress.

The early stages of Róman history are here presented according to what the author believes to be the most plausible and scientific views. The pupil should, of course, understand that the history of Rome, previous to the destruction of the city by the Gauls, is based largely upon traditions and upon inferences drawn from archaeological investigations. He should know that there are different views regarding the significance of these traditions, and that many views which are accepted today may be rejected or modified tomorrow. But it can hardly be expected that the beginner can enter upon a critical examination of the sources and credibility of early Róman history, a work which must be reserved for more advanced students.

In tracing the growth of the Róman people, the effort has been made to keep clearly and prominently in view that which has given to this people their distinctive place in history: the genius for organization. The kingdom, the republic, and the empire are seen to be successive stages in the growth of a policy to bring together and organize the various elements of the ancient world. Attention is paid to the life and customs of the Róman people: their houses, meals, dress, marriage and other customs, education, etc.; but these have not been made so prominent as to lead the pupil to believe that the study of antiquities can take the place of the study of history in the proper sense of the word.

Special attention is called to the maps, which are intended to show the location of every place mentioned in the text. The series of "progressive maps" shows in a clear way the gradual expansion of the Róman dominion. For the purpose of encouraging the reading of other books, each chapter is supplemented by two short lists of reading references, the one applying to the general subject matter of the chapter, under the name of "Selections for Reading"; and the other constituting a "Special Study" upon some especially important or interesting topic. A classified list of the most valuable and available books in the English language upon Róman history will be found in the appendix to this volume. Every experienced teacher knows that history cannot be adequately taught by means of any single book, and that too much importance cannot be attached to the use of suitable bibliographical aids. [Editor's Note: The original maps and images have been replaced for greater legibility and image quality. The references mentioned by Dr. Morey have been replaced by the Florilegium.]

W. C. M.
University of Rochester
Rochester, New York

CHAPTER I

INTRODUCTION: THE LAND AND THE PEOPLE

The Character of Róman History, I.—The Geography of Ítaly, II.—The Peoples of Ítaly, III.

I. THE CHARACTER OF RÓMAN HISTORY

Importance of Róman History.—As we begin the study of Róman history, we may ask ourselves the question, Why is this subject important and worthy of our attention? It is because Rome was one of the greatest powers of the ancient world and has also exercised a great influence upon nearly all modern nations. There are a few great peoples, like the Hébrews, the Greeks, and the Rómans, who have done much to make the world what it is. If these peoples had never existed, our life and customs would no doubt be very different from what they are now. In order, then, to understand the world in which we live today, we must study these world peoples, who may have lived many centuries ago, but who have given to us much that makes us what we are — much of our language, our literature, our religion, our art, our government and law.

Rome and the Ancient World.—We often think of the Rómans as the people who conquered the world. But Rome not only conquered the most important countries of the old world; she also made of these different countries one united people, so that the ancient world became at last the Róman world. The old countries which bordered upon the Mediterránean Sea, Cárthage and Égypt, Pálestine and Sýria, Greece and Macedónia, all became parts of the Róman Empire. The ideas and customs, the art and institutions, of these countries were taken up and welded together into what we call Róman civilization. We may, therefore, say that Rome was the highest product of the ancient world.

Rome and the Modern World.—If Rome held such an important relation to the ancient world, she has held a still more important relation to the modern world. When the Róman Empire fell and was broken up into fragments, some of these fragments became the foundation of modern states: Ítaly, Spain, France, and Éngland. Rome is thus the connecting link between ancient and modern history. She not only gathered up the products of the ancient world, she also transmitted these products to modern times. What she inherited from the past she bequeathed to the future, together with what she herself created. On this account we may say that Rome was the foundation of the modern world.

Phases of Róman History.—As we approach the study of Róman history, we shall find that we can look at it from different points of view; and it will present to us different phases.

In the first place, we may look at the external growth of Rome. We shall then see her territory gradually expanding from a small spot on the Tíber, until it takes in the whole peninsula of Ítaly, and finally all the countries on the Mediterránean Sea. Our attention will then be directed to her generals, her armies, her battles, her conquests. We may trace on the map the new lands and new peoples which she gradually brought under her sway. Looked at from this point of view, Rome will appear to us as the great *conquering* nation of the world.

Again, we may look at the way in which Rome ruled her subjects, the way in which she built up, from the various lands and peoples that she conquered, a great state, with its wonderful system of government and law. We shall then see the work of her statesmen and lawgivers, her

1

magistrates, her senate, and her assemblies. From this point of view she will seem to us the great *governing* nation of the world.

Finally, we may look at the way in which the Rómans were themselves improved in their manners and customs as they came into contact with other peoples: how they learned lessons even from those whom they conquered, and were gradually changed from a rude, barbarous people to a highly civilized and cultivated nation. We shall see the straw-thatched huts of early times giving place to magnificent temples and theaters and other splendid buildings. We shall see the rude speech of the early Rómans growing into a noble language, capable of expressing fine, poetic feeling and lofty sentiments of patriotism. We shall also see Rome giving the fruits of her culture to the less favored peoples whom she takes under her control; and when she passes away, we shall see her bequeathing her treasures to future generations. From this point of view Rome will appear to us as the great *civilizing* nation of the world.

In order to understand the Rómans well, we should look at them in all these phases. We should study their conquests, their government, and their civilization.

II. THE GEOGRAPHY OF ÍTALY

The Itálian Peninsula.—The study of Róman history properly begins with the geography of Ítaly; because it was in Ítaly that the Róman people had their origin, and it was here that they began their great career. It was only when the Rómans had conquered and organized Ítaly that they were able to conquer and govern the world. If we look at the map, we shall see that the position of the Itálian peninsula was favorable to the growth of the Róman power. It was situated almost in the center of the Mediterránean Sea, on the shores of which had flourished the greatest nations of antiquity: Égypt, Cárthage, Phœnícia, Judéa, Greece, and Macedónia. By conquering Ítaly, Rome thus obtained a commanding position among the nations of the ancient world.

Boundaries and Extent of Ítaly.—In very early times, the name "Ítaly" was applied only to the very southern part of the peninsula. But from this small area it was extended so as to cover the whole peninsula which actually projects into the sea, and finally the whole territory south of the Alps. The peninsula is washed on the east by the Adriátic or Upper Sea, and on the west by the Tyrrhénian or Lower Sea. Ítaly lies for the most part between the parallels of thirty-eight degrees and forty-six degrees north latitude. It has a length of about 720 miles; a width varying from 330 to 100 miles; and an area of about 91,000 square miles.

The Mountains of Ítaly.—There are two famous mountain chains which belong to Ítaly, the Alps and the Ápennines. (1) The *Alps* form a semicircular boundary on the north and afford a formidable barrier against the neighboring countries of Éurope. Starting from the sea at its western extremity, this chain stretches toward the north for about 150 miles, when it rises in the lofty peak of Mt. Blanc, 15,000 feet in height; and then continues its course in an easterly direction for about 330 miles, approaching the head of the Adriátic Sea, and disappearing along its coast. It is crossed by several passes, through which foreign peoples have sometimes found their way into the peninsula. (2) The *Ápennines*, beginning at the western extremity of the Alps, extend through the whole length of the peninsula, forming the backbone of Ítaly. From this main line are thrown off numerous spurs and scattered peaks. Sometimes the Ápennines have furnished to Rome a kind of barrier against invaders from the north.

The Rivers of Ítaly.—The most important river of Ítaly is the Po, which, with its hundred tributaries, drains the fertile valley in the north, lying between the Alps and the Ápennines. The eastern slope of the peninsula proper is drained by a large number of streams, the most noted of which are the Rúbicon, the Metáurus, the Frénto, and the Áufidus. On the western slope the most important river is the Tíber, with its tributary, the Ánio.

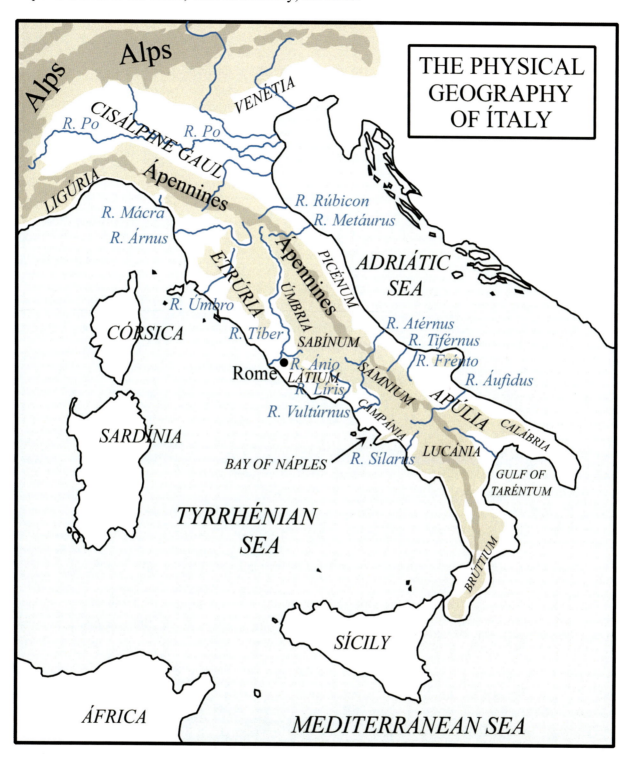

Climate and Products.—The climate of Ítaly varies greatly as we pass from the north to the south. In the valley of the Po the winters are often severe, and the air is chilled by the neighboring snows of the Alps. In central Ítaly the climate is mild and agreeable, snow being rarely seen south of the Tíber, except on the ranges of the Ápennines; while in southern Ítaly we approach a climate almost tropical, the land being often swept by the hot south wind, the *sirócco*, from the plains of África.

The soil of Ítaly is generally fertile, especially in the plains of the Po and the fields of Campánia. The staple products in ancient times were wheat, the olive, and the vine. For a long period Ítaly took the lead of the world in the production of olive oil and wine. The production of wheat declined when Rome, by her conquests, came into commercial relation with more fertile countries, such as Égypt.

The Divisions of Ítaly.—For the purpose of convenience and to aid us in our future study, we may divide ancient Ítaly into three divisions: northern, central, and southern.

(1) *Northern* Ítaly comprised the whole continental portion from the Alps to a line drawn from the river Mácra on the west to the Rúbicon on the east. It contained three distinct countries: Ligúria toward the west, Cisálpine Gaul in the center, and Venétia toward the east.

(2) *Central* Ítaly comprised the northern part of the peninsula proper, that is, the territory between the line just drawn from the Mácra to the Rúbicon, and another line drawn from the Sílarus on the west to the Frénto on the east. This territory contained six countries, namely, three on the western coast—Etrúria, Látium, and Campánia—and three on the eastern coast and along the Ápennines—Úmbria, Picénum, and what we call the Sabéllian country, which included many mountain tribes, chief among which were the Sábines, the Frentáni, and the Sámnites.

(3) *Southern* Ítaly comprised the rest of the peninsula and contained four countries, namely, two on the western coast, Lucánia and Brúttium, extending into the toe of Ítaly; and two on the eastern coast, Apúlia and Calábria (or Iapýgia), extending into the heel of Ítaly.

III. THE PEOPLES OF ÍTALY

The Settlement of Ítaly.—Long before Rome was founded, every part of Ítaly was already peopled. Many of the peoples living there came from the north, around the head of the Adriátic, pushing their way toward the south into different parts of the peninsula. Others came from Greece by way of the sea, settling upon the southern coast. It is of course impossible for us to say precisely how Ítaly was settled. It is enough for us at present to know that most of the earlier settlers spoke an Índo-Európéan language, and that when they first appeared in Ítaly they were scarcely civilized, living upon their flocks and herds and just beginning to cultivate the soil.

The Itálic Tribes.—The largest part of the peninsula was occupied by a number of tribes which made up the so-called Itálic race. We may for convenience group these tribes into four divisions: the Látins, the Óscans, the Sabéllians, and the Úmbrians.

(1) The *Látins* dwelt in central Ítaly, just south of the Tíber. They lived in villages scattered about Látium, tilling their fields and tending their flocks. The village was a collection of straw-thatched huts; it generally grew up about a hill, which was fortified, and to which the villagers could retreat in times of danger. Many of these Látin villages or hill-towns grew into cities, which were united into a league for mutual protection, and bound together by a common worship (of *Júpiter Latiáris*); and an annual festival which they celebrated on the Álban Mount, near which was situated Álba Lónga, their chief city.

(2) The *Óscans* were the remnants of an early Itálic people which inhabited the country stretching southward from Látium, along the western coast. In their customs they were like the Látins, although perhaps not so far advanced. Some authors include in this branch the Æquians, the Hérnicans, and the Vólscians, who carried on many wars with Rome in early times.

(3) The *Sabéllians* embraced the most numerous and warlike peoples of the Itálic stock. They lived to the east and south of the Látins and Óscans, extending along the ridges and slopes of the Ápennines. They were devoted not so much to farming as to the tending of flocks and herds. They lived also by plundering their neighbors' harvests and carrying off their neighbors' cattle. They were broken up into a great number of tribes, the most noted of which were the Sámnites, a hardy race which became the great rival of the Róman people for the possession of central Ítaly. Some of the Sámnite people in very early times moved from their mountain home and settled in the fertile plain of Campánia.

(4) The *Úmbrians* lived to the north of the Sabéllians. They are said to have been the oldest people of Ítaly. But when the Rómans came into contact with them, they had become crowded into a comparatively small territory, and were easily conquered. They were broken up into small tribes, living in hill-towns and villages, and these were often united into loose confederacies.

The Etrúscans.—Northwest of Látium dwelt the Etrúscans, in some respects the most remarkable people of early Ítaly. Their origin is shrouded in mystery. In early times they were a powerful nation, stretching from the Po to the Tíber, and having possessions even in the plains of Campánia. Their cities were fortified, often in the strongest manner, and also linked together in confederations. Their prosperity was founded not only upon agriculture, but also upon commerce. Their religion was a gloomy and weird superstition, in which they thought that they could discover the will of the gods by means of augury, that is, by watching the flight of birds and by examining the entrails of animals. The Etrúscans were great builders; and their massive walls, durable roads, well-constructed sewers, and imposing sepulchers show the greatness of their civilization.

The Greeks in Ítaly.—But the most civilized and cultivated people in Ítaly were the Greeks, who had planted their colonies at Taréntum, and on the western coast as far as Náples (*Neápolis*) in Campánia. So completely did these coasts become dotted with Greek cities, enlivened with Greek commerce, and influenced by Greek culture, that this part of the peninsula received the name of Great Greece (*Mágna Grǽcia*).

The Gauls.—If the Greeks in the extreme south were the most civilized people of Ítaly, the Gauls or Celts, in the extreme north, were the most barbarous. Crossing the Alps from western Éurope, they had pushed back the Etrúscans and occupied the plains of the Po; hence this region received the name which it long held, Cisálpine Gaul. They held this territory against the Ligúrians on the west and the Véneti on the east and for a long time were the terror of the Itálian people.

CHAPTER II

THE BEGINNINGS OF ROME

Traditions of the Early Kings, I.—The Situation of Rome, II.—The Origin of the City, III.

I. TRADITIONS OF THE EARLY KINGS

The Early Legendary History.—In its beginnings, the history of Rome, like that of all other ancient peoples, is made up largely of traditions. But we must not suppose on this account that the early history of Rome is a mere blank. Like all other traditions, these stories have in them some elements of truth. They show to us the ideas and the spirit of the Róman people; and they show how the Rómans used to explain the origin of their own customs and institutions. While we may not believe all these stories, we cannot ignore them entirely; because they have a certain kind of historical value, and have become a part of the world's literature.

Ænéas Bearing Anchíses from Troy (1729)
Carle van Loo (1705-1765), Louvre Museum, Paris

Foundation of the City.—According to the Róman legends, the origin of the city was connected with Álba Lónga, the chief city of Látium; and the origin of Álba Lónga was traced to the city of Troy in Ásia Mínor. After the fall of that famous city, it is said that the Trójan hero, Ænéas, fled from the ruins, bearing upon his shoulder his aged father, Anchíses, and leading by the hand his son, Ascánius. Guided by the star of his mother, Vénus, he landed on the shores of Ítaly with a band of Trójans, and was assured by omens that Látium was to be the seat of a great empire. He founded the city of Lavínium, and after his death his son Ascánius transferred the seat of the kingdom to Álba Lónga. Here his descendants ruled for three hundred years, when the throne was usurped by a prince called Amúlius. To secure himself against any possible rivals,

this usurper caused his brother's daughter, Rhéa Sílvia, to take the vows of a véstal virgin. But she became the mother of twin children, Rómulus and Rémus; their father was Mars, the god of war. The wicked Amúlius caused the children to be thrown into the Tíber; but they remained under the guardianship of the gods. Drifting ashore at the foot of the Pálatine hill, they were nursed by a she-wolf, and were brought up at the home of a neighboring shepherd. And when they had grown to manhood, they founded (753 B.C.) the city of Rome on the Pálatine, where they had been providentially rescued. In a quarrel between the two brothers, Rémus was killed, and Rómulus became the king of the new city.

Rómulus and Rémus Fed by She-Wolf (early 2nd Century A.D.)
Altar to Mars and Vénus, Palazzo Massimo alle Terme, Rome

6

The Reign of Rómulus.—Rómulus was looked upon by the Rómans not only as the founder of their city, but as the creator of their social and political institutions. He is said to have peopled his new town by opening an asylum for refugees; and when he wanted wives for his people he captured them from the Sábines. After a war with the Sábines peace was made; and the two peoples became bound together into one city under the two kings, Rómulus and Títus Tátius. After the death of Títus, Rómulus reigned alone and gave laws to the whole people. He made many wars upon the neighboring towns, and after a reign of thirty-seven years he was translated to heaven and worshiped under the name of Quirínus.

The Abduction of the Sábine Women (ca. 1634), Nicolas Poussin (1594-1665), Metropolitan Museum of Art

Núma Pompílius.—After a year's interregnum a Sábine named Núma Pompílius was elected as the second king of Rome. He is said to have been a very wise and pious man, and to have taught the Rómans the arts of peace and the worship of the gods. Núma is represented in the legends as the founder of the Róman religion. He appointed priests and other ministers of religion. He divided the lands among the people, placing boundaries under the charge of the god Términus. He is also said to have divided the year into twelve months, and thus to have founded the Róman calendar. After a peaceful reign of forty-two years, he was buried under the hill Janículum, across the Tíber.

Túllus Hostílius.—The third king, Túllus Hostílius, was chosen from the Rómans. His reign was noted for the conquest of Álba Lónga. In accounts of this war with Álba Lónga, the famous story is told of the Horátii and the Curiátii, three brothers in each army, who were selected to decide the contest by a combat, which resulted in favor of the Horátii, the Róman champions. Álba Lónga thus became subject to Rome. Afterward, Álba Lónga was razed to the ground, and

7

all its people were transferred to Rome. Túllus, it is said, neglected the worship of the gods, and was at last, with his whole house, destroyed by the lightnings of Jove (Júpiter).

The Oath of the Horátii (1784), Jacques-Louis David (1748-1825)

Áncus Mártius.—After the reign of Túllus the people elected Áncus Mártius, a Sábine and a grandson of Núma Pompílius. He is said to have published the sacred laws of his grandfather, and to have tried to restore the arts of peace. But, threatened by the Látins, he conquered many of their cities, brought their inhabitants to Rome, and settled them upon the Áventine hill. He fortified the hill Janículum, on the other side of the Tíber, to protect Rome from the Etrúscans, and built across the river a wooden bridge (the *Pons Sublícius*). He also conquered the lands between Rome and the sea and built the port of Óstia at the mouth of the Tíber.

Cápitoline She-Wolf (5th Century B.C.)
With Rómulus and Rémus (A.D. 15th Century)
Musei Capitolini, Rome

Credibility of the Legends.—These are in substance the stories which, decorated by many fanciful and miraculous incidents, the Rómans were proud to relate as explaining the beginnings of their city and the work of their early kings. These traditions have been shown to be unworthy of belief in many particulars. It is of course impossible, in a small book like this, even to suggest the many and various opinions which have been expressed regarding the credibility of early Róman history. It is enough to say that, while we need not believe all the incidents and details contained in these stories, we may find in them references to facts and institutions which really existed; and with the aid of other means, we may put these facts together so as to explain in a rational way the origin and growth of the famous city on the Tíber.

The Hills of Rome.—To obtain a more definite knowledge of the birth of Rome than we can get from the traditional stories, we must study that famous group of hills which may be called the "cradle of the Róman people." By looking at these hills, we can see quite clearly how Rome must have come into being, and how it became a powerful city. The location of these hills was favorable for defense, and for the beginning of a strong settlement. Situated about eighteen miles from the mouth of the Tíber, they were far enough removed from the sea to be secure from the attacks of the pirates that infested these waters; while the river afforded an easy highway for commerce.

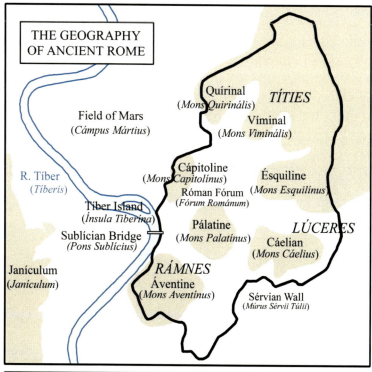

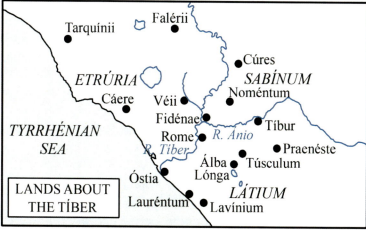

Their Relation to One Another.—To understand the relation of these hills to one another, we may consider them as forming two groups, the northern and the southern. The southern group comprised three hills: the Pálatine (*Mons Palatínus*), the Cælian (*Mons Cǽlius*), and the Áventine (*Mons Aventínus*), arranged in the form of a triangle, with the Pálatine projecting to the north. The northern group comprised four hills, arranged in the form of a crescent or semicircle, in the following order, beginning from the east: the Ésquiline (*Mons Esquilínus*), the Víminal (*Mons Viminális*), the Quírinal (*Mons Quirinális*), and the Cápitoline (*Mons Capitolínus*)—the last being a sort of spur of the Quírinal. These two groups of hills became, as we shall see, the seats of two different settlements. Of all the hills on the Tíber (*Tíberis*), the Pálatine occupied the most central and commanding position. It was, therefore, the people of the Pálatine settlement who would naturally become the controlling people of the seven-hilled city.

Their Relation to Neighboring Lands.—By looking at the neighboring lands about the Tíber we see that Rome was located at the point of contact between three important countries. On the south and east was Látium, the country of the Látins, already dotted with a number of cities, the most important of which was Álba Lónga. On the north was the country of the Sábines, a branch of the Sabéllian stock. On the northwest was Etrúria, with a large number of cities organized in confederacies and inhabited by the most civilized and enterprising people of central Italy. The peoples of these three different countries were pushing their outposts in the direction of the seven hills. It is not difficult for us to see that the time must come when there would be a struggle for the possession of this important locality.

III. THE ORIGIN OF THE CITY

The Látin Settlement on the Pálatine.—So far as we know, the first people to get a foothold upon the site of Rome were the Látins, who formed a settlement about the Pálatine hill. This Látin settlement was at first a small village. It consisted of a few farmers and shepherds who were sent out from Látium (perhaps from Álba Lónga) as a sort of outpost, both to protect the Látin frontier and to trade with the neighboring tribes. The people who formed this settlement were called *Rámnes*. They dwelt in their rude straw huts on the slopes of the Pálatine, and on the lower lands in the direction of the Áventine and the Cǽlian. The outlying lands furnished the fields which they tilled and used for pasturage. In order to protect them from attacks, the sides of the Pálatine hill were strengthened by a wall built of rude but solid masonry. This fortified place was called *Róma Quadráta*, or "Square Rome." It formed the citadel of the colony, into which the settlers could drive their cattle and conduct their families when attacked by hostile neighbors.

The Sábine Settlement on the Quírinal.—Opposite the Pálatine settlement there grew up a settlement on the Quírinal hill. This Quírinal settlement seems to have been an outpost or colony of the Sábine people, just as the Pálatine settlement was a Látin colony. The Sábines were pushing southward from beyond the Ánio. The settlers on the Quírinal were called *Títies*; their colony formed a second hill-town, similar in character and nearly equal in extent to the Pálatine town.

Union of the Rómans and the Sábines.—The two hill-towns which thus faced each other naturally became rivals for the possession of the lands near the Tíber; but being so nearly of equal strength, neither could conquer the other. If these settlements had not been so close together, they might have indulged in occasional strife and still remained separate; but being near to each other, they were obliged to be constantly at war, or else to come to some friendly understanding. They chose the latter course, and after forming an alliance, were united by a permanent league, and really became a single city. To celebrate this union, the intervening space was dedicated to the two-faced god, Jánus, who watched the approaches of both towns, and whose temple was said to have been built by Núma. The Cápitoline hill was chosen as the common citadel. The space between the two towns was used as a common market place (*fórum*), and also as a place for the common meeting of the people (*comítium*). This union of the Pálatine and Quírinal towns into one community, with a common religion and government, was an event of great importance. It was, in fact, the first step in the process of "incorporation" which afterward made Rome the most powerful city of Látium, of Ítaly, and finally of the world.

The Third Settlement, on the Cǽlian.—The union of the Rómans (*Rámnes*) and the Sábines (*Títies*) was followed by the introduction of a third people, called the *Lúceres*. This people was probably a body of Látins who had been conquered and settled upon the Cǽlian hill, although they are sometimes regarded as having been Etrúscans. Whatever may have been their origin, it is quite certain that they soon came to be incorporated as a part of the whole city community. The city of the early Róman kings thus came to be made up of three divisions, or "tribes" (*tríbus*, a third part, from *tres*, three). The evidence of this threefold origin was preserved in many institutions of later times. The three settlements were gradually united into a single city-state with common social, political, and religious institutions. By this union the new city became strong and able to compete successfully with its neighbors.

CHAPTER III

THE INSTITUTIONS OF EARLY ROME

The Early Róman Society, I.—The Early Róman Government, II.—The Early Róman Religion, III.

I. THE EARLY RÓMAN SOCIETY

The Social Institutions.—We have thus far traced the origin of the Róman city, according to what seem to be the most reasonable and generally accepted views. Various writers on early Róman history, of course, differ upon many matters of detail; but they are fairly well agreed that the Róman city grew out of a settlement of Látin shepherds and farmers on the Pálatine hill; and that this first settlement slowly expanded by taking in and uniting with itself the settlements established on the other hills. But to understand more fully the beginnings of this little city-state, we must look at the way in which the people were organized, that is, how they were arranged in social groups; how they were ruled; and how their society and government were held together and made strong by a common religion. Let us look first at the early social institutions.

The Róman Family.—The smallest group of Róman society was the family, which the early Rómans regarded as the most important and sacred of all human institutions. At its head was the household father (*paterfamílias*). He was supreme ruler over all the members of the household; his power extended to life and death. He had charge of the family worship and performed the religious rites about the sacred fire, which was kept burning upon the family altar. Around the family hearth were gathered the sons and daughters, grandsons and granddaughters, and also, the adopted children, all of whom remained under the power of the father as long as he lived. The family might also have dependent members, called "clients," who looked up to the father as their "patron"; and also slaves, who served the father as their master. Every Róman looked with pride upon his family and the deeds of his ancestors; and it was regarded as a great calamity for the family worship to become extinct.

The Róman Gens.—A number of families which were supposed to be descended from a common ancestor formed a clan, or *gens*. Like the family, the gens was bound together by common religious rites. It was also governed by a common chief or ruler (*decúrio*), who performed the religious rites, and led the people in war.

The Róman Cúria.—A number of *géntes* formed a still larger group, called a *cúria*. In ancient times, when different people wished to unite, it was customary for them to make the union sacred by worshiping some common god. So the cúria was bound together by the worship of a common deity. To preside over the common worship, a chief (*cúrio*) was selected, who was also the military commander in time of war, and chief magistrate in time of peace. The chief was assisted by a council of elders; and upon the most important questions he consulted the members of the cúria in a common place of meeting (*comítium*). So that the cúria was a small confederation of géntes, and made what we might call a little state.

The Róman Tribes.—There was in the early Róman society a still larger group than the cúria; it was what was called the tribe. It was a collection of *cúriæ* which had united for purposes of common defense and had come to form quite a distinct and well organized community, like that which had settled upon the Pálatine hill, and also like the Sábine community which had settled upon the Quírinal. Each of these settlements was therefore a tribe. Each had its chief, or king

11

(*rex*), who was priest of the common religion, military commander in time of war, and civil magistrate to settle all disputes. Like the cúria, it had also a council of elders and a general assembly of all people capable of bearing arms. Three of such tribes formed the whole Róman people.

II. THE EARLY RÓMAN GOVERNMENT

The Growth of the Róman Government.—It will now be easy for us to understand how the government of the whole united city came into existence. Each of the tribes, as we have seen, had its own king, its council of elders, and its general assembly. When the tribes on the Pálatine and Quírinal hills united and became one people, their governments were also united and became one government. For example, their two kings were replaced by one king chosen alternately from each tribe. Their two councils of one hundred members each were united in a single council of two hundred members. Their two assemblies, each one of which was made up of ten cúriæ, were combined into a single assembly of twenty cúriæ. And when the third tribe is added, we have a single king, a council of elders made up of three hundred members, and an assembly of the people composed of thirty cúriæ.

The Róman King.—The Róman king was the chief of the whole people. He was elected by all the people in their common assembly and inaugurated under the approval of the gods. He was in a sense the father of the whole nation, the chief priest of the national religion, and the military commander of the people, whom he called to arms in time of war. He administered law and justice, and like the father of the household had the power of life and death over all his subjects.

The Róman Senate.—The council of elders for the united city was called the sénate (from *sénex*, an old man). It was composed of the chief men of the géntes, chosen by the king to assist him with their advice. It comprised at first one hundred members, then two hundred, and finally three hundred, the original number having been doubled and tripled, with the addition of the second and third tribes. The senate at first had no power to make laws, only the power to give advice, which the king might accept or not, as he pleased.

The Comítia Curiáta.—All the people of the thirty cúriæ, capable of bearing arms, formed a general assembly of the united city, called the *comítia curiáta*. In this assembly each cúria had a single vote, and the will of the assembly was determined by a majority of such votes. In a certain sense the comítia curiáta was the ultimate authority in the state. It elected the king and passed a law conferring upon him his power. It ratified or rejected the most important proposals of the king regarding peace and war. The early city-state of Rome may then be described as a democratic monarchy, in which the power of the king was based upon the will of the people.

III. THE EARLY RÓMAN RELIGION

The Growth of the Early Religion.—Like the Róman government, so the early Róman religion grew up with the union of the various settlements into one community. When the different tribes came together into the Róman city, they selected Júpiter and Mars as their common gods to be worshiped upon the Cápitoline hill, together with Quirínus on the Quírinal. As the fire was kept burning on the family hearth, so the sacred fire of the city was kept burning in the temple of Vésta. The Róman people were filled with religious ideas. All power, from that of the household father to that of the king, was believed to come from above. In peace and in war they lived in the presence of the gods, and sought to remember them by worship and festivals.

Left: Bas-Relief of Minérva from Ruins of Herculáneum; Left Center: Statue of Mars, Villa of Hádrian; Right Center: Colossal Statue of Céres, Róman Goddess of Grain, Vátican Museums; Right Flóra, Róman Goddess of Flowers, Cápitoline Museum, Rome

Bronze Statue of Júpiter Státor (1st Century A.D.)
Musée d'Evreux

The Early Róman Deities.—To the ancestral gods which were worshiped in the family and gens, were added the gods of nature, which the Rómans saw everywhere. These earliest deities were those which naturally sprang from the imagination of a pastoral and agricultural people. In their gods they saw the protectors of their flocks and herds, and the guardians of the weather, the seasons, and the fruits of the soil. Jove (Júpiter) was the god of the sky and the elements of the air, the thunder and the lightning. Téllus was the goddess of the earth, and the mother of all living things; Sáturn, the god of sowing; and Céres, the goddess of the harvest; Minérva, the goddess of olives; Flóra, of flowers; and Líber, the god of wine.

The Religious Officers.—The king was the supreme religious officer of the state; but he was assisted by other persons, whom he appointed for special religious duties. To each of the three great national gods, Júpiter, Mars, and Quirínus, was assigned a special priest, called a *flámen*. To keep the fires of Vésta always burning, there were appointed six véstal virgins, who were regarded as the consecrated daughters of the state. Special pontiffs, under the charge of a *póntifex máximus*, had charge of the religious festivals and ceremonies; and the *fetiáles* were entrusted with the formality of declaring war.

Flámen (3rd Century A.D.), Louvre Museum, Paris

13

Relief of Véstal Virgin (2nd Century A.D.)
Antiquarium of the Pálatine

Priestess with Censer and Sacrificing Man (1st Century A.D.)
Glyptothek Museum, Munich

The Religious Observances.—The Rómans showed their remembrance of the gods in their prayers, offerings, and festivals. The prayers were addressed to the gods for the purpose of obtaining favors, and were often accompanied by vows. The religious offerings consisted either of the fruits of the earth, such as flowers, wine, milk, and honey; or the sacrifices of domestic animals, such as oxen, sheep, and swine. The festivals which were celebrated in honor of the gods were very numerous and were scattered through the different months of the year. The old Róman calendar contained a long list of these festival days. The new year began with March and was consecrated to Mars and celebrated with war festivals. Other religious festivals were devoted to the sowing of the seed, the gathering of the harvest, and similar events which belonged to the life of an agricultural people such as the early Rómans were.

Preparation of a Sacrifice (Early 2nd Century A.D.)
Louvre Museum, Paris

Jánus, Vátican Museums, Rome

14

CHAPTER IV

THE ETRÚSCAN KINGS OF ROME

The Traditions of the Later Kings, I.—The Etrúscan Influence, II.—The Growth of the City, III.

I. THE TRADITIONS OF THE LATER KINGS

The Later Kingdom.—As we come to the later kingdom, we shall see that many changes took place which made Rome quite different from what it was in the early period. The history is still based upon legends; but these legends are somewhat more trustworthy than the older ones. We shall see that Rome now came under foreign princes; and that the city was greatly improved, and its institutions were changed in many respects. These new kings, instead of being Rómans or Sábines, were Etrúscans, who gave to Rome something of the character of an Etrúscan city.

Tarquínius Príscus.—The first of these new kings, it is said, came from the Etrúscan city of Tarquínii, from which he derived his name. The story is told that, as he approached the city, an eagle came from the sky, and, lifting his cap from his head, replaced it. His wife, who was skilled in the Etrúscan art of augury, regarded the eagle as a messenger from heaven, and its act as a sign that her husband was to acquire honor and power. At the death of Áncus Mártius, Tarquínius became king. He carried on many wars with the neighboring peoples, the Látins and the Sábines. He was great in peace as well as in war. He drained the city, improved the Fórum, and founded a temple to Júpiter on the Cápitoline hill. After a reign of thirty-eight years, he was treacherously slain by the sons of Áncus Mártius.

Sérvius Túllius.—The next king was Sérvius Túllius, who is said to have been the son of a slave in the royal household, and whom the gods favored by mysterious signs. He proved a worthy successor to the first Tárquin. He made a treaty with the Látins, by which Rome was acknowledged as the head of Látium; and as a sign of this union, he built a temple to Diána on the Áventine hill. He enlarged the city and enclosed the seven hills within a single wall. After a reign of forty-four years, he was murdered by his own son-in-law, who became the next king.

Tarquínius Supérbus.—Tradition represents the last king, Tarquínius Supérbus, as a cruel despot. He obtained the throne by murder, and ruled without the consent of the senate or the people. He loved power and pomp. He continued the wars with the Látins. He also waged war with the Vólscians on the southern borders of Látium; and with the spoils there obtained he finished the temple of Júpiter on the Cápitoline hill. Although he scorned religion, it is related that he was induced to buy the Síbylline books from the inspired prophetess of Cúmæ. It is also said that later in life he was frightened by strange dreams, and sent his two sons, with his nephew Brútus, to consult the Greek oracle at Délphi. To one question asked the oracle, the response was given that the person who first kissed his mother should succeed to the power of Tárquin. Brútus showed that he was the person intended, by falling and kissing the earth, the common mother of all. The traditions tell us how at last the proud Tárquin was driven from the throne and the kingdom was ended.

Lúcius Június Brútus Kisses the Earth (1700-1704)
Sebastiano Ricci (1659-1734), National Gallery, Padua

Significance of the Legends.—We cannot of course accept these stories as real history. We can yet see in them the evidence that Rome was becoming different from what it had been under the early kings. We can see that Rome came under the power of the Etrúscans; that it was much improved by the construction of great public works and buildings; and that it acquired a dominant power over the neighboring land of Látium.

II. THE ETRÚSCAN INFLUENCE

The Kingly Power.—One of the most important features of the Etrúscan dynasty was the increase of the kingly power. All the Etrúscan kings were represented as powerful rulers. Although they could not change the spirit and character of the people, they gave to Rome a certain kind of strength and influence which it did not have before. This great power of the Etrúscan kings was at first used for the good of the people; but finally it became a tyranny which was oppressive and hateful.

Relief of a Líctor Bearing the Fásces, Archeological Museum of Verona

The Insignia of Power.—From the Etrúscans came the royal insignia, that is, the symbols of power which were intended to make the person of the king more dignified and respected. These insignia consisted of a golden crown, an ivory scepter, an ivory chair called the "cúrule chair," a white robe with a purple border (*tóga prætéxta*), and twelve líctors, or royal attendants, each carrying a bundle of rods (*fásces*) enclosing an ax. This last symbol was a sign of the absolute power of the king.

16

The Harúspices.—From Etrúria also came the art of the harúspices, or soothsayers, who interpreted the will of the gods. These persons were supposed to ascertain the divine will by observing the lightning and other phenomena of nature, and also by examining the internal organs of animals offered in sacrifice, and even by watching the sacred chickens as they ate their food. The Etrúscan soothsayers were supposed to be better versed in divine things than the Róman áugurs; and the senate is said to have provided for the perpetual cultivation of the Etrúscan ritual.

Public Works.—The buildings and other public works of the later kings bear the marks of Etrúscan influence. The massive and durable style of architecture, especially as seen in the walls and the sewers constructed at this time, shows that they were the works of great and experienced builders, The name of the "Túscan Street" (*vícus Túscus*) which opened into the Fórum, preserved the memory of this foreign influence in the Róman city.

Top: Funerary Relief Depicting Cúrule Chair
Bottom: Etrúscan Bridge at Vúlci

III. THE GROWTH OF THE CITY

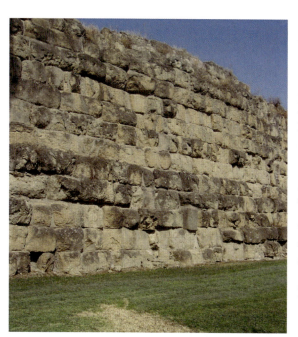

The Sérvian Walls.—The expansion of the city under the Tárquins is shown, in the first place, by the construction of the new and larger walls which are ascribed to Sérvius Túllius, and which received his name. Previous to this time the principal city wall was on the Pálatine. Some of the other hills were partly fortified. But now a single fortification was made to encircle all the seven hills, by joining the old walls and by erecting new defenses. The walls were generally built of large, rectangular blocks of stone, and so durable were they that they remained the only defenses of the city for many hundreds of years; and parts of them may be seen at the present day.

Modern Remains of the Sérvian Walls

The New Temples.—Under the Tárquins, the temples of the city assumed a more imposing architectural appearance. Before this the places of worship were generally altars, set up on consecrated places, and perhaps covered with a simple roof. The Etrúscan kings gave a new dignity to the sacred buildings. The most imposing example of the new structures was the temple dedicated to Júpiter Óptimus Máximus, on the Cápitoline hill, which contained shrines set apart for the worship of Júno and Minérva. Other new temples were the one dedicated to Sáturn at the foot of the Cápitoline near the Fórum, and one dedicated to Diána on the Áventine.

The Cloáca Máxima.—Among the most remarkable works of the Tárquins were the sewers which were constructed to drain the city. The most important of these was the famous *Cloáca Máxima*, or great drain, which ran under the Fórum and emptied into the Tíber. It was said to be large enough to admit a hay cart, and one could sail down it in a boat. It was strongly built of stone, in the form of a semicircular arch, such as the Etrúscans had used, and its mouth is still visible on the shore of the Tíber.

The Círcus Máximus.—For the amusement of the people, games were introduced from Etrúria, and a great circus, called the *Círcus Máximus*, was laid out between the Áventine and the Pálatine hill. Here the people assembled once every year, to witness chariot races and boxing and other sports, which were celebrated in honor of the gods who were worshiped on the Cápitoline.

Left: *The Outlet of the Cloáca Máxima* (ca. 1880)
       Ettore Roesler Franz (1845-1907), Museum of Rome

Below: Modern Remains of the Círcus Máximus

CHAPTER V

THE REORGANIZATION OF THE KINGDOM

The Introduction of the Plebéians, I.—The Reformed Constitution, II.—The Supremacy of Rome in Látium, III.

I. THE INTRODUCTION OF THE PLEBÉIANS

The Reforms of the Tárquins.—We must not suppose that the work of the Etrúscan kings was simply to give to Rome better buildings and more durable public works. However important these may have been, the Tárquins did something which was of still greater benefit to the Róman people. The first Tárquin and Sérvius Túllius are described as great reformers, who made the little Róman state stronger and more compact than it had been before. Let us see why the Róman state needed to be reformed, and how this reform was brought about.

The Patrícian Aristocracy.—We have already seen that the early Róman people was made up of three tribes, that is, the three old communities which were settled on the Róman hills. We have also seen that these tribes were made up of cúriæ; and these cúriæ of géntes; and lastly, that these géntes were composed of the old families. It is therefore evident that no person could be a member of the state unless he was a member of some old Róman family. It was only the descendants of the old families who could vote in the assembly or could be chosen to the senate. And it was they only who were called upon to serve in the army. These old families and their descendants were called patricians; and the state was in reality a patrícian state. As all other persons were excluded from political rights and privileges, the patricians formed an aristocratic class, exclusive and devoted to their own interests.

The Growth of the Plebéians.—But in the course of time there grew up by the side of the patrícians a new class of persons. Though living at Rome, they were not members of the old families, and hence had no share in the government. These persons were called plebéians. There were no doubt many of these persons under the early kings; but they became more numerous under the later kings. They consisted largely of people of other cities who had been conquered and brought to Rome, and of people who had escaped from other cities and found refuge at Rome. They thus became subjects, but not citizens. They could not hold office, nor vote; nor could they marry into the patrícian families; although they were allowed to hold property of their own. But as they became more numerous, and as some of them became wealthy, they desired to be made equal with the patrícians.

The New Plebéian Géntes.—It was Tarquínius Príscus, the first Etrúscan king, who, it is said, took the first step toward introducing the plebéians into the state. He did this by introducing into each one of the tribes a number of the more wealthy plebéian families, under the name of lesser géntes (*géntes minóres*); while the old patrician gentes were called by the more honorable name of greater géntes (*géntes maióres*). In this way the line of separation between the patrícians and the plebéians began to be broken down, but it was many years after this time before the two classes became entirely equal.

II. THE REFORMED CONSTITUTION

The New Local Tribes.—More important than the reforms of Tarquínius Príscus were the reforms which are said to have been made by Sérvius Túllius. The previous changes had affected only a small part of the plebéian class; the great body of the plebéians remained just where they were before. Now Sérvius saw that Rome would be stronger and more able to compete with her enemies if the plebéians were called upon to serve in the army and pay taxes, just like the patrícians. He therefore made a new division of the people, based not upon their birth and descent, like the old division into tribes, but upon their domicile, that is, the place where they lived. He divided the whole Róman territory, city and country, into local districts, like wards and townships. There were four of these in the city, and sixteen in the country, the former being called "city tribes" (*tríbus urbánæ*), and the latter "rural tribes" (*tríbus rústicæ*). All persons, whether patrícians or plebéians, who had settled homes (*assídui*), were enrolled in their proper tribes and were made subject to military service and the tribal tax (*tribútum*).

The New Classes and Cénturies.—The next step which Sérvius took was to reorganize the Róman army, so that it should include all persons who resided in the Róman territory and were enrolled in the new local tribes. First came the cavalry (*équites*), made up of young wealthy citizens, and arranged in eighteen cénturies, or companies. Next came the infantry (*pédites*), which comprised all the rest of the men capable of bearing arms. In ancient times every man was obliged to furnish his own weapons. Now as all the people could not afford to obtain the heavier armor, they were subdivided into "classes" according to their wealth, and according to the armor it was supposed they could afford to furnish. The first class consisted of eighty cénturies, and was made up of the wealthiest men, who could afford a full armor: a brass shield carried on the left arm, greaves which covered the legs, a cuirass to protect the breast, and a helmet for the head, together with a sword and a spear. The second class had in place of the brass shield a wooden shield, covered with leather. The third class omitted the greaves, and the fourth class omitted also the cuirass and the helmet, carrying only the wooden shield, spear, and sword. The fifth class was made up of the poorest citizens, who fought only with darts and slings. Each of these classes, except the first, was arranged in twenty cénturies, or companies. One half of the cénturies in each class were composed of the younger men (*iunióres*), who might be called out at any time. The other half were composed of the older men (*senióres*), who were called out only in times of great danger. Besides, there were fifteen cénturies of musicians, carpenters, and substitutes, We may perhaps get a clearer idea of this new military arrangement by the following:

I.	Cavalry (*Équites*):	18 cénturies
II.	Infantry (*Pédites*), 1st class (40 *iunióres*, 40 *senióres*):	80 cénturies
	Infantry (*Pédites*), 2nd - 5th classes (10 *iunióres*, 10 *senióres*):	10 cénturies each
	Musicians, Carpenters, Substitutes	15 cénturies

The New Assembly, Comítia Centuriáta.—This arrangement of the people was first intended for a military purpose; but it soon came to have a political character also. There was every reason why the important questions relating to war, which had heretofore been left to the old body of armed citizens, should now be left to the new body of armed citizens. As a matter of fact, the new fighting body became a new voting body; and there thus arose a new assembly, called the assembly of the cénturies (*comítia centuriáta*). But this new assembly did not lose its original military character. For example, it was called together, not by the voice of the líctor, like the old assembly, but by the sound of the trumpet. Again, it did not meet in the Fórum, where the old assembly met, but in the Field of Mars (*Cámpus Mártius*), outside of the city. It also voted by cénturies, that is, by military companies. After a time the *comítia centuriáta* became a real political and legislative body, of greater importance than the old *comítia curiáta*.

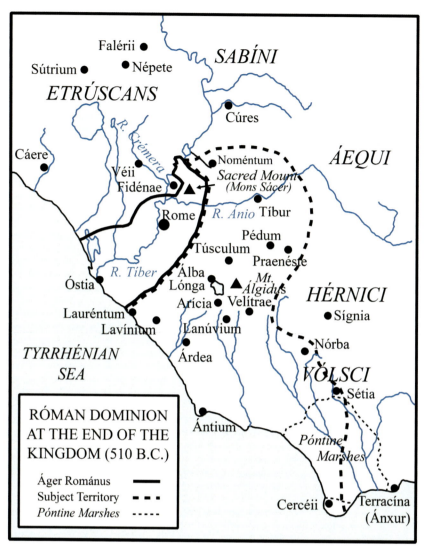

Conquests in Látium.—While Rome was thus becoming strong, and her people were becoming more united and better organized, she was also gaining power over the neighboring lands. The people with whom she first came into contact were the Látins. A number of Látin towns were conquered and brought under her power, and were made a part of the Róman domain (*áger Románus*). She also pushed her conquests across the Ánio into the Sábine country, and across the Tíber into Etrúria. So that before the fall of the kingdom, Rome had begun to be a conquering power. But her conquests at present were limited, for the most part, to Látium, and it was from this conquered land in Látium that she had created the rural tribes already mentioned.

Rome and the Látin League.—Outside of this conquered territory were the independent Látin cities, united together into a strong confederacy. When Álba Lónga was conquered, Rome succeeded to the headship of this confederacy of thirty cities. The people of these cities were not made Róman citizens; but they were given the right to trade and to intermarry with Rómans. The Látin league was bound to Rome by a treaty, which made it partly subject to her; because it could not wage war without her consent, and it must assist her in her wars.

Review of the Róman Kingdom.—In the various ways which we have described, Rome had come to be a strong city, and was growing into something like a new nation, with a kind of national policy. If we should sum up this policy in two words, these words would be *expansion* and *incorporation*. By "expansion" is meant the extension of Róman power over neighboring territory, whether by conquest or by alliance. By "incorporation" we mean the taking of subject people into the political body. For example, Rome had first incorporated the Sábine settlement on the Quírinal, then the Látin settlement on the Cǽlian, and finally the plebéian class, which had grown up by the side of the patrícian class. By pursuing this kind of policy, Rome had come to be, at the end of the kingdom, a compact and well organized city-state with a considerable territory of her own (*áger Románus*) about the Tíber, and having a control over the cities of Látium.

CHAPTER VI

THE STRUGGLE AGAINST THE KINGSHIP

The Expulsion of the Kings, I.—The New Republican Government, II.

I. THE EXPULSION OF THE KINGS

The Transition to the Republic.—We have seen how Rome came into existence, and how it gradually grew in extent and power under the regal government. We are now to consider how the Róman kingdom was changed into a republic; and to look at the different struggles by which this change was brought about. The change from the Róman kingdom to the republic was due to the tyranny of the last Tárquin; so that the first struggle for Róman liberty was a struggle against the kingship. When the rule of Tarquínius Supérbus became intolerable, he was expelled from Rome, with his whole family (510 B.C.). But with the aid of the Etrúscans and Látins he tried to regain his lost power; and the first days of the republic were, therefore, days full of strife and trouble. The stories of this period tell us of many deeds of Róman virtue and patriotism. In them we see the heroic efforts made by a liberty-loving people to rid themselves of a despotic king, and to form a freer government.

The Story of Brútus and Collatínus.—The legends first tell how the king was driven from Rome. This was brought about by the efforts of two patriotic men, Brútus and Collatínus, who determined to avenge the dishonorable deeds of Tarquínius Supérbus and his family. These patriots aroused the Róman people, and led them to pass a law to banish Tárquin and his corrupt household. The gates of the city were ordered to be closed against him. The soldiers saluted Brútus as the deliverer of their country. The people declared that the kingship should be abolished forever; and they elected Brútus and Collatínus to rule over them for a year.

Bronze Bust of Lúcius Június Brútus
4th to 3rd centuries B.C.
Cápitoline Museum, Rome

The Conspiracy of Brútus' Sons.—The banished king then sent messengers to Rome to ask that his property be restored to him. While engaged on this mission, the messengers formed a plot to bring back the king to his throne; and the two sons of Brútus joined in the treacherous scheme. But a slave who happened to hear the plan of the conspirators exposed the whole affair. When Brútus found that his own sons were engaged in this act of treason, he did not allow his feelings as a father to prevent him from doing his duty as a patriot, but condemned them to death as traitors to their country.

The Líctors Bring to Brútus the Bodies of His Sons (1789)
Jacques-Louis David (1748-1825), Louvre Museum, Paris

The Attempts of the Etrúscans to restore Tarquínius.—When the plot at Rome failed, Tarquínius appealed for help to the Etrúscan cities of Véii and Tarquínii, which raised an army to assist him. In a fierce battle which followed, Brútus was slain by the king's son. The battle, which had been long in doubt, was decided by the god Sylvánus, whose voice was heard in the forest proclaiming that the Rómans had won. Tarquínius next appealed to Lars Porséna, king of Clúsium, and the most powerful prince of Etrúria. Collecting his army, Porséna suddenly seized the Janículum, the hill just across the Tíber, and Rome was saved only by the heroism of Horátius Cócles, who, with two companions, withstood the whole Etrúscan army while the wooden bridge was destroyed. Porséna was thus prevented from entering the city. After ravaging the surrounding country he soon made peace with the Rómans and gave no further aid to the Tárquins.

The Attempt of the Látins.—The Tárquins then turned for aid to the Látins. The thirty Látin cities revolted and joined the cause of the banished king. The danger was so great that the Rómans appointed a dictator to lead their armies into the field. Then was fought the noted battle of Lake Regíllus, which, according to the old story, was decided by the aid of two gigantic youths, who rode upon snow-white horses in the Róman ranks, and whom the Rómans recognized as the twin gods Cástor and Póllux. A temple to these gods was built in the Fórum in memory of this deliverance.

23

Battle of Lake Regíllus, Tommaso Laureti (1530-1602), Capitoline Museums, Rome

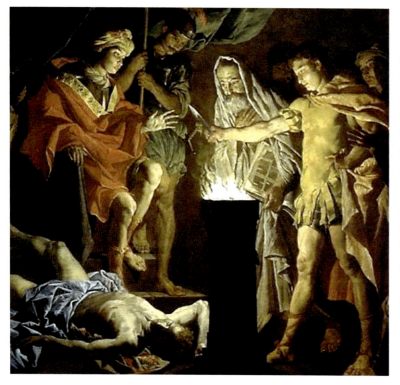

Múcius Scǽvola in the Presence of Lars Porséna (Early 1640's)
Matthias Stomer (ca. 1600 - unknown), Art Gallery of New South Wales

Significance of the Legends.— While we cannot believe everything contained in these romantic stories, we can yet see in them the record of a great historical event. We can see that the government of the kings was overthrown. We can also see that this change was not a peaceful change, but was attended by a severe struggle. We can see, finally, that the Rómans honored the heroic virtues of courage and patriotism; and that they believed their destiny was in the hands of the gods.

II. THE NEW REPUBLICAN GOVERNMENT

The Two Cónsuls.—When the kingdom came to an end, the power of the kings was put into the hands of two cónsuls (at first called prǽtors), elected by the people. The cónsular power, though derived from the old kingly power, was yet different from it in many respects. In the first place, the power of the king had been a lifelong power; but the power of the cónsuls was limited to one year. Again, the royal power had been held by one person; but the cónsular power was held by two persons, so that each was a restraint upon the other. Moreover, the power of the king had been absolute, that is, it had extended to life and death over all citizens at all times; the power of the cónsuls, on the other hand, was limited, since they could not exercise the power of life and death, except outside of the city and over the army in the field. The cónsuls retained the old insignia of the king; but when in the city, the ax was withdrawn from the fásces. In this way the chief authority, which was placed in the hands of the cónsuls, was shorn of its worst features. It must also be noted that the priestly power of the king was not given to the cónsuls, but to a special officer, called king of the sacrifices (*rex sacrórum*); and the management of the finances was put in charge of two *quéstors* elected by the people.

The Dictatorship.—The Rómans were wise enough to see that in times of great danger the power of the cónsuls might not be strong enough to protect the state. To meet such an emergency a dictator was appointed, who was a sort of temporary king. He had entire control of the city and the army. He was even given the power of life and death over citizens; and his líctors retained the ax in the *fásces*. But this extraordinary power could be held for only six months, after which time the cónsuls resumed their regular authority as chief magistrates. With the dictator there was generally appointed another officer, who was second in authority, called the master of horse; but over him, as over everyone else, the dictator was supreme.

The New Senators.—When the cónsuls were elected, it is said that one of their first acts was to fill up the senate to the number of three hundred members. The last king had practically ruled without the senate, and he had no reason to fill the vacancies when they occurred. But the new cónsuls wished the help of the senate, and therefore desired to keep its numbers complete. The new senators who were enrolled were called *conscrípti*; and the whole body of senators became known as *pátres conscrípti*.

The Popular Assemblies.—With the establishment of the republic, the two assemblies with which we are already acquainted, the *comítia curiáta* and the *comítia centuriáta*, both remained. But the former lost a great deal of its old power, which became transferred to the latter. The assembly of the centuries was therefore the body in which the people generally expressed their will. Here they elected the officers, and passed the most important laws. It was this assembly which became the chief legislative body during the early republic.

The Laws of Valérius Poplícola.—It is said that after the death of Brútus, his colleague Valérius (who had succeeded Collatínus) did not call an assembly to elect another cónsul. This aroused the fear that Valérius wished to make himself king. But it was soon found that instead of aiming to be king, he was preparing a set of laws which would prevent anyone from becoming king, and would also protect the people from the arbitrary power of their magistrates. One of these laws declared that any person who assumed the chief power without the people's consent should be condemned as a traitor. Another law granted to every citizen the right of an appeal to the people, in case he was condemned for a crime. These laws, known as the Valérian laws, may be called the "first charter of Róman liberty," because they protected the people from the exercise of arbitrary power. So highly honored was Valérius that he was surnamed Poplícola, or the People's Friend.

The Loss of Róman Territory.—We remember how extensive were the lands which were acquired by the Rómans under the kings. But they had lost many of these lands during the struggles against the last Tárquin. They had lost their conquests in Etrúria, and much of their land in Látium; and the thirty Látin cities had reasserted their independence. So that the authority of the new government was now reduced to a comparatively small strip of territory south of the Tíber, together with the Janículum on the Etrúscan side.

CHAPTER VII

THE STRUGGLE FOR ECONOMIC RIGHTS

The Grievances of the Plebs, I.—The First Secession and Its Results, II.
Wars with the Vólscians, Æquians, and Etrúscans, III.

I. THE GRIEVANCES OF THE PLEBS

The Power of the Patrícians.—The patrícians and plebéians had united in their efforts to drive out the kings; but when the struggle against the kingship was ended, the chief fruits of the victory fell to the patrícians. The plebéians could, it is true, still vote in the *comítia centuriáta*; but they could not hold any of the new offices, nor could they sit in the senate. Rome became a republic, but it was an aristocratic, and not a democratic republic; that is, the chief power rested not in the whole people, but in a particular class. The plebéians might perhaps have submitted to the government of the patrícians, if it had not been exercised in a selfish and oppressive manner. But the patrícian rule proved to be as despotic as that of the kings; and a long and fierce struggle ensued between the two orders. As the patrícians were generally more wealthy than the plebéians, the conflict became at first a struggle between the rich and the poor, a contest for a more equal distribution of wealth.

Poverty and Distress of the Plebéians.—The late wars had left the plebéians in a very dependent and deplorable condition. The wealthy patrícians, for the most part, lived in the city; and their property was protected by the city walls. But the homes of the plebéians were generally in the country. Accordingly, when they were serving in the army, their little farms were neglected, or ravaged by the enemy, their families were driven away, and their property was destroyed. In this way, while serving their country, they were deprived of their houses and fields, and of the means of subsistence, and so were reduced to a condition of poverty and great distress.

The Unjust Law of Debt.—The sorest burden which now rested upon the plebéians was the harsh law of debt. Having lost their property by the misfortunes of war, they were obliged to borrow money of the rich patrícians; and they were thus reduced to the condition of a debtor class. But a debtor in the early days of Rome was especially wretched. If he could not pay his debt, he was liable to be arrested, thrown into a dungeon, and made the slave of his creditor. His lot was chains, stripes, and slavery.

The law of debt was not only harsh in itself, but its effect was to keep the poor in a continual state of poverty, from which they could not easily escape.

The Unequal Division of the Public Land.—Another cause which kept the plebéians in a state of poverty was the unjust distribution of the public land (*áger públicus*) which had been acquired in war. This land properly belonged to all the people, and might have been used to relieve the distress of the poor. But the government was in the hands of the patrícians, and they disposed of this land for their own benefit; they allowed it to be "occupied," at a nominal rent, by members of their own order. As long as the land remained public, it could not be sold by the occupants; but the longer the rich patrícians retained the occupation of this land, the more they would look upon it as their own property, and ignore the fact that it belonged to the whole Róman people. So that the common people were deprived of their just share of the land which they had helped to conquer.

First Secession of the Plebéians.—It was the hard law of debt which first drove the plebéians to revolt. As there was no legal way to redress their wrongs, they decided that they would no longer serve in the army, but leave the patrícians to fight their own battles. They therefore deserted their general, marched in full array to a hill beyond the Ánio, which they called the Sacred Mount (*Mons Sácer*), and proposed to form an independent city (494 B.C.). The patrícians saw that the loss of the plebéian army would be the destruction of Rome. They were therefore compelled to make a solemn compact to the effect that the debts of all persons who were insolvent should be canceled; and that those who had been imprisoned on account of debt should be released.

The Secession of the Plebéians to the Sacred Mount (1849), Engraving of B. Barloccini

The Tríbunes of the People.—But the most important result of the first secession was the creation of a new office, that of tríbune of the people. In order to protect the plebéians from any further oppressive acts on the part of the patrícian magistrate, it was agreed to appoint two tríbunes from among the plebéians themselves. These new officers were given the power to "veto," that is, to forbid, the act of any magistrate which bore unjustly upon any citizen. In order that the tríbunes might exercise their authority without hindrance, their persons were made "inviolable," which means that they could not be arrested, and that anyone who interfered with them in the exercise of their lawful duty could be put to death. The tríbunes were assisted by two *ædiles*, who were also chosen from the plebéian body.

The Plebéian Assembly.—The meetings which the plebéians had occasionally held before this time now assumed the character of a permanent assembly (*concílium plébis*). This assembly could be called together by the tríbunes, who were permitted to address the people in regard to their interests; and no magistrate was allowed to interrupt them while speaking or to disperse this assembly (*lex Icília*, 492 B.C.). The assembly could also pass resolutions (*plebiscíta*), which were binding upon the plebéians, but not as yet upon the whole people. It was not many years before the plebéian assembly was given the right to elect their own tríbunes and ædiles (*lex Publília*, 472 B.C.). In this way the plebéians acquired a position in the state which they had never before held.

The Agrarian Law of Spúrius Cássius.—The second great cause of complaint was, as we have seen, the unjust distribution of the public land. To remove this injustice was the effort of the cónsul Spúrius Cássius. This man was both a patriot and a statesman. He loved the people, and he labored to protect their interests. In order to strengthen Rome against her foreign enemies, he first of all made a new treaty with the Látin towns, and a treaty with the neighboring Hérnicans.

But the most famous act of Sp. Cássius was the proposal of the first "agrarian law," that is, a law intended to reform the division of the public land (486 B.C.). It was not his purpose to take away any private land which legally belonged to the patrícians; but to make a more just distribution of the land which properly belonged to the whole state. When this law was brought forward, the patrícians used their influence to prevent its passage. After his year of office had expired, Sp. Cássius was charged with treason and with the attempt to make himself king. He was tried, condemned, scourged, and beheaded; and thus one of Rome's greatest patriots suffered the doom of a traitor. But the people remembered Sp. Cássius, and his name was inscribed upon a tablet and placed in the Fórum, where it remained for many generations.

III. WARS WITH THE VÓLSCIANS, ÆQUIANS, AND ETRÚSCANS

The Foreign Enemies of Rome.—While these struggles were going on to relieve the distress of the poor plebéians, the frontiers were continually threatened by foreign enemies. The chief enemies of Rome at this time were the Vólscians, the Æquians, and the Etrúscans. The Vólscians occupied the southern plains of Látium, near the seacoast. The Æquians held the slopes of the Ápennines on the northeast. The Etrúscans held all their original territory on the right bank of the

Tíber, except the hill Janículum. On every side Rome was beset by foes; and for many years her armies fought in defense of their homes, and almost within sight of the city. By the treaties which Sp. Cássius had formed, the Rómans, the Látins, and the Hérnicans made common cause in repelling these attacks. There is no continuous history of these frequent wars, but the Róman historians have preserved the memory of them in certain legends, which were sacred to the Rómans themselves, and which we should not forget if we would understand the character and spirit of the Róman people.

The Family of Coriolánus (after 1771)
Joseph-Marie Vien (1716-1809)

Coriolánus and the Vólscians.—The Vólscian wars have left us the story of Coriolánus, which tells us that this young patrícian opposed the distribution of grain among the plebéians; that he was threatened by the common people and fled to the Vólscians, and led an army against his native city; that his mother and his wife went to the Vólscian camp and pleaded with him to cease his wars upon Rome; that Rome was thus saved, and a temple was built to commemorate the patriotism of the Róman women.

Cincinnátus and the Æquians.—The memory of the Æquian wars is preserved in the story of the Róman patriot Cincinnátus, who was called from his country home to rescue the Róman army, which was surrounded by the Æquians, and threatened with destruction in a narrow defile in Mt. Álgidus, near the Álban hills and who with great speed and skill defeated the Æquian army, compelling it to "pass under the yoke" as a sign of submission, and then returned the next evening to Rome in triumph. The "yoke" consisted of a spear supported in a horizontal position by two spears fixed upright in the ground.

Cincinnátus Leaves the Plow for the Róman Dictatorship (ca. 1806)
Juan Antonio Ribera (1779-1860), Museo del Prado, Madrid

The Fábii and the Etrúscans.—With the Etrúscan wars is linked the story of the Fábian gens, which was one of the greatest patrícian houses of Rome; and which, having volunteered to carry on the war against the Etrúscans at its own expense, was, with the exception of one person, utterly destroyed by the enemy. The Fábian gens was therefore honored for having sacrificed itself in the defense of Rome.

These stories should be read, not as an accurate narration of facts, but because they show the kind of virtues that the early Rómans most admired.

CHAPTER VIII

THE STRUGGLE FOR EQUAL LAWS

The Demand for Written Laws, I.—Decémvirs and the XII. Tables, II.—Second Secession and Its Results, III.

I. THE DEMAND FOR WRITTEN LAWS

Proposals of Terentílius Hársa (462 B.C.).—The conflict between the two orders had been going on for nearly fifty years; and yet no real solution had been found for their difficulties. The plebéians were at a great disadvantage during all this time, because the law was administered solely by the patricians, who kept the knowledge of it to themselves, and who regarded it as a precious legacy from their ancestors, too sacred to be shared with the lowborn plebéians. The laws had never been written down or published. The patricians could therefore administer them as they saw fit. This was a great injustice to the lower classes. It was clear that there was not much hope for the plebéians until they were made equal before the law. It was also clear that they could not be equal before the law as long as they themselves had no knowledge of what the law was. Accordingly one of the tríbunes, Gáius Terentílius Hársa, proposed that a commission be appointed to gather up the law, and to publish it to the whole people. This proposal, though both fair and just, was bitterly opposed by the patricians, and was followed by ten years of strife and dissension.

Concessions to the Plebéians.—To rescue the city from these troubles, the senate tried to conciliate the plebéians by making certain concessions to them. For example, the number of tríbunes was increased from two to five, and then to ten. This was supposed to give them greater protection than they had had before. Then it was decided to give up to them the public land on the Áventine hill, and thus to atone for not carrying out the agrarian law of Sp. Cássius. Finally, the amount of fine which any magistrate could impose was limited to two sheep and thirty oxen. It was thought that such concessions would appease the discontented people and divert their minds from the main point of the controversy.

Compromise between the Orders.—But these concessions did not satisfy the plebéians, who still clung to their demand for equal rights before the law. The struggle over the proposal of Terentílius, which lasted for nearly ten years, was ended only by a compromise. It was finally agreed that a commission of ten men, called decémvirs, should be appointed to draw up the law, and that this law should be published and be binding upon patricians and plebéians alike. It was also agreed that the commissioners should all be patricians; and that they should have entire control of the government while compiling the laws. The patricians were thus to give up their cónsuls and quǽstors; and the plebéians were to give up their tríbunes and ǽdiles. Both parties were to cease their quarreling, and await the work of the decémvirs.

II. DECÉMVIRS AND THE XII. TABLES

The Commission to Greece.—It is said that a commission of three men was sent to Greece, to consult the laws of Sólon and other Greek codes. However true this story may be, it is not likely that the Rómans intended to borrow the laws of another country by which to govern their own. The complaint of the plebéians was not that they did not have any laws, but that the laws which they had were unwritten and known only to the patricians. What they wanted was that the unwritten laws should be published; so that they could know what they were, and whether they were properly administered or not.

Formation of the XII. Tables (450 B.C.).—The first body of commissioners, or the First Decémvirate, entered upon the work assigned to it, gathered together the law which had hitherto been kept secret, and inscribed it on ten tables of brass. These tables were erected in the Fórum, where they could be seen by everyone, and were declared binding on all the people. At the close of the year, a Second Decémvirate was appointed to complete the code, and two more tables were added. This whole body of law was called the Twelve Tables, and formed the basis of the most remarkable system of law that the world has ever seen. There was nothing strange, however, in the XII. Tables themselves. They contained nothing especially new. The old law of debt remained as it was, and the distinction between patrícians and plebéians was not destroyed. The XII. Tables were important, because they put the law before the eyes of the people; and plebéians, as well as patricians, could know what were their rights. So highly valued was this code that it formed a part of Róman education, and the boys in school were obliged to commit it to memory.

Contents of the XII. Tables:

Table I.	Court and Trial Procedure
Table II.	Trials and Laws Governing Theft
Table III.	Laws Concerning Debt
Table IV.	Rights of the Father (*Paterfamílias*)
Table V.	Legal Guardianship and Inheritance
Table VI.	Acquisition and Possession
Table VII.	Land Rights and Crimes
Table VIII.	Laws of Injury (Torts and Delicts)
Table IX.	Public Law
Table X.	Sacred Law
Table XI.	First Supplement
Table XII.	Second Supplement

Tyranny of the Second Decémvirate.—Although the second body of decémvirs had the honor of completing the XII. Tables, the way in which they exercised their power brought them into dishonor. With all their professed love of equal laws, they still hated the plebéians and used their authority in an oppressive manner. They appeared in the Fórum each with twelve líctors, carrying the axes in the *fásces* as a sign that they claimed the power of life and death over every citizen. At the close of their year of office, they refused to resign, and continued their oppressive rule under the leadership of Áppius Cláudius. The story goes, whether true or not, that Áppius Cláudius attempted to gain possession of Vergínia, who was the beautiful daughter of a plebéian soldier, and who was killed by her own father to save her from dishonor. The repeated acts of tyranny committed by the second body of decémvirs at last made their rule intolerable.

III. SECOND SECESSION AND ITS RESULTS

Second Secession of the Plebs.—The tragic death of Vergínia, it is said, aroused the people to vengeance. With his bloody knife in hand, Vergínius rushed to the camp outside of the city and called upon the soldiers to resist the infamous power of the decémvirs. With the memory of the Sacred Mount still in mind, the army once more seceded from the city, and, followed by a multitude of citizens, took up their station again on this hill, determined no longer to fight in defense of tyranny. The Róman state seemed again on the point of ruin, and the decémvirs were forced to resign. The old government was restored. Two new cónsuls were elected, both of whom were friendly to the plebéians. These were Valérius and Horátius, names which the Róman people ever delighted to honor.

The Death of Vergínia, Heinrich Friedrich Füger (1751-1818), Staatsgalerie, Stuttgart

The Valério-Horátian Laws (448 B.C.).—The second secession of the plebéians resulted in the overthrow of the decémvirate and the restoration of the cónsulship; but it also resulted in making the plebéians more respected than they had been before. The patrícians were becoming more and more convinced that the plebéians were not only brave in fighting the enemies of Rome, but were also determined to defend their own liberties. The new cónsuls, Valérius and Horátius, came forward as their champions. Two of the rights of the people had been continually disregarded, namely, the right of appeal to the people, and the right of the tríbunes to be sacredly protected in the exercise of their duties. These two rights were now solemnly reaffirmed. But what was quite as important, the assembly of the plebéians (*concílium plébis*) was now given power to make laws binding upon the whole people. It is supposed that this assembly had by this time been reorganized and based upon the tribal districts so as to include the patrícians as well as the plebéians. This newly organized assembly came to be known as the *comítia tribúta*, and we shall see it grow in influence and dignity, until it becomes the most important assembly of the republic. These laws of Valérius and Horátius we may call the "second charter of Róman liberty."

The Right of Intermarriage.—The patrícians and plebéians had long lived side by side; but they had been kept socially distinct because it was not legal for them to intermarry. This prejudice was now passing away, as the plebéians were showing a spirit worthy of the patrícians themselves. A great step toward equalizing the classes was now taken by the passage of a law (*lex Canuléia*, 445 B.C.) which granted the right of intermarriage between the two orders. This insured their social and civil equality, and paved the way for their political equality, and finally their union into a harmonious people.

CHAPTER IX

THE STRUGGLE FOR POLITICAL EQUALITY

The Contest for the Cónsulship, I.—Wars with Véii and the Gauls, II.—The Equalization of the Orders, III.

I. THE CONTEST FOR THE CÓNSULSHIP

Successes of the Plebéians.—Never before had the cause of the plebéians seemed so hopeful as it did at this time. The tyranny of the decémvirs had brought to their aid the better class of patricians. And the passage of the recent laws led them to look forward to still greater victories. They had already gained great successes, but there was still something else for them to obtain, in order to have full equality in the state. We may, perhaps, better understand just what the plebéians had gained, and what was still to be gained, if we look at the following table, which contains a list of the various rights possessed by a full Róman citizen:

The Rights of Citizenship: (cívitas)	I. Public Rights: (iúra púbica)	1. Rights of Holding Office (honóres)
		2. Rights of Voting (suffrágium)
	II. Private Rights: (iúra priváta)	1. Rights of Intermarriage (conúbium)
		2. Rights of Property and Contract (commércium)

The plebéians already possessed the lowest right, the *commércium*; they could hold property and carry on trade just like any other Róman citizens. They had just now obtained the *conúbium*, or the right of contracting a legal marriage with a patrician. They had also the *suffrágium*, or the right of voting, in the assemblies of the centuries and of the tribes. As regards the *honóres*, or the right of holding office, they could be elected to the lower offices, that is, could be chosen tríbunes of the people and ædiles; but could not be elected to the higher offices, that is, could not be chosen cónsuls and quæstors. What the plebéians now wanted was a share in the higher offices, especially in the cónsulship.

The Military Tríbunes, with Cónsular Power (444 B.C.).—Instead of allowing the plebéians a direct share in the cónsulship, the patricians agreed to the appointment of certain new officers, something like the cónsuls, who could be elected from either the patricians or the plebéians. These new officers were called "military tríbunes with cónsular power," and were to be elected in the *comítia centuriáta*, where the plebéians as well as the patricians were allowed to vote. But it was also provided that cónsuls might still be elected instead of the new military tríbunes, if the senate thought such a course was best for the state. We can easily see how this plan would work. The patrícians, who had control of the senate, could decide at any time that cónsuls were needed; or else they might control the election and choose the military tríbunes from their own number. As a matter of fact, the senate, for some years after this, decided that cónsuls should be elected. But later the election of military tríbunes became the rule, and the plebéians gradually grew in political influence and power.

The Cénsorship and the New Quæstors.—As the patricians saw that the plebéians were growing stronger, they resorted to a new plan to keep as much power as possible in their own hands. To do this, they created another new office, the cénsorship (443 B.C.), and transferred to the two cénsors some of the most important powers hitherto exercised by the cónsuls. The cénsors were to draw up the cénsus, that is, to make an estimate of every man's property, to assign each man to a proper class in the cénturies, whether he belonged to the *équites* or the *pédites*, and to designate who was entitled to sit in the senate. The new cénsors were to be elected every five years, from the patrícian class. But to offset this advantage, the patricians agreed that there should be two new quǽstors (421 B.C.), to be elected from the plebéians. So it was that the period following the decémvirate was a period full of adroit schemes and compromises; but the plebéians were steadily gaining new rights and privileges.

The Fate of Spúrius Mǽlius.—That the patricians were not entirely reconciled to the growing influence of the plebéians, is shown by the story told of Sp. Mǽlius. While a severe famine was raging in Rome, and many poor citizens sought relief in suicide, Sp. Mǽlius, a wealthy plebéian, purchased grain at his own expense and distributed it to the suffering poor. His generosity so won the hearts of the people, that the patricians felt alarmed at his popularity, and charged him with the design of making himself king. It was claimed that secret meetings were held at his house, and that the republic was in danger. Hence a dictator was demanded. The aged Cincinnátus, who had rescued the beleaguered army at Mt. Álgidus, was selected; and Servílius Ahála was appointed his second in command, or master of horse. Mǽlius was then summoned to appear before the dictator, to answer the charge of treason. But foreseeing his danger, he implored the protection of the people; whereupon Servílius Ahála drew a dagger and stabbed him to the heart. The fate of Mǽlius at first terrified the people, but they were soon excited to vengeance, and Servílius was driven into exile. The name of Sp. Mǽlius was thus associated with that of Sp. Cássius, the author of the first agrarian law. These men were accused of aiming to be king; and both suffered death as the reward of their generous deeds.

II. WARS WITH VÉII AND THE GAULS

Recovery of Róman Territory.—The reforms which had been carried on since the fall of the decémvirs gave fresh hope to the plebéians, and inspired the whole Róman people with new life and vigor. The armies in the field also began to be successful, and Rome recovered much of her lost ground in Látium. The triple league formed by Spúrius Cássius between the Rómans, Látins, and Hérnicans, had resulted in checking the Vólscians and Ǽquians. The Rómans now felt encouraged to attack the Etrúscans in the hope of recovering the territory which they had lost years before, when the Tárquins were expelled. Fidénæ, the Etrúscan city a few miles north of Rome, was captured, and the way was opened to attack Véii, the strongest city of Etrúria.

Siege and Capture of Véii (405-396 B.C.).—The people of Véii were not disposed to meet the Rómans in the open field, but retreated within their walls. It therefore became necessary to lay siege to the city. The great Etrúscan walls were too strong to be taken by assault; and the Róman armies stationed themselves around the city for the purpose of starving the people into submission. The Róman soldiers were not permitted to return home and cultivate their farms, as they were wont to do; and so, for the first time, they were given regular pay for their services. For ten years the siege continued, when it was brought to a close by Camíllus, who was appointed dictator. Véii was deprived of its inhabitants, and its walls enclosed a vacant city. The capture of Véii was the greatest victory which the Rómans had yet achieved, and Camíllus was given a splendid triumph, when he returned to Rome. The lands of southern Etrúria also fell into the hands of the Rómans; and four new rural tribes were added to the Róman domain.

Destruction of Rome by the Gauls (390 B.C.).—If the capture of Véii was the greatest victory which the Rómans had ever achieved, we now approach one of the greatest disasters which they ever suffered. One reason why Rome was able to capture Véii was the fact that the great body of the Etrúscans were obliged to face a new enemy on the northern frontier, an enemy whom they feared more than the Rómans on the south. This enemy was the Gauls, the barbarous nation which held the valley of the Po, and which now swept south across the Ápennines like a hurricane. News of this invasion reached Rome, and it was resolved to aid the Etrúscans in repelling the common foe. The Róman army met the Gauls near the little river Állia, about eleven miles north of Rome, and suffered a terrible defeat. The Gauls pressed on to Rome. They entered, plundered, and burned the city. Only the Cápitol remained. This was besieged for seven months, and, according to the legend, was at one time saved by M. Mánlius, who was aroused by the cackling of the sacred geese just in time to resist a night assault. At last the Gauls, sated with plunder, and induced by a large bribe, retreated unmolested or, as one legend says, were driven from the city by Camíllus, the hero of the Véientine war. The destruction of Rome by the Gauls was a great disaster, not only to Rome, but to all the world; because in it the records of the ancient city perished, leaving many things in the early history of ancient Rome dark and obscure.

Camíllus Rescuing Rome from Brénnus (1716), Sebastiano Ricci (1659-1734), Detroit Institute of Arts

The Restoration of Rome.—Such a disastrous event as the Gállic invasion would have disheartened almost any other people; but Rome bent before the storm and soon recovered after the tempest was past. Many of the people desired to abandon the city of ashes, and transfer their homes to the vacant town of Véii. But it was decided that Rome was the place for Rómans. The city rose so quickly from its ruins that little care was taken in the work of rebuilding, so that the new streets were often narrow and irregular.

The Rómans seemed to be in haste to resume the work of extending their power, which had been so favorably begun with the conquest of Véii, but which had been interrupted by the defeat on the Állia. Rome raised new armies and quickly defeated her old enemies, the Vólscians, Æquians, and Etrúscans, who tried to take advantage of her present distress. The hero Camíllus added fresh laurels to his fame. The southern part of Etrúria was recovered, and its towns garrisoned by military colonies. Many towns of Látium also were brought into subjection, and

35

they afforded homes for the poor people. Rome seemed almost ready to enter upon a career of conquest; but the recurrence of poverty and distress demanded the attention of the government, and showed the need of further reforms.

The Triumph of Fúrius Camíllus (1545), Fresco by Francesco Salviati (1510-1563), Palazzo Vechio, Florence

III. THE EQUALIZATION OF THE ORDERS

Desire for Union.—It became more and more evident that the power of Rome depended upon the union of her people; that harmony, and not discord, was the source of her strength. The two orders had begun to feel that their interests were one and the same. There had been of late little severity in the application of the law of debt; there had been a disposition even to give the plebéians some right in the conquered land; and some progress had been made in opening to them the public offices. But the great loss of property and the devastation resulting from the Gállic invasion were sorely felt by the poorer classes, and led once more to a general state of poverty and distress. The old grievances were revived, and a new set of reformers appeared.

The Attempt of M. Mánlius.—The first attempt to relieve the distress of the poor was that of Márcus Mánlius, the defender of the Cápitol. It is said that he rescued more than four hundred of his fellow-citizens from imprisonment by lending them money without interest. He sold his estates and devoted the proceeds to the relief of debtors. But from being a philanthropist, Mánlius soon became a social agitator, and by his harangues sought to inflame the people against the government. The patrícians therefore sought to crush him. He was charged with conspiracy against the state, and was finally condemned to death. Although his motives and methods were not above reproach, his admirers placed him by the side of Sp. Cássius and Sp. Mǽlius as a friend of the people who was unjustly condemned on the charge of aspiring to be king.

36

The Licínian Laws (367 B.C.).—The continuation of distress among the lower classes showed how useless it was to try to abolish poverty by mere acts of charity, or by exciting the populace. A more thorough mode of reform was adopted under the able leadership of the two tríbunes, C. Licínius Stólo and L. Séxtius. These men were able and broad-minded statesmen. It was not mere relief, but reformation, which they sought.

In the first place, they saw that some relief must be given to the helpless debtor class. But instead of confiscating all debts, they proposed that the interest already paid upon debts should be deducted from the principal; and that for the payment of the rest of the principal three years' time should be allowed.

In the next place, they saw that some definite regulation should be made in the distribution of the public land, which by right belonged to the plebéians as well as to the patrícians. They therefore provided that the occupation of the public land should be thrown open equally to all classes; that no person should receive and hold more than five hundred iúgera (about three hundred acres); and that the number of slaves employed on estates should be limited, thus giving an opportunity for the poor freemen to earn something for themselves.

Finally, they saw that the plebéians could not receive full justice until they were admitted to the highest offices of the state. They provided that the new "military tríbunate" should be done away with, and that cónsuls should hereafter always be elected, one of whom must be a plebéian.

It was natural that such an important scheme of legislation as this should meet with much opposition, but after a few years of strife, these proposals became laws. This noble body of law may be called the "third charter of Róman liberty."

The Prætor and Cúrule Ædiles.—The patricians were yet loath to lose everything; and so the judicial power was taken away from the cónsuls and given to a new officer, called the prætor (367 B.C.), who must still be a patrícian; also it was provided that there should be two patrícian ædiles (called cúrule ædiles), to police the city, and to offset the plebéian ædiles. Although complete equality was not even yet reached, the struggle was practically ended; and the great Camíllus, who had been appointed dictator and had done much to reconcile the people, consecrated a temple to Concord.

Final Equality of the Orders.—After the passage of the Licínian laws, there were a few offices which still remained in the possession of the patrícians. These were the dictatorship, the cénsorship, the prætorship, and the cúrule ædileship. But it was not many years before these offices also were open to the plebéians, and the last barrier between the two orders was thus broken down. There was then no longer any civil or political distinction between the patrícian and the plebéian. The old Róman aristocracy, which depended upon family relationship, passed away with the Licínian legislation and the laws which soon followed it. The union of patrícians and plebéians into one compact body of citizens was a triumph for Rome greater than the conquest of Véii, or any other foreign victory. By it she conquered herself. She destroyed for a time the elements of discord within her own borders, and prepared herself to become the ruler of the world.

CHAPTER X

THE CONQUEST OF LÁTIUM

Beginning of the Róman Conquest, I.—The Great Látin War (340-338 B.C.), II.—The Pacification of Látium, III.

I. BEGINNING OF THE RÓMAN CONQUEST

Character of the New Period.—The next period of Róman history is that in which Rome began her great career of conquest, in which she extended her dominion from the banks of the Tíber to the shores of the Itálian peninsula. We are now to see how Rome became the great conquering nation of the world. The years which lie before us are therefore years which are filled with the clash of arms and the stories of battles. But they are also years in which Rome learned new lessons of government and law; and in which she came into contact with more civilized peoples, and became herself more civilized.

Róman Territory about the Tíber.—To understand the course of the Róman conquests, we should first keep in mind the extent of her territory at the beginning of this period. Much of the land about the Tíber, which she had lost with the expulsion of the kings, she had gradually recovered. So that now her territory included lands not only in Látium, but also in Etrúria toward the north, and in the Vólscian country toward the south. The Róman territory at the beginning of this period was not large, but it was compact and well organized into twenty-seven local tribes, twenty-three in the country and four in the city. The most formidable and dangerous neighbors of Rome at this time were the Etrúscans on the north and the Sámnites on the south.

The First Sámnite War in Campánia (343-341 B.C.).—In extending their territory, the Rómans first came into contact with the Sámnites, the most warlike people of central Ítaly. But the first Sámnite war was, as we shall see, scarcely more than a prelude to the great Látin war and the conquest of Látium. The people of Sámnium had from their mountain home spread to the southwest into the plains of Campánia. They had already taken Cápua from the Etrúscans, and Cúmæ from the Greeks. Enamored with the soft climate of the plains and the refined manners of the Greeks, the Sámnites in Campánia had lost their primitive valor, and had become estranged from the old Sámnite stock. In a quarrel which broke out between the old Sámnites of the mountains and the Campánians, the latter appealed to Rome for help, and promised to become loyal Róman subjects. Although Rome had previously made a treaty with the Sámnites, she did not hesitate to break this treaty, professing that she was under greater obligations to her new subjects than to her old allies. In this way began the first contest between Rome and Sámnium for supremacy in central Ítaly, a contest which took place on the plains of Campánia.

Battles of Mt. Gáurus and Suéssula.—Very little is known of the details of this war. According to a tradition, which is not very trustworthy, two Róman armies were sent into the field, the one for the protection of Campánia, and the other for the invasion of

Sámnium. The first army, it is said, met the Sámnites at Mt. Gáurus, near Cúmæ, and gained a decisive victory. The Sámnites retreated toward the mountains, and rallied at Suéssula, where they were again defeated by the two Róman armies, which had united against them. So brilliant was the success of the Rómans that the Carthagínians, it is said, sent to them a congratulatory message and a golden crown. Although these stories may not be entirely true, it is quite certain that the Rómans obtained control of the northern part of Campánia.

Mutiny of the Róman Légions.—This success, however, was marred by a mutiny of the Róman soldiers, who were stationed at Cápua for the winter, and who threatened to take possession of the city as a reward for their services. They submitted only on the passage of a solemn law declaring that every soldier should have a just share in the fruits of war, regular pay, and a part of the booty; and that no soldier should be discharged against his will.

Rome withdraws from the War.—The discontent of the soldiers in the field soon spread to the Látin allies. The Látins had assisted the Rómans and had taken a prominent part in the war; and while the Róman army was in a state of mutiny, they were the chief defenders of Campánia against the Sámnites. The Campánians, therefore, began to look to the Látins instead of the Rómans, for protection; and they too shared in the general defection against Rome. Under these circumstances, Rome saw the need of subduing her own allies before undertaking a war with a foreign enemy. She therefore made a treaty with the Sámnites, withdrew from the war, and prepared for the conquest of Látium.

II. THE GREAT LÁTIN WAR (340-338 B.C.)

The Demands of the Látins.—The relations between Rome and the Látin cities had been different at different times. In very early times, we remember, Rome was at the head of the Látin confederacy. Later she was united to the Látin league by a treaty of equal alliance, formed by Sp. Cássius. This treaty had been dissolved, and was afterward renewed. But the Látins believed that Rome wished to resume her old position as head of Látium; and this they were not willing to permit. They therefore decided that the time had now come to demand absolute equality with Rome; and if this were refused, to declare their independence. They at first sent an embassy to Rome, demanding that Rómans and Látins should be united in one republic, on terms of perfect equality, and that one cónsul and half of the senate be chosen from the Látins. This proposal was scornfully rejected. One senator, Mánlius, declared that he would stab the first Látin who was admitted to the senate. Meeting with such a rebuff, the Látins renounced their allegiance to the "Róman Júpiter" and commenced their war for independence.

The Parties to the War.—When Rome withdrew from the first Sámnite war, and formed a treaty with Sámnium, the Látins continued to fight in behalf of the Campánians. The Látins and Campánians, therefore, continued their friendly relations, and became the common enemies of Rome and Sámnium. By such a curious turn of fortune, Rome was able to fight her previous allies, the Látins, with the aid of her previous enemy, the Sámnites.

Battle of Mt. Vesúvius and the Defeat of the Látins.—As Látium was now a hostile country, the Róman armies, under Mánlius Torquátus and Décius Mus, were obliged to march around the northeastern boundaries of Látium, to join the Sámnite forces. When they had formed a union in Sámnium, they invaded Campánia. They soon gained a decisive victory near Mt. Vesúvius. Driven from Campánia, the Látins continued the war with resolute courage, but without avail. Tíbur, Prænéste, Arícia, Lanúvium, Velítræ, and Ántium were conquered in succession; and in the third year the last city, Pédum, also surrendered, and the Látin revolt was at an end.

Stories of Mánlius and Décius.—There are two famous stories which are told in connection with this war, and which illustrate two traits of the Róman character: stern authority and patriotic devotion. The first story is told of Títus Mánlius, the son of the cónsul commanding the army. The young Mánlius, contrary to his father's orders, left the ranks to fight a single combat with one of the enemy's champions. The enemy was slain, and Mánlius carried the spoils in triumph to his father. But the father, instead of congratulating his son on his success, condemned him to death for disobedience of orders. From this time the "Mánlian orders" became a synonym for the severest discipline. The other story is told of Décius Mus, the cónsul, who, in response to a vision, sacrificed his own life that the Róman army might prevail.

III. THE PACIFICATION OF LÁTIUM

Rome's Policy of Pacification.—The chief result of the great Látin war was the breaking up of the Látin confederacy, and the adoption of a more efficient method of governing the Látin towns. The repeated revolts of the Látins had shown the danger of dealing with a number of towns united in a league, or confederacy. The only safety seemed to lie in destroying the league and dealing with each city by itself. This was the Róman policy of *isolation*. It was also evident that all the cities were not equally fit to exercise the right of Róman citizenship; and upon this was based the distinction between perfect and imperfect citizenship. The subject towns of Látium and those of Campánia were thus treated in various ways.

Towns fully Incorporated.—In the first place, many of the towns of Látium were fully adopted into the Róman state. Their inhabitants became full Róman citizens, with all the private and public rights, comprising the right to trade and intermarry with Rómans, the right to vote in the assemblies at Rome, and the right to hold any public office. Their lands became a part of the Róman domain. The ncw territory was organized into two new tribes, making now the total number twenty-nine.

Towns partly Incorporated.—But most of the towns of Látium. received only a part of the rights of citizenship. To their inhabitants were given the right to trade and the right to intermarry with Róman citizens, but not the right to vote or to hold office. This imperfect, or qualified, citizenship (which had before been given to the town of Cære) now became known as the "Látin right."

Látin and Róman Colonies.—In order to keep in subjection a refractory town, or to form an outpost on the frontier, it was customary to send out a body of citizen soldiers, who occupied the town. These were known as military, or Látin, colonies, and were made up of persons who possessed the Látin right. At the same time Rome established on the seacoast maritime, or Róman, colonies, as they were called, composed entirely of full Róman citizens.

Dependent Allies.—There were certain other towns which were not incorporated with Rome at all. They were allowed to retain their local government, but were compelled to make a treaty, by which they were obliged to cede their public lands to Rome, and to lend their support in time of war.

This wise method of treating the various subject communities cemented more closely the Látin cities to Rome; and was the beginning of an important policy, which was more fully carried out in the subsequent organization of Ítaly and of the Mediterránean world.

40

CHAPTER XI

THE CONQUEST OF CENTRAL ÍTALY

The Second Sámnite War (326-304 B.C.), I.—The Third Sámnite War (298-290 B.C.), II.
Results of the Sámnite Wars, III.

I. THE SECOND SÁMNITE WAR (326-304 B.C.)

Renewal of the Struggle for Central Ítaly.—The question as to who should be supreme in central Ítaly, Rome or Sámnium, was not yet decided. The first struggle had been interrupted by the Látin war; and a twelve years' peace followed. The Sámnites saw that Rome was becoming stronger and stronger. But they could not prevent this, because they themselves were threatened in the south by a new enemy. Alexánder of Epírus, the uncle of Alexánder the Great, had invaded Ítaly to aid the people of Taréntum, and also with the hope of building up a new empire in the West. Rome also regarded Alexánder as a possible enemy, and hastened to make a treaty with him against the Sámnites. But the death of Alexánder left the Tárentines to shift for themselves, and left the Sámnites free to use their whole force against Rome in the decisive struggle now to come for the mastery of central Ítaly.

Cause of the War again in Campánia.—The direct cause of the second Sámnite war, like that of the first, grew out of troubles in Campánia. Here were situated the twin cities of Palæpolis (the old city) and Neápolis (the new city), which were still in the hands of the Greeks, but under the protection of the Sámnites. Many disputes arose between the people of these cities and the Róman settlers in Campánia. Palæpolis appealed to the Sámnites for help, and a strong garrison was given to it. The Rómans demanded that this garrison should be withdrawn. The Sámnites refused. The Rómans then declared war and laid siege to Palæpolis, which was soon captured by Q. Publílius Phílo.

The Rómans Passing Under the Yoke (1858)
Marc-Charles-Gabriel Gleyre, (1806-1874)
Musée Cantonal des Beaux-Arts de Lausanne

Battle at the Cáudine Forks (321 B.C.).—In the early part of the war the Rómans were nearly everywhere successful. They formed alliances with the Apúlians and Lucánians on the south, and they also took the strong city of Lucéria in Apúlia; so that the Sámnites were surrounded by the Róman army and their allies. But in spite of these successes, the great Sámnite general, Póntius, inflicted upon the Rómans one of the most humiliating defeats that they ever suffered. The Róman cónsuls in Campánia, deceived by the false report that Lucéria was besieged by the whole Sámnite force, decided to hasten to its relief by going directly through the heart of the Sámnite territory. In passing through a defile in the mountains near Cáudium, called the "Cáudine Forks," the whole Róman force was entrapped by Póntius and obliged to surrender. The army was compelled to pass under the yoke; and the cónsuls were forced to make a treaty, yielding up all the territory conquered from the Sámnites. But the Róman senate refused to ratify this treaty, and delivered up the offending cónsuls to the Sámnites. Póntius, however, refused to accept the cónsuls as a compensation for the broken treaty; and demanded that the treaty should be kept, or else that the whole Róman army should be returned to the Cáudine Forks, where they had surrendered. Rome refused to do either, and the war was continued.

Uprising of the Etrúscans.—After breaking this treaty and recovering her army, Rome looked forward to immediate success. But in this she was disappointed. Everything seemed now turning against her. The cities in Campánia revolted, the Sámnites conquered Lucéria in Apúlia and Fregéllæ on the Líris, and gained an important victory in the south of Látium near Ánxur. To add to her troubles, the Etrúscans came to the aid of the Sámnites and attacked the Róman garrison at Sútrium. The hostile attitude of the Etrúscans aroused Rome to new vigor. Under the leadership of Q. Fábius Máximus Rulliánus, the tide was turned in her favor. Many victories were gained over the Etrúscans, closing with the decisive battle at Lake Vadimónis, and the submission of Etrúria to Rome.

Capture of Boviánum and End of the War.—Rome now made desperate efforts to recover her losses in the south. Under the cónsul L. Papírius Cúrsor, who was afterward appointed dictator, the Rómans recaptured Lucéria and Fregéllæ. The Sámnites were defeated at Cápua and driven out of Campánia. The war was then carried into Sámnium, and her chief city, Boviánum, was captured. This destroyed the last hope of the Sámnites. They sued for peace and were obliged to give up all their conquests and to enter into an alliance with Rome.

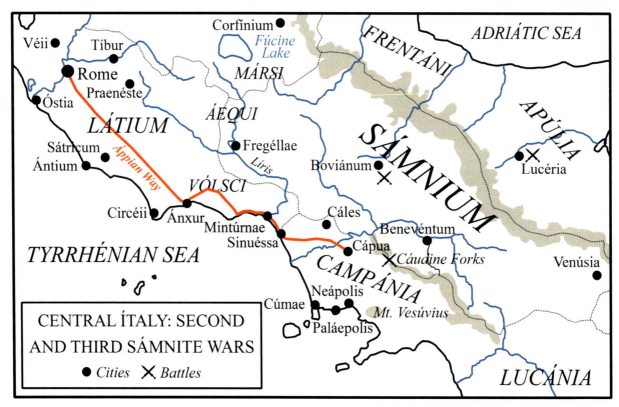

II. THE THIRD SÁMNITE WAR (298-290 B.C.)

The Itálian Coalition against Rome.—Although Rome was successful in the previous war, it required one more conflict to secure her supremacy in central Ítaly. This war is known as the third Sámnite war, but it was in fact a war between Rome and the principal nations of Ítaly: the Sámnites, the Úmbrians, the Etrúscans, and the Gauls. The Itálians saw that either Rome must be subdued, or else all Ítaly would be ruled by the city on the Tíber. This was really a war for Itálian independence.

Cause of the War in Lucánia.—Rome and Sámnium both saw the need of strengthening themselves for the coming conflict. Rome could depend upon the Látins, the Vólscians, and the Campánians in the south. She also brought under her power the Æquians and the Mársians on the east. So that all her forces were compact and well in hand. The Sámnites, on the contrary, were obliged to depend upon forces which were scattered from one end of the peninsula to the other. They determined first to win over to their side the Lucánians, who were their nearest neighbors on the south, but who had been the allies of Rome in the previous war. This attempt of the Sámnites to get control of Lucánia led to the declaration of war by Rome.

Sámnite Soldiers from Frieze at Nóla
(4th Century B.C.)

The War carried into Etrúria.—The Sámnites now made the most heroic efforts to destroy their hated rival. Three armies were placed in the field, one to defend Sámnium, one to invade Campánia, and the third to march into Etrúria. This last army was expected to join the Úmbrians, the Etrúscans, and the Gauls, and to attack Rome from the north. This was a bold plan, and alarmed the city. Business was stopped, and all Róman citizens were called to arms. The Róman forces moved into Etrúria under the cónsuls Q. Fábius Rulliánus and Décius Mus, the son of the hero who sacrificed himself in the battle at Mt. Vesúvius. The hostile armies were soon scattered, and the Sámnites and Gauls retreated across the Ápennines to Sentínum.

Battle of Sentínum (295 B.C.).—Upon the famous field of Sentínum was decided the fate of Ítaly. Fábius was opposed to the Sámnites on the right wing; and Décius Mus was opposed to the Gauls on the left. Fábius held his ground; but the Róman left wing under Décius was driven back by the terrible charge of the Gállic war chariots. Décius, remembering his father's example, devoted himself to death, and the Róman line was restored. The battle was decided in favor of the Rómans; and the hope of a united Ítaly under the leadership of Sámnium was destroyed.

End of the Itálian Coalition.—After the great battle of Sentínum, the Gauls dispersed; Úmbria ceased its resistance; and the Etrúscans made their peace in the following year. But the Sámnites continued the hopeless struggle in their own land. They were at last compelled to submit to Cúrius Dentátus, and to make peace with Rome. Another attempt to form a coalition against Rome, led by the Lucánians, failed; and Rome was left to organize her new possessions.

The Consecration of Décius Mus (1616-1617)
Peter Paul Rubens (1577-1640), Liechtenstein Museum, Vienna

III. RESULTS OF THE SÁMNITE WARS

Rome's Position in Central Ítaly.—The great result of the Sámnite wars was to give Rome the controlling position in central Ítaly. The Sámnites were allowed to retain their own territory and their political independence. But they were compelled to give up all disputed land, and to become the subject allies of Rome. The Sámnites were a brave people and fought many desperate battles; but they lacked the organizing skill and resources of the Rómans. In this great struggle for supremacy Rome succeeded on account of her persistence and her great fortitude in times of danger and disaster; but more than all else, on account of her wonderful ability to unite the forces under her control.

Increase of the Róman Territory.—As a result of these wars, the Róman territory was extended in two directions. On the west side of the peninsula, the greater part of Campánia was brought into the Róman domain; and the Lucánians became the subject allies of Rome. On the east side the Sábines were incorporated with Rome, receiving the partial right of citizenship, which in a few years was extended to full citizenship. Úmbria was also subdued. The Róman domain now stretched across the Itálian peninsula from sea to sea. The inhabitants of Picénum and Apúlia also became subject allies.

The New Colonies.—In accordance with her usual policy, Rome secured herself by the establishment of new colonies. Two of these were established on the west side, one at Mintúrnæ at the mouth of the Líris River, and the other at Sinuéssa in Campánia. In the south a colony was placed at Venúsia, which was the most powerful garrison that Rome had ever established, up to this time. It was made up of twenty thousand Látin citizens, and was so situated as to cut off the connection between Sámnium and Taréntum.

44

CHAPTER XII

THE CONQUEST OF SOUTHERN ÍTALY

Rupture between Rome and Taréntum, I.—War with Pýrrhus (280-275 B.C.), II.—Final Reduction of Ítaly, III.

I. RUPTURE BETWEEN ROME AND TARÉNTUM

Greek Cities in Southern Ítaly.—All the peninsular portion of Ítaly was now under the practical dominion of Rome, except the Greek cities in the south. These cities were the centers of Greek art and culture. Situated upon the coast, they had engaged in commerce, and on account of their wealth they were subject to the depredations of their less civilized neighbors, the Lucánians and Brúttians. With no great capacity for organization, they were accustomed, when assailed, to appeal to some stronger power for help. They had sometimes looked to Greek princes, as in the case of Alexánder of Epírus. But now, when Thúrii was threatened by the Lucánians, this city threw itself upon the mercy of Rome. Rome promptly interfered, and placed garrisons not only in Thúrii, but also in other cities along the coast, as Cróton, Lócri, and Rhégium.

Rome and Taréntum.—The most important of the Greek cities of Ítaly was Taréntum. This city was now alarmed at the rapid advances made by Rome on the southern coast. Hemmed in on all sides by the Róman outposts, Taréntum found it necessary to decide whether she should open her gates to Rome, or maintain her independence with the aid of some Greek ally. She had already a commercial treaty with Rome, which prevented the ships of the latter power from passing the Lacínian promontory. But this treaty would not prevent the Róman armies from threatening the city by land.

Cause of the Rupture.—While this question was yet undecided, a Róman war fleet, on its way to the coast of Úmbria, anchored in the harbor of Taréntum. The people were angered by this breach of the treaty, and immediately attacked the fleet. Five of the Róman vessels were captured, and the crews were either put to death or sold into slavery. A Róman embassy which was sent to Taréntum to demand reparation was grossly insulted. The Rómans thereupon declared war, and sent an army to subdue the insolent city.

Pýrrhus of Epírus, Museo Archeologico Nazionale, Náples

Taréntum calls upon Pýrrhus.—There was now but one course open to the people of Taréntum, and that was to appeal to Greece for protection. Pýrrhus was at this time king of Epírus. He was a brilliant and ambitious leader, and aspired to found an empire in the West. When Taréntum appealed to him for help, he was ready not only to aid this city, but to rescue all the Greek cities of Ítaly from Rome, and also all the cities of Sícily from the power of Cárthage. The war which the Rómans began against Taréntum was thus turned into a war against Pýrrhus, who was the ablest general of his time.

Pýrrhus lands in Ítaly.—Pýrrhus landed in Ítaly, bringing with him a mercenary army raised in different parts of Greece, consisting of twenty-five thousand men and twenty elephants. Taréntum was placed under the strictest military discipline. Rome, on her part, made the greatest preparations to meet the invader. Her garrisons were strengthened. One army was sent into Etrúria, to prevent an uprising in the north; and the main army, under the cónsul Valérius Lævínus, was sent to southern Ítaly.

Battle of Heacléa (B. C. 280).—The first battle between the Itálian and Greek soldiers occurred at Heacléa, not far from Taréntum. It was here that the Róman légion first came into contact with the Macedónian phálanx. The légion was drawn up in three separate lines, in open order; and the soldiers, after hurling the javelins, fought at close quarters with the sword. The phálanx, on the other hand, was a solid mass of soldiers in close order, with their shields touching, and twenty or thirty ranks deep. Its weapon was a long spear, so long that the points of the first five ranks all projected in front of the first rank. Pýrrhus selected his ground on the open plain. Seven times the Róman légions charged against his unbroken phálanxes. After the Róman attack was exhausted, Pýrrhus turned his elephants upon the Róman cavalry, which fled in confusion, followed by the rest of the Róman army. The Rómans, though defeated in this battle, displayed wonderful courage and discipline, so that Pýrrhus exclaimed, "With such an army I could conquer the world!"

Embassy of Cíneas.—The great losses which Pyrrhus suffered convinced him that the Rómans could not be conquered with the forces which he had under his command; and that he had better turn his attention to the Carthagínians in Sícily. He therefore resolved to use his victory as a means of obtaining an honorable peace with the Rómans. His most trusted minister, Cíneas, who is said to have conquered more nations with his tongue than Pýrrhus had with his sword, was sent to Rome with the proposal to make peace, on condition that the Rómans should relinquish their conquests in southern Ítaly. So persuasive were the words of Cíneas, that the Róman senate seemed ready to consider his offer. But the charm of his speech was broken by the stern eloquence of Áppius Cláudius, the blind old cénsor, who called upon the senate never to make peace with an enemy on Róman soil. Failing in his mission, Cíneas returned to his master with the report that the Róman senate was "an assembly of kings." To give force to the claims of Cíneas, Pýrrhus had pushed his army into Campánia, and even into Látium; but finding the cities loyal to Rome, he withdrew again to Taréntum.

Áppius Cláudius Entering the Senate, Cesare Maccari (1840-1919), Villa Madama, Rome

Battle of Ásculum (279 B.C.).—In southern Ítaly, Pýrrhus received the support of the Greek cities, of the Brúttians, the Lucánians, and even the Sámnites. In the next year he marched into Apúlia, in the direction of the Róman stronghold Lucéria. The hostile armies met at Ásculum, a few miles south of Lucéria. The battle of Ásculum was a repetition of Heracléa. The Róman légions charged in vain against the Greek phálanxes; and were then routed by the elephants, which they could not withstand. But again, although the Rómans were defeated, the great losses of Pýrrhus prevented him from following up his victory.

Coin of Pýrrhus
Kóre (obverse), Athéna Álkis (reverse)

Pýrrhus in Sícily (278-276 B.C.).—Pýrrhus resolved to turn his back upon Ítaly, where his victories had been so barren, and go to the rescue of the Greek cities in Sícily, which were subject to Cárthage. Leaving his general, Mílo, at Taréntum, he crossed over to Sýracuse, and gained many victories over the Carthagínians. He drove them to their stronghold in Lilybǽum, at the western extremity of the island; but this city he failed to capture. He then called upon the people of Sícily to build a fleet, but they murmured at his severe command. Believing that such a people was unworthy of his aid, he returned to Taréntum. In the meantime the Rómans had recovered nearly all their lost ground in southern Ítaly.

Battle of Benevéntum and Departure of Pýrrhus (275 B.C.).—Before abandoning Ítaly, Pýrrhus determined once more to try the fortunes of war. One of the cónsular armies, under Cúrius Dentátus, lay in a strong position near Benevéntum in the hilly regions of Sámnium. Pýrrhus resolved to attack this army before it could be reinforced. He stormed the Róman position, and was repulsed. The Róman cónsul then pursued him to the plains and gained a complete victory. Baffled and disappointed, Pýrrhus retreated to Taréntum; and leaving a garrison in that city under his lieutenant, Mílo, he led the remnants of his army back to Greece.

MÁGNA GRÁECIA: WAR WITH PÝRRHUS

47

III. FINAL REDUCTION OF ÍTALY

Fall of Taréntum (272 B.C.).—After the departure of Pýrrhus, Rome had no real rival left in Ítaly. The complete reduction of the peninsula speedily followed. Taréntum was besieged, and after a stubborn resistance of four years, Mílo agreed to surrender, on condition of being allowed to withdraw his garrison to Epírus (272 B.C.). The city was allowed to retain its local government, but was obliged to pay an annual tribute to Rome.

The Lucánians, Brúttians, and Sámnites.—Some of the people in the south of Ítaly were still loath to accept the supremacy of Rome, and kept up a kind of guerrilla warfare for some time. But the Lucánians and Brúttians were soon obliged to submit, and all the cities on the coast finally came under the Róman power. A temporary revolt of the Sámnites was also crushed. The Róman power in the south was secured by strong colonies, planted at Pæstum in Lucánia (273 B.C.) and at Benevéntum in Sámnium (268 B.C.).

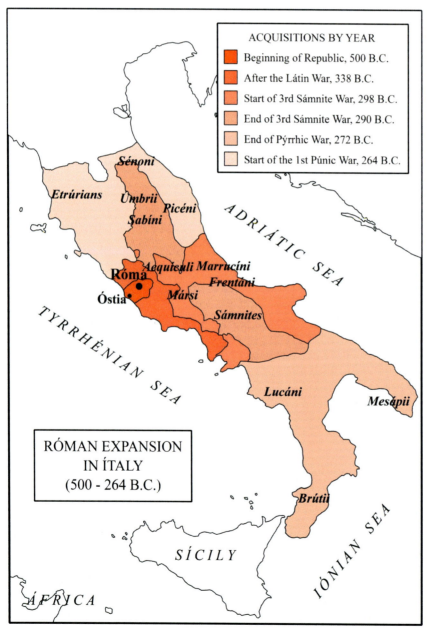

ACQUISITIONS BY YEAR
Beginning of Republic, 500 B.C.
After the Látin War, 338 B.C.
Start of 3rd Sámnite War, 298 B.C.
End of 3rd Sámnite War, 290 B.C.
End of Pýrrhic War, 272 B.C.
Start of the 1st Púnic War, 264 B.C.

RÓMAN EXPANSION IN ÍTALY (500 - 264 B.C.)

Picénum and Úmbria.—With the south pacified, Rome soon brought into submission the Itálian remnants on the eastern coast. The chief city of Picénum, Ancóna, was taken by storm (268 B.C.), and the whole country was reduced. Farther to the north, the chief city of Úmbria, Aríminum, was also taken (266 B.C.), and the territory yielded to Rome.

Reduction of Etrúria.—A spirit of defection still existed in some parts of Etrúria. The most haughty of the Etrúscan cities was Volsínii, which was selected as an example. Its walls were razed to the ground, and its works of art were transferred to Rome. After the fall of this city, all the other towns not already allied to Rome were willing to submit; and Rome ruled supreme from the Rúbicon and Mácra to the Sicílian strait.

48

CHAPTER XIII

SUPREMACY OF ROME IN ÍTALY

The Sovereign Róman State, I.—The Subject Communities, II.—The Military System, III.

I. THE SOVEREIGN RÓMAN STATE

The Sovereign and Subject Communities.—To understand properly the history of Rome, we must study not only the way in which she conquered her territory, but also the way in which she organized and governed it. The study of her wars and battles is less important than the study of her policy. Rome was always learning lessons in the art of government. As she grew in power, she also grew in political wisdom. With every extension of her territory, she was obliged to extend her authority as a sovereign power. If we would comprehend the political system which grew up in Ítaly, we must keep clearly in mind the distinction between the people who made up the sovereign body of the state, and the people who made up the subject communities of Ítaly. Just as in early times we saw two distinct bodies, the patrícian body, which ruled the state, and the plebéian body, which was subject to the state; so now we shall see, on the one hand, a ruling body of citizens, who lived in and outside the city upon the Róman domain (*áger Románus*), and on the other hand, a subject body of people, living in towns and cities throughout the rest of Ítaly. In other words, we shall see a part of the territory and people incorporated into the state, and another part unincorporated, the one a sovereign community, and the other comprising a number of subject communities.

Extent of the Róman Domain.—The Róman domain proper, or the *áger Románus*, was that part of the territory in which the people became incorporated into the state, and were admitted to the rights of citizenship. It was the sovereign domain of the Róman people. This domain land, or incorporated territory, had been gradually growing while the conquest of Ítaly was going on. It now included, speaking generally, the most of Látium, northern Campánia, southern Etrúria, the Sábine country, Picénum, and a part of Úmbria. There were a few towns within this area, like Tíbur and Prænéste, which were not incorporated, and hence not a part of the domain land, but retained the position of subject allies.

The Thirty-three Tribes.—Within the Róman domain were the local tribes, which had now increased in number to thirty-three. They included four urban tribes, that is, the wards of the city, and twenty-nine rural tribes, which were like townships in the country. All the persons who lived in these tribal districts and were enrolled, formed a part of the sovereign body of the Róman people, that is, they had a share in the government, in making the laws, and in electing the magistrates.

The Róman Colonies.—The colonies of citizens sent out by Rome were allowed to retain all their rights of citizenship, being permitted even to come to Rome at any time to vote and help make the laws. These colonies of Róman citizens thus formed a part of the sovereign state; and their territory, wherever it might be situated, was regarded as a part of the áger Románus. Such were the colonies along the seacoast, the most important of which were situated on the shores of Látium and of adjoining lands.

The Róman Municípia.—Rome incorporated into her territory some of the conquered towns under the name of *municípia*, which possessed all the burdens and some of the rights of citizenship. At first, such towns (like Cære) received the private but not the public rights (*cívitas síne suffrágio*) and the towns might govern themselves or be governed by a prefect sent from Rome. In time, however, the municípia obtained not only local self-government but also full Róman citizenship; and this arrangement was the basis of the Róman municipal system of later times.

II. THE SUBJECT COMMUNITIES

The Subject Territory.—Over against this sovereign body of citizens living upon the *áger Románus*, were the subject communities scattered throughout the length and breadth of the peninsula. The inhabitants of this territory had no share in the Róman government. Neither could they declare war, make peace, form alliances, or coin money, without the consent of Rome. Although they might have many privileges given to them, and might govern themselves in their own cities, they formed no part of the sovereign body of the Róman people.

The Látin Colonies.—One part of the subject communities of Ítaly comprised the Látin colonies. These were the military garrisons which Rome sent out to hold in subjection a conquered city or territory. They were generally made up of veteran soldiers, or sometimes of poor Róman citizens, who were placed upon the conquered land and who ruled the conquered people. But such garrisons did not retain the full rights of citizens. They lost the political rights, and generally the *conúbium*, but retained the *commércium*. These colonies, scattered as they were throughout Ítaly, carried with them the Látin language and the Róman spirit, and thus aided in extending the influence of Rome.

The Itálian Allies.—The largest part of the subject communities were the Itálian cities which were conquered and left free to govern themselves, but which were bound to Rome by a special treaty. They were obliged to recognize the sovereign power of Rome. They were not subject to the land tax which fell upon Róman citizens, but were obliged to furnish troops for the Róman army in times of war. These cities of Ítaly, thus held in subjection to Rome by a special treaty, were known as federated cities (*civitátes fœderátæ*), or simply as allies (*sócii*); they formed the most important part of the Itálian population not incorporated into the Róman state.

This method of governing Ítaly was, in some respects, based upon the policy which had formerly been adopted for the government of Látium. The important distinction between Rómans, Látins, and Itálians continued until the "social war".

III. THE MILITARY SYSTEM

The Róman Army.—The conquest of Ítaly was due, in great measure, to the efficiency of the Róman army. The strength of the Róman government, too, depended upon the army, which was the real support of the civil power. By their conquests the Rómans became a nation of warriors. Every citizen between the ages of seventeen and forty-five was obliged to serve in the army, when the public service required it. In early times the wars lasted only for a short period, and consisted in ravaging the fields of the enemy; and the soldier's reward was the booty which he was able to capture. But after the siege of Véii, the term of service became longer, and it became necessary to give to the soldiers regular pay. This pay, with the prospect of plunder and of a share in the allotment of conquered land; furnished a strong motive to render faithful service.

Divisions of the Army.—In case of war it was customary to raise four légions, two for each cónsul. Each légion was composed of thirty mániples, or companies, of heavy-armed troops, twenty mániples consisting of one hundred and twenty men each, and ten mániples of sixty men each, making in all three thousand heavy-armed troops. There were also twelve hundred light-armed troops, not organized in mániples. The whole number of men in a légion was therefore forty-two hundred. To each légion was usually joined a body of cavalry, numbering three hundred men. After the reduction of Látium and Ítaly, the allied cities were also obliged to furnish a certain number of men, according to the terms of the treaty.

Above: Róman Military Standards
Below: Stéle of Róman Warrior

Order of Battle.—In ancient times the Rómans fought in the manner of the Greek phálanx, in a solid square. This arrangement was well suited to withstand an attack on a level plain, but it was not adapted to aggressive warfare. About the time of Camíllus, the Rómans introduced the more open order of "mániples." When drawn up in order of battle, the légion was arranged in three lines: first, the *hastáti*, made up of young men; second, the *príncipes*, composed of the more experienced soldiers; and third, the *triárii*, which comprised the veterans, capable of supporting the other two lines. Each line was composed of ten mániples, those of the first two lines consisting of one hundred and twenty men each, and those of the third line consisting of sixty men each; the mániples, or companies, in each line were so arranged that they were opposite the spaces in the next line, as follows:

1. *Hastáti* — — — — — — — — — —
2. *Príncipes* — — — — — — — — — —
3. *Triárii* — — — — — — — — — —

This arrangement enabled the companies in front to retreat into the spaces in the rear, or the companies in the rear to advance to the spaces in front. Behind the third line usually fought the light-armed and less experienced soldiers (*rorárii* and *accénsi*). Each mániple carried its own ensign; and the légion carried a standard surmounted with a silver eagle.

51

Armor and Weapons.—The defensive armor of all the three lines was alike: a coat of mail for the breast, a brass helmet for the head, greaves for the legs, and a large oblong shield carried upon the left arm. For offensive weapons, each man carried a short sword, which could be used for cutting or thrusting. The soldiers in the first two lines each had also two javelins, to be hurled at the enemy before coming into close quarters; and those of the third line each had a long lance, which could be used for piercing. It was with such arms that the Róman soldiers conquered Ítaly.

Military Rewards and Honors.—The Rómans encouraged the soldiers with rewards for their bravery. These were bestowed by the general in the presence of the whole army. The highest individual reward was the "civic crown," made of oak leaves, given to him who had saved the life of a fellow-citizen on the battlefield. Other suitable rewards, such as golden crowns, banners of different colors, and ornaments, were bestowed for singular bravery. When a general slew the general of the enemy, the captured spoils (*spólia opíma*) were hung up in the temple of Júpiter Ferétrius. The highest military honor which the Róman state could bestow was a triumph, a solemn procession, decreed by the senate, in which the victorious general, with his army, marched through the city to the Cápitol, bearing in his train the trophies of war.

Military Roads.—An important part of the military system of Rome was the network of military roads by which her armies and munitions of war could be sent into every part of Ítaly. The first military road was the Áppian Way (*vía Áppia*), built by Áppius Cláudius during the Sámnite wars. It connected Rome with Cápua, and was afterward extended to Benevéntum and Venúsia, and finally as far as Brundísium. This furnished a model for the roads which were subsequently laid out to other points in Ítaly. The Látin Way (*vía Latína*) ran south into the Sámnite country and connected with the Áppian Way near Cápua and at Benevéntum. The Flamínian Way (*vía Flamínia*) ran north through eastern Etrúria and Úmbria to Aríminum. From this last-mentioned place, the Æmílian Way (*vía Æmília*) extended into Cisálpine Gaul as far as Placéntia on the river Po. Another important road, the Cássian Way (*vía Cássia*) ran through central Etrúria to Arrétium, and connected with the Æmílian Way in Cisálpine Gaul. Along the western coast of Etrúria ran the Aurélian Way (*vía Aurélia*). These were the chief military roads constructed during the time of the republic and were so durable that their remains exist today.

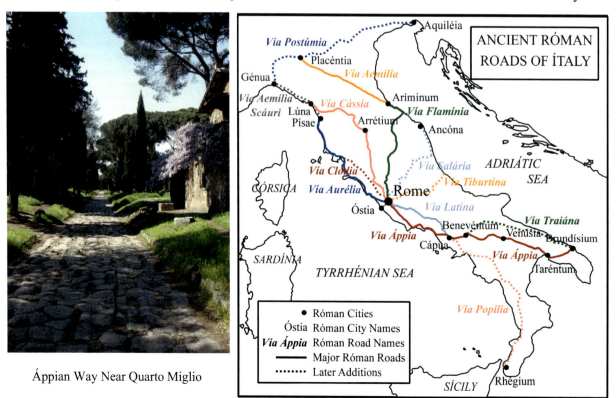

Áppian Way Near Quarto Miglio

52

CHAPTER XIV

THE FIRST PÚNIC WAR (264-241 B.C.)

Cárthage and Rome, I.—Operations of the First Púnic War, II.—Events Following the War (241-218 B.C.), III.

I. CÁRTHAGE AND ROME

Beginning of Foreign Conquests.—The ambition and the resources of Rome were not exhausted with the conquest of Ítaly. It was but a step from the Greek cities of Ítaly to the Greek cities of Sícily. But when Rome ventured to cross the Sicílian Strait, she was drawn into a struggle which was not ended until she was mistress of the Mediterránean. In passing beyond the limits of her own peninsula, she became one of the great world powers. The strength which she had acquired in her wars with the Látins and Etrúscans and Sámnites, she was now to use in the greater conflicts with Cárthage and Macedónia and Sýria.

The Death of Dído, Andrea Sacchi (1599-1661)
Musée des Beaux-Arts, Caen

The Origin of Cárthage.—The first foreign power with which Rome came in contact, outside of Ítaly, was Cárthage. This city was originally a colony of Tyre, and had come to be the capital of a great commercial empire on the northern coast of África. The origin of Cárthage, like that of Rome, is almost lost in the clouds of tradition. An old story tells us how Queen Dído was driven from Tyre and landed in África, as Ænéas did in Ítaly, with a band of fugitives. It is said that Dído purchased from the Áfrican princes as much land as an oxhide would cover; and cunningly cut the hide into thin strips and encircled enough land, upon which to found a city. Vérgil has told us the romantic story of Dído and Ænéas, and the death of the queen. But all we really know of the origin of this city is that it was settled by Phœnícians from Tyre, and early acquired dominion over the native races of África, the Lýdians and the Numídians.

Government of Cárthage.—When Cárthage came into conflict with Rome, it had in some respects the same kind of government as the Róman republic. It had two chief magistrates (called *suffétes*), corresponding to the Róman cónsuls. It had a council of elders, called the "hundred," which we might compare to the Róman senate. It had also an assembly something like the Róman *comítia*. But while the Carthagínian government had some outward similarity to the Róman, it was in its spirit very different. The real power was exercised by a few wealthy and prominent families. The Carthagínians, moreover, did not understand the Róman method of incorporating their subjects into the state; and hence did not possess a great body of loyal citizens, as did Rome. But one great advantage of the Carthagínian government was the fact that it placed the command of the army in the hands of a permanent able leader, and not in the hands of its civil magistrates, who were constantly changing as were the cónsuls at Rome.

The Civilization of Cárthage.—Cárthage brought into the western Mediterránean the ideas and civilization which the Phœnícians had developed in the East. Her power was based upon trade and commercial supremacy. She had brought under her control the trading colonies of northern África and many of the Greek cities of Sícily. She was, in fact, the great merchant of the Mediterránean. She had grown wealthy and strong by buying and selling the products of the East and the West: the purple of Tyre, the frankincense of Arábia, the linen of Égypt, the gold of Spain, the silver of the Baléaric Isles, the tin of Brítain, and the iron of Élba. She had formed commercial treaties with the chief countries of the world. She coveted not only the Greek cities of Sícily, but the Greek cities of Ítaly as well. We can thus see how Rome and Cárthage became rivals for the possession of the countries bordering upon the western Mediterránean Sea.

Remains of the Circular Port of Cárthage (1958)

Rome and Cárthage Compared.—In comparing these two great rivals of the West, we might say that they were nearly equal in strength and resources. Cárthage had greater wealth, but Rome had a better organization. Cárthage had a more powerful navy, but Rome had a more efficient army. Cárthage had more brilliant leaders, while Rome had a more steadfast body of citizens. The main strength of Cárthage rested in her wealth and commercial resources, while that of Rome depended upon the character of her people and her well-organized political system. The greatness of the Carthagínians was shown in their successes, while the greatness of the Rómans was most fully revealed in the dark hours of disaster and trial.

II. OPERATIONS OF THE FIRST PÚNIC WAR

Outbreak of the War in Sícily (264 B.C.).—The first conflict between Rome and Cárthage, which is known as the first Púnic war, began in Sícily; and really came to be a contest for the possession of that island. Sícily was at this time divided between three powers. (1) Cárthage held all the western part of the island, with the important cities of Agrigéntum on the south, Panórmus on the north, and Lilybæum at the extreme point. (2) The southeastern part of the island was under the control of the king of Sýracuse, who ruled not only this city, but also some of the neighboring towns. (3) The northeastern corner of the island was in the possession of a body of Campánian soldiers, who had been in the service of the king of Sýracuse, and who, on returning home, had treacherously seized the city of Messána.

These Campánian mercenaries, who called themselves Mámertines, or Sons of Mars, murdered the inhabitants and ravaged the surrounding country. The king of Sýracuse attacked them, laid siege to their city, and reduced them to such an extremity that they felt obliged to look for help. The choice lay between Rome and Cárthage. They finally decided to call upon Rome for help. The Róman senate hesitated to help these robbers against Sýracuse, which was a friendly power. But when the question was left to the assembly, the people fearing that Cárthage would be called upon if they refused, it was decided to help the Mámertines, and thus prevent the Carthagínians from getting possession of this part of Sícily. In this way began the first Púnic war.

Capture of Messána and Agrigéntum.—A Róman army, under Áppius Cláudius, was dispatched to Sícily, and gained a foothold upon the island. But the Mámertines, during the delay of the Rómans, had already admitted a Carthagínian garrison into the city. This seemed to the Róman general to be a breach of faith. He accordingly invited the Carthagínian commander, Hánno, to a friendly conference, and then treacherously ordered him to be seized. Whereupon the latter, in order to regain his liberty, agreed to give up the city. Thus the Rómans got possession of Messána. The king of Sýracuse then formed an alliance with the Carthagínians to drive the Rómans out of the island; but both their armies were defeated. When the Rómans had thus shown their superiority, the king of Sýracuse changed his policy and formed an alliance with the Rómans to drive the Carthagínians out of the island. Town after town fell before the Róman army; and in the second year of the war, the important city of Agrigéntum was captured, after a siege of seven months (262 B.C.).

Rome becomes a Naval Power.—The Rómans now learned that Cárthage, to be overcome, must be met upon the sea, as well as upon the land. When the Carthagínian fleet first appeared, it recovered most of the coastal cities which had been lost to the Rómans. It ravaged the coasts of Ítaly, and by its command of the sea made it difficult for Rome to send fresh troops to Sícily. The Rómans had, it is true, a few ships; but these were tríremes, or ships with only three banks of oars, and were unable to cope with the great Carthagínian vessels, which were quínquiremes, or ships with five banks of oars. The Rómans saw that they must either give up the war, or else build a fleet equal to that of the Carthagínians. Taking as a model a Carthagínian vessel which had been wrecked on the Itálian shore, they constructed, it is said, a hundred vessels like it in sixty days. In the meantime their soldiers were trained into sailors by practicing the art of rowing upon rude benches built upon the land and arranged like the banks of a real vessel. The Rómans knew that their soldiers were better than the Carthagínians in a hand-to-hand encounter. To maintain this advantage, they provided their ships with drawbridges which could be used in boarding the enemy's vessels. Thus equipped with a fleet, Rome ventured upon the sea as a rival of the first naval power of the world.

Victory of Duílius at Mýlæ (260 B.C.).—The new Róman fleet was put under the command of the cónsul Duílius. The Carthagínians were now plundering the northern coast of Sícily near Mýlæ. Without delay Duílius sailed to meet them. As the fleets came together, the Rómans dropped their drawbridges upon the enemy's ships and quickly boarded them. In the hand-to-hand encounter, the Rómans proved their superiority. The Carthagínians were routed; and fifty of their vessels were either sunk or captured. This was a most decisive victory. The Rómans had fought and gained their first great battle upon the sea. Duílius was given a magnificent triumph, and to commemorate the victory, a column was erected in the Fórum, adorned with the beaks of the captured vessels (*Colúmna Rostráta*).

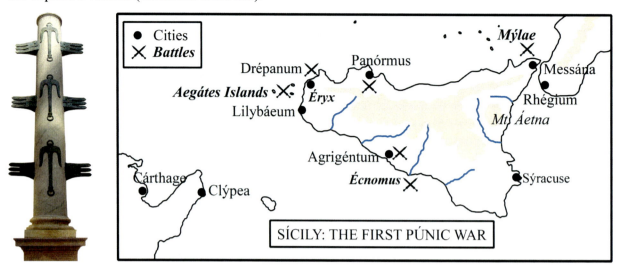

Left: Reproduction of the Colúmna Rostráta of Duílius

Invasion, of África by Régulus, (256 B.C.).—Elated by this success, the Rómans felt prepared to carry the war into África. With a still larger fleet, they defeated the Carthagínian squadron which attempted to bar their way on the southern coast of Sícily, off the promontory of Écnomus. Two légions, under L. Mánlius Vúlso and Régulus, landed on the coast of África east of Cárthage, and laid waste the country. So easily was this accomplished that the Rómans decided that one cónsul, with his army, would be enough to finish the work in África. Vúlso was therefore recalled, and Régulus remained. The Carthagínians attempted in vain to make peace; and in despair, it is said, even threw some of their children into the flames to propitiate their god Móloch. They then placed their army in the hands of a Spártan soldier named Xanthíppus. This general defeated the Róman légions with great slaughter, and made Régulus a prisoner. A fleet was then sent from Ítaly to rescue the survivors, but this fleet on its return was wrecked in a storm. Thus ingloriously closed the war in África.

The War Confined to Sícily (255-241 B.C.).—For several years after this, the war languished in Sícily. The long series of Róman disasters was relieved by the capture of Panórmus on the northern coast, which was soon followed by a second victory over the Carthagínians at the same place. It is said that the Carthagínians, after this second defeat, desired an exchange of prisoners, and sent Régulus to the Róman senate to advocate their cause, under the promise that he would return if unsuccessful. But Régulus, it is said, persuaded the senate not to accept the offer of the Carthagínians; and then, in spite of the tears and entreaties of his friends, went back to Cárthage. Whether this story is true or not, it illustrates the honor and patriotism of the true Róman.

After the Róman victories at Panórmus, the Carthagínians were pushed into the extreme western part of the island. The Rómans then laid siege to Lilybǽum, the stronghold of the Carthagínian power. Failing to capture this place, the Róman cónsul, P. Cláudius, determined to destroy the enemy's fleet lying near Drépanum; but he was defeated with the loss of over ninety ships. The superstitious Rómans believed that this defeat was due to the fact that Cláudius had impiously disregarded the auguries; when the sacred chickens had refused to eat, he had in a fit of passion thrown them into the sea. The cónsul was recalled by the senate, and a dictator was appointed in his place. After the loss of other fleets by storms, and after fruitless campaigns against the great Carthagínian soldier, Hamílcar Bárca, the Róman cause seemed a failure.

Márcus Atílius Régulus Departs for Carthage (1832), Michael Ghislain Stapleaux (1799-1881)

Victory at the Ægátes Islands (241 B.C.).—It is in the midst of such discouraging times as these that we are able to see the strong elements of the Róman character: patriotism, fortitude, and steadfast perseverance. With a loss of one sixth of their population and a vast amount of treasure, they still persisted in the attempt to conquer Sícily. Wealthy citizens advanced their money to build a new fleet. In this way two hundred ships were built and placed under the cónsul C. Lutátius Cátulus. A decisive victory was gained at the Ægátes Islands, off the western extremity of Sícily. The Carthagínians were unprepared for the terrible defeat which they suffered, and were obliged to sue for peace. They were obliged to give up Sícily; release all the Róman prisoners without ransom; and pay to the Rómans 3,200 talents, within ten years. Thus ended the first Púnic war, which had lasted for twenty-three years. During this time Rome had shown her ability to fight upon the sea and had fairly entered the lists as one of the great powers of the world. But this first contest with Cárthage, severe as it was, was merely a preparation for the more terrible struggle which was yet to come.

III. EVENTS FOLLOWING THE WAR (241-218 B.C.)

Sícily becomes the First Róman Province.—In the interval between the first and second Púnic wars, both Rome and Cárthage sought to strengthen and consolidate their power. They knew that the question of supremacy was not yet decided, and sooner or later another contest must come. Rome found herself in possession of a new territory outside of Ítaly, which must be organized. She had already three kinds of territory: (1) the Róman domain (*áger Románus*), where all were, generally speaking, full citizens; (2) the Látin colonies, in which the people had a part of the rights of citizens; and (3) the Itálian land, in which the people were not citizens, but were half independent, having their own governments, but bound to Rome as allies in war. In Sícily a new system was introduced. The people were made neither citizens nor allies, but subjects. The land was generally confiscated, and the inhabitants were obliged to pay a heavy tribute. The whole island, except Sýracuse, which remained independent, was governed by a prætor sent from Rome. By this arrangement Sícily became a "province," which is another name for a conquered territory outside of Ítaly.

Annexation of Sardínia and Córsica.—Besides Sícily, there were in the Mediterránean two other islands which seemed by nature to belong to Ítaly. These were Sardínia and Córsica. While Cárthage was engaged in suppressing a revolt of her own soldiers, which is known as the "mercenary war" in África, Rome saw a favorable opportunity to get possession of Sardínia. Cárthage protested against such an act; and Rome replied by demanding the cession of the island, and also the payment of a fine of 1200 talents. Cárthage was obliged to submit to this unjust demand; but she determined to avenge herself in the future. As Sardínia came to her so easily, Rome proceeded to take Córsica also, and the two islands were erected into a second Róman province. Rome thus obtained possession of the three great islands of the western Mediterránean.

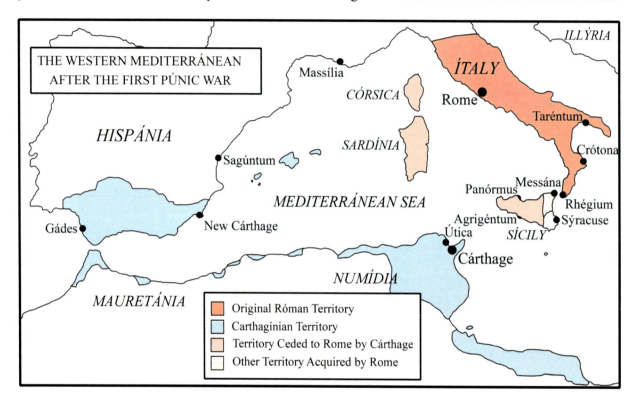

Suppression of the Illýrian Pirates.—The attention of Rome was soon directed to the eastern coast of the Adriátic Sea. An appeal came from the Greek cities for protection against the pirates of the Adriátic. These pirates were the people of Illýricum, who made their living by plundering the ships and ravaging the coasts of their Greek neighbors. With a fleet of two hundred ships, Rome cleared the Adriátic Sea of these pirates. She then took the Greek cities under her protection; Rome thus obtained a foothold upon the eastern coast of the Adriátic, which brought her into friendly relations with Greece, and afterward into hostile relations with Macedónia.

Conquest of Cisálpine Gaul.—As Rome began to be drawn into foreign wars, she became aware that her position at home could not be secure so long as the northern part of Ítaly remained unconquered. The Alps formed the natural boundary of Ítaly; and to this boundary she felt obliged to extend her power. She planted colonies upon the Gállic frontier, and in these towns made a large assignment of lands to her own citizens. The Gauls resented this as an encroachment upon their territory; they appealed to arms, invaded Etrúria, and threatened Rome. The invaders were defeated and driven back, and the war was continued in the valley of the Po until the whole of Cisálpine Gaul was finally subdued. The conquered territory was secured by new colonies, and Rome was practically supreme to the Alps. Her people were made more devoted to her by the share which they received in the new land. Her dominions were now so well organized, and her authority so secure, that she felt prepared for another contest with Cárthage.

CHAPTER XV

THE SECOND PÚNIC WAR (218-201 B.C.)

From Sagúntum to Cánnæ (218-216 B.C.), I.—From Cánnæ to the Metáurus (216-207 B.C.), II.
From the Metáurus to Záma (207-201 B.C.), III.

I. FROM SAGÚNTUM TO CÁNNÆ (218-216 B.C.)

Beginning of the War in Spain.—The second Púnic war, which now followed, was to decide the fate of Rome, and perhaps of Éurope. Its real cause was the growing rivalry between the two great powers that were now struggling for supremacy in the western Mediterránean. But it was directly brought about by the rapid growth of the Carthagínian dominion in Spain. While Rome was adding to her strength by the conquest of Cisálpine Gaul and the reduction of the islands in the sea, Cárthage was building up a great empire in the Spánish peninsula. Here she expected to raise new armies, with which to invade Ítaly. This was the policy of Hamílcar Bárca, her greatest citizen and soldier. The work was begun by Hamílcar himself, and then continued by his son-in-law, Hásdrubal, who founded the city of New Cárthage as the capital of the new province.

Rome began to be alarmed, as she saw the territory of her rival extending toward the north. She induced Cárthage to make a treaty not to extend her conquests beyond the river Ibérus (Ébro), in the northern part of Spain. Rome also formed a treaty of alliance with the Greek city of Sagúntum, which, though south of the Ibérus, was up to this time free and independent. Cárthage continued the work of conquering the southern part of Spain, without infringing upon the rights of Rome, until Hásdrubal died. Then Hánnibal, the young son of the great Hamílcar, and the idol of the army, was chosen as commander. This young Carthagínian, who had in his boyhood sworn an eternal hostility to Rome, now felt that his mission was come. He marched from New Cárthage and proceeded to attack Sagúntum, the ally of Rome; and after a siege of eight months, captured it. The Rómans sent an embassy to Cárthage to demand the surrender of Hánnibal. The story is told that Quíntus Fábius, the chief Róman envoy, lifted up a fold of his toga and said to the Carthagínian senate, "Here we bring you peace and war; which do you choose?" "Give us either," was the reply. "Then I offer you war," said Fábius. "And this we accept," shouted the Carthagínians. Thus was begun the most memorable war of ancient times.

Hánnibal and Rome.—Rome was now at war, not only with Cárthage, but with Hánnibal. The first Púnic war had been a struggle with the greatest naval power of the Mediterránean, but the second Púnic war was to be a conflict with one of the greatest soldiers that the world has ever seen. As a military genius, no Róman could compare with him. If the Rómans could have known what ruin and desolation were to follow in the train of this young man of Cárthage, they might have hesitated to enter upon this war. But no one could know the future. While Cárthage placed her cause in the hands of a brilliant captain, Rome felt that she was supported by a courageous and steadfast people. It will be interesting for us to follow this contest between a great man and a great nation.

Bust of Hánnibal, Museo Nazionale, Náples

59

Hánnibal's Invasion of Ítaly.—Even at the beginning of the war Hánnibal showed his great genius as a soldier. The Rómans formed an excellent plan to send two armies into the enemy's country—one into África under Semprónius, and the other into Spain under P. Cornélius Scípio. But Hánnibal, with the instinct of a true soldier, saw that Cárthage would be safe if Ítaly were invaded and Rome threatened. Leaving his brother Hásdrubal to protect Spain, he crossed the Pýrenees with fifty thousand infantry, nine thousand cavalry, and a number of elephants. Without delay he pushed on to the river Rhône; outflanked the barbarians, who were trying to oppose his passage; and crossed the river above, just as the Róman army (which had expected to meet him in Spain) had reached Massília (Marseilles). When the Róman commander, P. Cornélius Scípio, found that he had been outgeneraled by Hánnibal, he sent his brother Cn. Scípio on to Spain with the main army, and returned himself to Cisálpine Gaul, expecting to destroy the Carthagínian if he should venture to come into Ítaly. Hánnibal in the meantime pressed on; and in spite of innumerable difficulties and dangers crossed the Alps. He finally reached the valley of the Po, with only twenty thousand foot and six thousand horse. Here he recruited his ranks from the Gauls, who eagerly joined his cause against the Rómans.

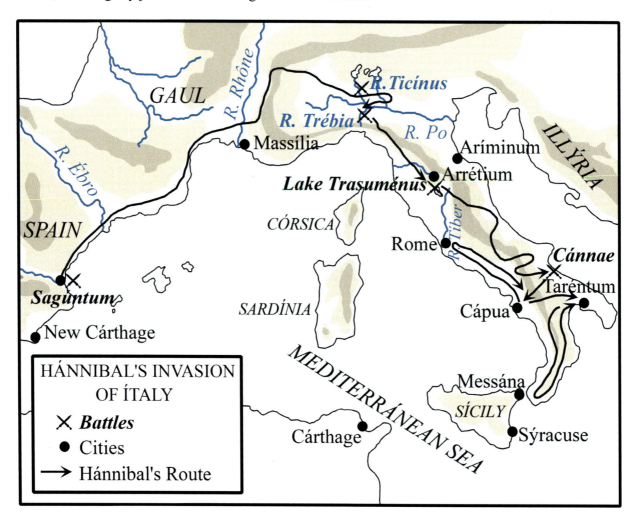

Hánnibal's Early Victories.—When the Rómans were aware that Hánnibal was really in Ítaly, they made preparations to meet and to destroy him. Semprónius was recalled with the army originally intended for África; and Scípio, who had returned from Massília, gathered together the scattered forces in northern Ítaly and took up his station at Placéntia on the Po. The cavalry of the two armies first met in a skirmish on the north side of the Po, near the little stream Ticínus. The Rómans were defeated, and Scípio himself was severely wounded. Hánnibal then crossed to the south of the Po. To prevent his advance, Scípio took up a strong position on the bank of the river Trébia. Scípio was soon joined by his colleague Semprónius, who came to him from Aríminum on the Adriátic coast. The two hostile armies were now separated by the river Trébia. Here again Hánnibal showed his great skill as a general. By a feigned attack he drew the Rómans over to his own side of the river. He then attacked them in front, upon the flank, and in the rear;

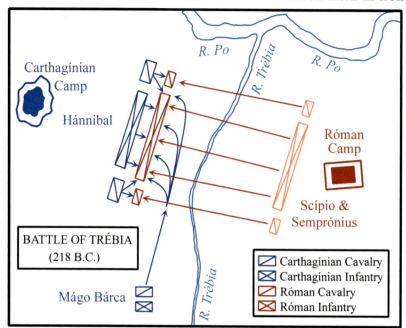

and the Róman army was nearly annihilated. The remnant of the army fled to Placéntia. This great disaster did not discourage the Rómans. They soon raised new armies with which to resist the invaders.

Battle of Lake Trasuménus (217 B.C.).—In the following spring, the new cónsul, Flamínius, placed his own army at Arrétium, in Etrúria, and his colleague's army at Aríminum, to guard the only roads upon which it seemed possible that Hánnibal could move, in order to reach Rome. But Hánnibal, instead of going by either of these roads on which he was expected to go, crossed the Ápennines and pushed on toward Rome through the marshy regions of Etrúria. He thus got between the Róman armies and the Róman capital. He knew that Flamínius would be obliged to hasten to Rome to protect the city. He also knew by what road Flamínius must go, and he determined to destroy the Róman army on its way. He posted his army on the heights near the northern shore of Lake Trasuménus (Trásimene), overlooking a defile through which the Róman army must pass. The Rómans approached this defile and entered it, not suspecting the terrible fate which awaited them. At a given signal, the soldiers of Hánnibal rushed to the attack. The Rómans were overwhelmed on every side, and those who escaped the fierce Gauls and the dreaded cavalry of Numídia were buried in the waters of the lake. Fifteen thousand Rómans and Itálians fell on that fatal field, with Flamínius, their leader. The Róman army was practically destroyed. Northern Ítaly was now at the mercy of Hánnibal, and Rome seemed an easy prey to the victorious Carthagínian.

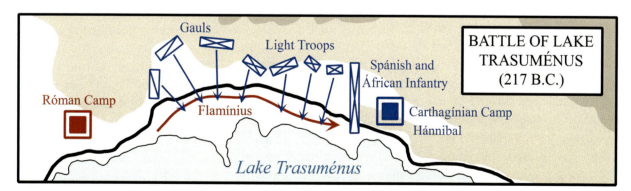

Fábius Máximus, Dictator.—"We have lost a great battle, our army is destroyed, Flamínius is killed!" was the simple announcement which the prǽtor made, after the frightful disaster at Lake Trasuménus. But this simple announcement brought consternation to the Róman people. They recalled the days of the Gauls and the battle on the Állia. But they were still determined to

61

defend their country. The times seemed to demand a dictator, and Q. Fábius Máximus was appointed. He was a member of that Fábian gens which had before proved its devotion to the country; and he was also that ambassador who had offered to Cárthage the choice between peace and war. He ordered new armies to be raised, and the city to be put in a state of defense.

Hánnibal did not see fit to attack Rome; but, turning to the east, he moved through Úmbria and Picénum into Apúlia, plundering the country as he went. He hoped to draw to his standard the allies of Rome in southern Ítaly, by showing that they were safe only under his protection. He also wished to provoke Fábius to a pitched battle. But Fábius had learned some lessons from the war; and he adopted the safe policy of harassing the army of Hánnibal and of avoiding a general engagement. On account of this cautious strategy he was called Fábius Cunctátor, or the Delayer. In order to irritate him to a conflict, Hánnibal marched through Sámnium into the rich fields of Campánia. Fábius then tried to shut Hánnibal up in this little territory by holding the mountain passes. But when Hánnibal was ready to go, he opened his way by a stratagem. He ordered his light-armed troops in the night to drive up the mountain side a herd of cattle, with lighted bundles tied to their horns. The Rómans who guarded the way, deceived or panic-stricken by this unusual demonstration, abandoned their post. Hánnibal marched through the unguarded pass, and was free again to plunder the countries of southern Ítaly. He moved eastward through Sámnium, and then descended into the region of Apúlia. During all this time the allied cities of Ítaly had remained faithful to Rome.

Battle of Cánnæ (216 B.C.).—The cautious strategy of Fábius soon became unpopular; and the escape of Hánnibal from Campánia especially excited the dissatisfaction of the people. Two new cónsuls were therefore chosen, who were expected to pursue a more vigorous policy. These were Teréntius Várro and Æmílius Páullus. Hánnibal's army was now in Apúlia, near the little town of Cánnæ on the Áufidus River. To this place the cónsuls led their new forces, consisting of eighty thousand infantry and six thousand cavalry, the largest army that the Rómans had, up to that time, ever gathered on a single battlefield; Hánnibal's army consisted of forty thousand infantry and ten thousand cavalry. But the brain of Hánnibal was more than a match for the forty thousand extra Rómans, under the command of less able generals. The Róman cónsuls took command on alternate days. Páullus was cautious; but Várro was impetuous and determined to fight Hánnibal at the first opportunity. As this was Hánnibal's greatest battle, we may learn something of his wonderful skill by looking at, its plan.

The Rómans drew up their heavy infantry in solid columns, facing to the south, to attack the center of Hánnibal's line. In front of the heavy-armed troops were the light-armed soldiers, to act as skirmishers. On the Róman right, near the river, were two thousand of the Róman cavalry, and on the left wing were four thousand cavalry of the allies. With their army thus arranged, the Rómans hoped to defeat Hánnibal. But Hánnibal laid his plan not simply to defeat the Róman army, but to draw it into such a position that it could be entirely destroyed. He therefore placed his weakest troops, the Spánish and Gállic infantry, in the center opposite the heavy infantry of the Rómans, and pushed them forward in the form of a crescent, with the expectation that they would be driven back and pursued by the Rómans. On either flank he placed an invincible body of Áfrican troops, his best and most trusted soldiers, drawn back in long, solid columns, so that they could fall upon the Rómans when the center had been driven in. On his left wing, next to the river, were placed four thousand Spánish and Gállic cavalry, and on the right wing his superb body of six thousand Numídian cavalry, which was to swing around and attack the Róman army in the rear, when it had become engaged with the Áfrican troops upon the right and left.

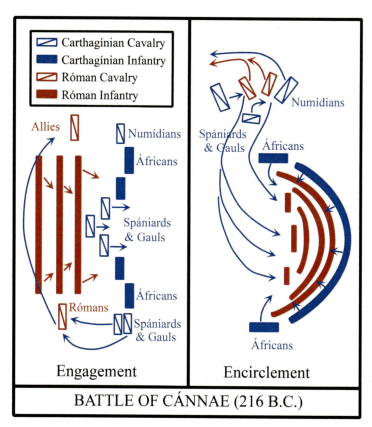

Carthagínian Cavalry
Carthagínian Infantry
Róman Cavalry
Róman Infantry

Allies

Numídians

Áfricans

Spániards & Gauls

Áfricans

Rómans

Spániards & Gauls

Engagement

Numídians

Spániards & Gauls

Áfricans

Áfricans

Encirclement

BATTLE OF CÁNNAE (216 B.C.)

The description of this plan is almost a description of the battle itself. When the Rómans had pressed back the weak center of Hánnibal's line, they found themselves engulfed in the midst of the Carthagínian forces. Attacked on all sides, the Róman army became a confused mass of struggling men, and the battle became a butchery. The army was annihilated; seventy thousand Róman soldiers are said to have been slain, among whom were eighty senators and the cónsul Æmílius. The small remnant of survivors fled to the neighboring towns, and Várro, with seventy horsemen, took refuge in the city of Venúsia. This was the most terrible day that Rome had seen since the destruction of the city by the Gauls, nearly two centuries before. Every house in Rome was in mourning.

II. FROM CÁNNÆ TO THE METÁURUS (216-207 B.C.)

Hánnibal's New Allies.—The battle of Cánnæ convinced the Itálian allies that it would be better to have the help, rather than the hostility, of such a man as Hánnibal. The Apúlians, the Lucánians, the Sámnites, the Brúttians, revolted and put themselves under his protection. But the Látin colonies and the Greek cities generally remained loyal to Rome. Cápua, however, the most important city in Ítaly, after Rome, opened her gates to Hánnibal; and Taréntum, which held a Róman garrison, was betrayed into his hands. The influence of Hánnibal's victory was also apparent outside of Ítaly. Sýracuse transferred her allegiance from Rome to Cárthage, and many other cities in Sícily threatened to revolt. Phílip V., the king of Macedónia, also made an alliance with Hánnibal, and threatened to invade Ítaly to assist him. Hánnibal at this time was at the height of his power.

Dismay and Fortitude of the Rómans.—During the period which followed the battle of Cánnæ, the Róman character was put to its severest test. The people feared the worst. Everything seemed turning against them. They were in dismay; but they did not despair. The popular excitement was soon allayed by the firmness of the senate. Under the wise counsels of Fábius Máximus, new plans were made for the recovery of Ítaly. But the problem now seemed greater than ever before. The war must be carried on, not only in Ítaly, to recover the revolted allies and to meet the continued attacks of Hánnibal; but also in Spain, to prevent reinforcements coming from Hásdrubal; and in Sícily, to prevent the cities of that province from following the example of Sýracuse; and finally in Greece, to prevent the king of Macedónia from interfering in the affairs of Ítaly. In the face of all discouragements, the Róman people, supported by the faithful Látin towns and colonies, remained firm; and with fixed resolution determined to prosecute the war with greater vigor than ever before.

The Turning of the Tide.—It was at this point that the fortunes of war began to turn in favor of the Rómans. The first ray of hope came from Spain, where it was learned that Hásdrubal had been defeated by the Scípios. Then Hánnibal's army met its first repulse in Campánia. The Rómans also, by forming a league with the Ætólian cities of Greece and sending them a few troops, were able to prevent Macedónia from giving any aid to Hánnibal. Soon Sýracuse was captured after a siege by the Róman prætor Marcéllus. Moreover, Hánnibal's forces were weakened by the need of protecting his new allies, scattered in various parts of southern Ítaly.

Recovery of Cápua.—The Rómans were greatly incensed by the revolt of Cápua, and determined to punish its citizens. Regular siege was laid to the city, and two Róman armies surrounded its walls. Hánnibal marched to the relief of the beleaguered city and attempted to raise the siege; but could not draw the Róman army from its entrenchments. As a last resort, he marched directly to Rome, hoping to compel the Rómans to withdraw their armies from Cápua for the defense of the capital. Although he plundered the towns and ravaged the fields of Látium, and rode about the walls of Rome, the fact that "Hánnibal was at the gates," did not entice the Róman army away from Cápua. Rome was well defended, and Hánnibal, having no means of besieging the city, withdrew again into the southern part of Ítaly. Cápua was soon taken by the Rómans; its chief citizens were put to death for their treason, many of the inhabitants were reduced to slavery, and the city itself was put under the control of a prefect. It was apparent that Hánnibal could not protect his Ítalian allies; and his cause seemed doomed to failure, unless he could receive help from his brother Hásdrubal, who was still in Spain.

The Scípios in Spain (218-212 B.C.); Battle of the Metáurus (207 B.C.).—Hásdrubal had been kept in Spain by the vigorous campaign which the Rómans had conducted in that peninsula under the two Scípios. Upon the death of these generals, the young Públius Cornélius Scípio was sent to Spain and earned a great name by his victories. But Hásdrubal was determined to go to the rescue of his brother in Ítaly. He followed Hánnibal's path over the Alps into the valley of the Po. Hánnibal had moved northward into Apúlia, and was awaiting news from Hásdrubal. There were now two enemies in Ítaly, instead of one. One Róman army under Cláudius Néro was, therefore, sent to oppose Hánnibal in Apúlia; and another army under Lívius Salinátor was sent to meet Hásdrubal, who had just crossed the river Metáurus, in Úmbria.

It was necessary that Hásdrubal should be crushed before Hánnibal was informed of his arrival in Ítaly. The cónsul Cláudius Néro therefore left his main army in Apúlia, and with eight thousand picked soldiers hurried to the aid of his colleague in Úmbria. The battle which took place at the Metáurus was decisive; and really determined the issue of the second Púnic war. The army of Hásdrubal was entirely destroyed, and he himself was slain. The first news which Hánnibal received of this disaster was from the lifeless lips of his own brother, whose head was thrown by the Rómans into the Carthagínian camp. Hánnibal saw that the death of his brother was the doom of Cárthage; and he sadly exclaimed, "O Cárthage, I see thy fate!" Hánnibal retired into Brúttium; and the Róman cónsuls received the first triumph that had been given since the beginning of this disastrous war.

Hánnibal Recognizes the Head of His Brother Hásdrubal
(ca. 1728-1739), Giovanni Battista Tiepolo (1697-1770),
Kunsthistorisches Museum, Vienna

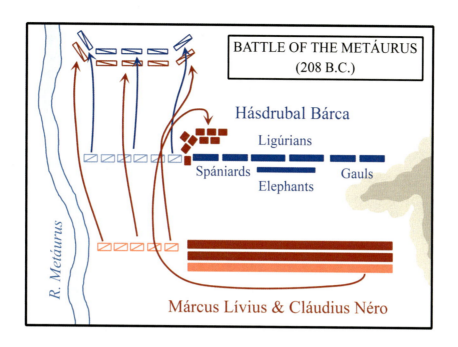

BATTLE OF THE METÁURUS
(208 B.C.)

Hásdrubal Bárca

Ligúrians

Spániards

Gauls

Elephants

R. Metáurus

Márcus Lívius & Cláudius Néro

III. FROM THE METÁURUS TO ZÁMA (207-201 B.C.)

Públius Scípio Africánus.—Of all the men produced by Rome during the Púnic wars, Públius Cornélius Scípio (afterward called Africánus) came the nearest to being a military genius. From boyhood he had, like Hánnibal, served in the army. At the death of his father and uncle, he had been entrusted with the conduct of the war in Spain. With great ability he had defeated the armies which opposed him, and had regained the entire peninsula, after it had been almost lost. With his conquest of New Cárthage and Gádes, Spain was brought under the Róman power. On his return to Rome, Scípio was unanimously elected to the cónsulship. He then proposed his scheme for closing the war. This plan was to keep Hánnibal shut up in the Brúttian peninsula, and to carry the war into África. Although this scheme seemed to the aged Fábius Máximus as rash, the people had entire confidence in the young Scípio, and supported him. From this time Scípio was the chief figure in the war, and the senate kept him in command until its close.

The War carried into África.—Scípio now organized his new army, which was made up largely of volunteers, and equipped by patriotic contributions. He embarked from Sícily and landed in África. He was assisted by the Numídian king, Masiníssa, whom he had previously met in Spain; and whose royal title was now disputed by a rival named Sýphax, an ally of Cárthage. The title to the kingship of Numídia thus became mixed up with the war with Cárthage. Scípio and Masiníssa soon defeated the Carthagínian armies in África, and the fate of Cárthage was sealed.

Bust of Scípio Africánus from Herculáneum
Museo Nazionale, Náples

Recall of Hánnibal.—While the war was progressing in África, Hánnibal still held his place in Brúttium like a lion at bay. In the midst of misfortune, he was still a hero. He kept control of his devoted army, and was faithful to his duty when all was lost. Cárthage was convinced that her only hope was in recalling Hánnibal to defend his native city. Hánnibal left Ítaly, the field of his brilliant exploits, and landed in África. Thus Rome was relieved of her dreaded foe, who had brought her so near to the brink of ruin.

65

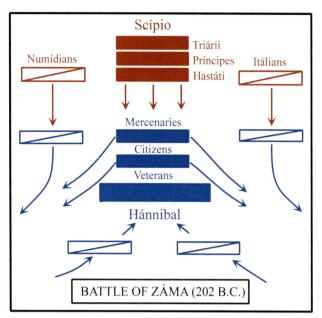

Battle of Záma and End of the War (201 B.C.).—The two greatest generals then living were now face to face upon the soil of África. The final battle of the war was fought (202 B.C.) near Záma. Hánnibal fought at a great disadvantage. His own veterans were reduced greatly in number, and the new armies of Cárthage could not be depended upon. Scípio changed the order of the légions, leaving spaces in his line, through which the elephants of Hánnibal might pass without being opposed. In this battle Hánnibal was defeated, and the Carthagínian army was annihilated. It is said that twenty thousand men were slain, and as many more taken prisoners. The great war was now ended, and Scípio imposed the terms of peace (201 B.C.).

These terms were as follows: (1) Cárthage was to give up the whole of Spain and all the islands between África and Ítaly; (2) Masiníssa was recognized as the king of Numídia and the ally of Rome; (3) Cárthage was to pay an annual tribute of 200 talents for fifty years; (4) Cárthage agreed not to wage any war without the consent of Rome.

Battle of Záma (ca. 1521), Giulio Romano (1499-1546), Pushkin Fine Arts Museum, Moscow

Rome was thus recognized as the mistress of the western Mediterránean. Cárthage, although not reduced to a province, became a dependent state. Sýracuse was added to the province of Sícily, and the territory of Spain was divided into two provinces, Hither and Farther Spain. Rome had, moreover, been brought into hostile relations with Macédonia, which paved the way for her conquests in the East.

CHAPTER XVI

THE CONQUESTS IN THE EAST (200-133 B.C.)

I. THE CONDITION OF THE EAST

The Divisions of the Empire of Alexánder.—At the time of the second Púnic war, the countries about the Mediterránean may be considered as forming two distinct worlds: the Western world, in which Rome and Cárthage were struggling for mastery; and the Eastern world, which was divided among the successors of Alexánder the Great. It was more than a century before this time that Alexánder had built up a great empire, extending from Greece to the middle of Ásia. By his conquests the ideals of Greek art and literature and philosophy had been spread into the eastern countries. But Alexánder had none of the genius for organization which the Rómans possessed, and so at his death his empire fell to pieces. The fragments were seized by his different generals, and became new and distinct kingdoms. At this time there were three of these kingdoms which were quite extensive and powerful. These were: (1) the kingdom of Egypt under the Ptólemies, in África; (2) the kingdom of Sýria under the Seleúcidæ, in Ásia; and (3) the kingdom of Macedónia under the direct successors of Alexánder, in southeastern Éurope.

Égypt under the Ptólemies.—Under the reign of the Ptólemies, Égypt had attained a remarkable degree of prosperity. Her territory not only included the valley of the Nile, but extended into Ásia, taking in Pálestine, Phœnícia, and the southern part of Sýria (Cœle-Sýria), besides Cýprus and some other islands. Its capital, Alexándria, was perhaps the most cultivated city of the world, where the learned men of all countries found their home. So devoted was Égypt to the arts of peace, that she kept aloof, as far as possible, from the great wars of this period. But she was an object of envy to the kings of Sýria and Macedónia; and toward the close of the second Púnic war, in order to protect herself, she had formed an alliance with Rome. The friendly relations between Rome and Égypt were preserved, while Rome carried on war with the other great powers of the East.

Sýria under Antíochus III.—The most important fragment of Alexánder's empire in Ásia was Sýria, or the kingdom of the Seleúcidæ, so called from the name of its founder, Seleúcus the Conqueror. It covered a large part of western Ásia, comprising the valley of the Euphrátes, upper Sýria, and portions of Ásia Minor. Its rulers included four kings by the name of Seleúcus, and eight by the name of Antíochus. These names also appear in the capital cities of the Sýrian empire, Seleúcia on the Tígris and Ántioch in upper Sýria. The most powerful of these kings was Antíochus III., surnamed the Great. He did much to enlarge and strengthen the empire. But he incurred the hostility of Rome by giving asylum to Rome's great enemy, Hánnibal, and also by attempting to make conquests in Éurope. There were a few small states in Ásia Minor, like Pérgamum, Bithýnia, Póntus, and the island republic of Rhodes, which were not included in the kingdom of Sýria and which were inclined to look to Rome for protection.

Macedónia and the Greek Cities.—The third great fragment of Alexánder's empire was Macedónia, which aspired to be supreme in eastern Éurope. A part of Greece fell under its authority. But many of the Greek cities remained free; and they united into leagues or confederations, in order to maintain their independence. One of these was the Achæan league, made up of the cities of southern Greece, or the Peloponnésus; and another was the Ætólian league, including a large number of cities in central Greece. When Phílip V. came to the throne of Macedónia, his kingdom was in a flourishing condition. The young ruler was ambitious to extend his power; and came into hostile relations with Rome, which espoused the cause of the Greek cities.

II. THE FIRST AND SECOND MACEDÓNIAN WARS

The First Macedónian War (215-206 B.C.).—It was the indiscreet alliance of Phílip of Macedónia with Hánnibal, during the second Púnic war, which we have already noticed, that brought about the first conflict between Rome and Macedónia. But Rome was then so fully occupied with her struggle with Cárthage that all she desired to do was simply to prevent Phílip from making his threatened invasion of Ítaly. Rome therefore sent a small force across the Adriátic, made friends with the Ætólians, and kept Phílip occupied at home. The Macedónian king was thus prevented from sending any force into Ítaly. The Ætólians, not satisfied with the support given to them by Rome, soon made peace with Phílip; and the Rómans themselves, who were about to invade África, were also willing to conclude a treaty of peace with him. Thus closed what is generally called the first Macedónian war, which was really nothing more than a diversion to prevent Phílip from giving aid to Hánnibal after the battle of Cánnæ.

Beginning of the Second Macedónian War (200-197 B.C.).—When the second Púnic war was fairly ended, Rome felt free to deal with Phílip of Macedónia, and to take a firm hand in settling the affairs of the East. Phílip had annoyed her, not only by making an alliance with Hánnibal, but afterward by sending a force to assist him at the battle of Záma. And now the ambitious schemes of Phílip were not at all to the liking of Rome. For instance, he made an agreement with Antíochus of Sýria to cut up the possessions of Égypt, a country which was friendly to Rome. He was also overrunning the coasts of the Ægéan Sea, and was threatening the little kingdom of Pérgamum in Ásia Minor, and the little republic of Rhodes, as well as the cities of Greece. When appeal came to Rome for protection, she espoused the cause of the small states, and declared war against Macedónia.

Battle of Cynoscéphalæ (197 B.C.).—The great hero of this war was T. Quínctius Flaminínus; and the decisive battle was fought near a hill in Théssaly called Cynoscéphalæ ("Dog's Heads"). Here Phílip was completely defeated, and his army was destroyed. Although Macedónia was not reduced to the condition of a province, it became practically subject to Rome. Macedónia was thus humbled, and there was no other power in Europe to dispute the supremacy of Rome.

Phílip V. of Mácedon

The Liberation of Greece (196 B.C.).—To complete her work in eastern Éurope, and to justify her position as defender of the Greek cities, Rome withdrew her garrisons and announced the independence of Greece. This was proclaimed by Flaminínus at the Ísthmian games, amid wild enthusiasm and unbounded expressions of gratitude. Rome was hailed as "the nation which, at its own expense, with its own labor, and at its own risk, waged war for the liberty of others, and which had crossed the sea that justice, right, and law should everywhere have sovereign sway."

Beginning of the War; the Ætólians.—There was now left in the world only one great power which could claim to be a rival of Rome. That power was Sýria, under its ambitious ruler, Antíochus III. A number of things led to the conflict between Rome and this great power in Ásia. But the direct cause of the war grew out of the intrigues of the Ætólians in Greece. This restless people stirred up a discord among the Greek cities, and finally called upon Antíochus to espouse their cause, and to aid them in driving the Rómans out of the country. Antíochus accepted this invitation, crossed the Héllespont, and landed in Greece with an army of 10,000 men (192 B.C.).

Battles of Thermópylæ and Magnésia.—Rome now appeared as the protector of Éurope against Ásia. She was supported by her previous enemy, Phílip of Macedónia; and she was also aided by the kingdom of Pérgamum and the republic of Rhodes. The career of Antíochus in Greece was short. He was defeated by Márcus Pórcius Cáto in the famous pass of Thermópylæ (191 B.C.), and was driven back across the sea into Ásia Minor. The next year the Rómans followed him, and fought their first battle upon the continent of Ásia. The Róman army was nominally under the command of the new cónsul, L. Cornélius Scípio, but really under the command of his famous brother, Scípio Africánus, who accompanied him. The decisive battle was fought at Magnésia (190 B.C.), not far from Sárdis in western Ásia Minor. Forty thousand of

Bust of Antíochus III. (So-Called), Louvre Museum, Paris

the enemy were slain, with a comparatively small loss to the Rómans. Scípio imposed the terms of peace, which required Antíochus (1) to give up all his possessions in Ásia Mínor, the most of which were added to the kingdom of Pérgamum, with some territory to the republic of Rhodes; (2) to give up his fleet and not to interfere in Európean affairs; (3) to pay the sum of 15,000 talents within twelve years; and (4) to surrender Hánnibal, who had taken an active part in the war.

Subjection of the Ætólians.—After the great victory of Magnésia, Rome turned her arms against the Ætólians, who were so foolish as to continue the struggle. Their chief city, Ambrácia, was taken; and they were soon forced to submit. Macedónia and all Greece, with the exception of the Achǽan league, were now brought into subjection to the Róman authority.

The Fate of Hánnibal.—To the Rómans it seemed an act of treachery that Hánnibal, who had been conquered in a fair field at Záma, should continue his hostility by fighting on the side of their enemies. But Hánnibal never forgot the oath of eternal enmity to Rome, the oath which he had sworn at his father's knee. When Antíochus agreed to surrender him, Hánnibal fled to Crete, and afterward took refuge with the king of Bithýnia. Here he continued his hostility to Rome by aiding this ruler in a war against Rome's ally, the king of Pérgamum. The Rómans still pursued him, and sent Flamínínus to demand his surrender. But Hánnibal again fled, and, hunted from the face of the earth, this great soldier, who had been the most terrible foe that Rome had ever encountered, took his own life by drinking poison. It is said that the year of his death was the same year (183 B.C.) in which died his great and victorious antagonist, Scípio Africánus.

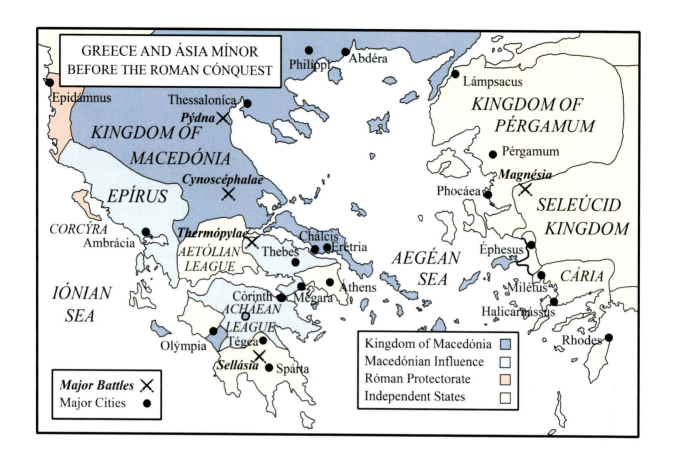

IV. THE THIRD MACEDÓNIAN WAR (171-168 B.C.)

Róman Policy in the East.—By the great battles of Cynoscéphalæ and Magnésia, Rome had reason to believe that she had broken the power of her rivals in the East. But she had not yet adopted in that part of the world the policy which she had previously employed in the case of Sícily and Spain, namely, of reducing the territory to the condition of provinces. She had left the countries of the East nominally free and independent; and had placed them in the condition of subject allies, or of tributary states. She had compelled them to reduce their armies, to give her an annual tribute, and to promise not to make a war without her consent. In this way she believed that Macedónia and Sýria would be obliged to keep the peace. Over the weaker powers, like the Greek cities, the kingdom of Pérgamum, and the republic of Rhodes, she had assumed the position of a friendly protector. But in spite of this generous policy, a spirit of discontent gradually grew up in the various countries, and Rome was soon obliged, as we shall see, to adopt a new and more severe policy, in order to maintain peace and order throughout her empire.

Beginning of the Third Macedónian War.—Phílip of Macedónia had been a faithful ally of Rome during the late war with Antíochus; but at its close he felt that he had not been sufficiently rewarded for his fidelity. He saw that the little states of Pérgamum and Rhodes had received considerable accessions to their territories, while he himself was apparently forgotten. On account of this seeming neglect, he began to think of regaining his old power. When he died, he was succeeded by his son, Pérseus, who continued the design of making Macedónia free from the dictation of Rome. Pérseus did what he could to develop the resources of his kingdom, and to organize and strengthen his army. He even began to be looked upon by the Greek cities as their champion against the encroachments of Rome. But the time soon came when he was obliged to answer for his arrogant conduct. The Rómans became convinced of the ambitious scheme of Pérseus, and entered upon a new war against Macedónia.

70

Battle of Pýdna (168 B.C.).—After three unsuccessful campaigns, the Rómans finally placed in command of their army an able general, Æmílius Páullus, the son of the cónsul who was slain at Cánnæ. The two armies met near Pýdna, and Pérseus suffered a crushing defeat. Here the Macedónian phálanx fought its last great battle, and the Róman légions gave a new evidence of their superior strength. Twenty thousand Macedónians were slain, and eleven thousand were captured. It is said that the spoils of this battle were so great that the citizens of Rome were henceforth relieved from the payment of taxes. Páullus received at Rome the most magnificent triumph that had ever been seen. For three days the gorgeous procession marched through the streets of Rome, bearing the trophies of the East. Through the concourse of exultant people was driven the chariot of the defeated king of Macedónia, followed by the victorious army adorned with laurels, and its successful commander decked with the insignia of Júpiter Capitolínus, with a laurel branch in his hand.

The Triumph of Æmílius Paúllus (1789), Carle Vernet (1758–1836), Metropolitan Museum of Art

The Settlement of Macedónia.—The question now arose as to what should be done with Macedónia, which had so many times resisted the Róman power. The Rómans were not yet ready to reduce the country to a province, and were not willing to have it remain independent. It was therefore split up into four distinct republics, which were to be entirely separated from one another, but which were to be dependent upon Rome. With a show of generosity, Rome compelled the people to pay as tribute only half of what had been previously paid to the Macedónian king. But the republics could have no relations with one another, either by way of commerce or intermarriage. All the chief men of Greece who had given any aid to the Macedónian king were transported to Ítaly, where they could not stir up a revolt in their native country. Among these Achæan captives was the famous historian, Polýbius, who during this time gathered the materials of his great work on Róman history.

CHAPTER XVII

REDUCTION OF THE RÓMAN CONQUESTS

Reduction of Macedónia and Greece, I.—Third Púnic War and Reduction of África (149-146 B.C.), II. Pacification of the Provinces, III.

I. REDUCTION OF MACEDÓNIA AND GREECE

Change of the Róman Policy.—We sometimes think that Rome started out upon her great career of conquest with a definite purpose to subdue the world, and with clear ideas as to how it should be governed. But nothing could be farther from the truth. She had been drawn on from one war to another, often against her own will. When she first crossed the narrow strait into Sícily at the beginning of the first Púnic war, she little thought that in a hundred years her armies would be fighting in Ásia; and when in early times she was compelled to find some way of keeping peace and order in Látium, she could not have known that she would, sooner or later, be compelled to devise a way to preserve the peace and order of the world. But Rome was ever growing and ever learning. She learned how to conquer before she learned how to govern. It was after the third Macedónian war that Rome became convinced that her method of governing the conquered lands was not strong enough to preserve peace and maintain her own authority. She had heretofore left the conquered states to a certain extent free and independent. But now, either excited by jealousy or irritated by the intrigues and disturbances of the conquered people, she was determined to reduce them to a more complete state of submission.

New Disturbances in Macedónia.—She was especially convinced of the need of a new policy by the continued troubles in Macedónia. The experiment which she had tried, of cutting up the kingdom into four separate states, had not been entirely successful. To add to the disturbances there appeared a man who called himself Phílip, and who pretended to be the son of Pérseus. He incited the people to revolt, and even defeated the Rómans in a battle; but he was himself soon defeated and made a prisoner.

Revolt of the Achǽan Cities.—The spirit of revolt, excited by the false Phílip, spread into Greece. The people once more began to feel that the freedom of Rome was worse than slavery. It is true that Rome had liberated the Achǽan captives who had been transported to Ítaly after the third Macedónian war; but these men, who had spent so much of their lives in captivity, carried back to Greece the bitter spirit which they still cherished. The Greek cities became not only unfriendly to Rome, but were also at strife with one another. Spárta desired to withdraw from the Achǽan league, and appealed to Rome for help. Rome sent commissioners to Greece to settle the difficulty; but the Achǽans came together in their assembly at Córinth and insulted the Róman commissioners, and were then rash enough to declare war against Rome herself.

Destruction of Córinth (146 B.C.).—The war which now followed, for the subjugation of Greece, was at first conducted by Metéllus; and afterward by Múmmius, an able general but a boorish man, who hated the Greeks and cared little for their culture. Córinth, the chief city of the Achǽan league, was captured; the art treasures, pictures and statues, the splendid products of Greek genius, were sent to Rome. The inhabitants were sold as slaves. And by the cruel command of the senate, the city itself was reduced to ashes. This was a barbarous act of war, such an act as no civilized nation has ever approved. That the Rómans were not yet fully civilized, and knew little of the meaning of art, is shown by the story told of Múmmius. This rude cónsul warned the sailors who carried the pictures and statues of Córinth to Rome, that "if they lost or damaged any of them, they must replace them with others of equal value."

Metéllus Raising the Siege (of Corinth), Armand-Charles Caraffe (1762-1822), Hermitage Museum, St. Petersburg

Macedónia reduced to a Province.—The time had now come for Rome to adopt her new policy in respect to Macedónia. The old divisions into which the kingdom had been divided were abolished, and each city or community was made directly responsible to the governor sent from Rome. By this new arrangement, Macedónia became a province. The cities of Greece were allowed to remain nominally free, but the political confederacies were broken up, and each city came into direct relation with Rome through the governor of Macedónia. Greece was afterward organized as a separate province, under the name of Acháia.

II. THIRD PÚNIC WAR AND REDUCTION OF ÁFRICA (149-146 B.C.)

Revival of Cárthage.—The new policy which Rome applied to Macedónia she also adopted with respect to Cárthage. Since the close of the second Púnic war, Cárthage had faithfully observed the terms of the treaty which Rome had imposed. She had abandoned war and devoted herself to the arts of peace. Her commerce had revived; her ships were again plying the waters of the Mediterránean; and she seemed destined to become once more a rich and prosperous city. But her prosperity was the cause of her ruin. The jealousy of Rome was aroused by the recovery of her former rival. The story is often told, that Cáto (the Cénsor) was sent to Cárthage on an embassy; that he was astonished at the wealth and prosperity which everywhere met his gaze; that he pictured the possibility of another struggle with that queen of the seas; and that he closed every speech in the senate with the words, "Cárthage must be destroyed."

Beginning of the Third Púnic War.—Whether Rome was really alarmed at the growth of Cárthage or only jealous of its commercial prosperity, the words of Cáto became the policy of the senate. The Rómans only waited for an opportunity to put this policy into effect. This they soon found in the quarrels between Cárthage and Numídia, whose king, Masiníssa, was an ally of Rome. After appealing in vain to the senate to protect their rights against Masiníssa, the Carthagínians were bold enough to take up arms to protect their own rights. But to Rome it was a deadly offense to take up arms against her ally. As a guaranty to keep the peace, the Carthagínians were commanded to give up three hundred of their noblest youths as hostages. The hostages were accordingly given up. The Carthagínians were then informed that, as they were then under the protection of Rome, they would not need to go to war; and that they must surrender all their arms and munitions. This hard demand was also complied with, and Cárthage became defenseless. The demand was now made that, as the city was fortified, it too must be given up, and the inhabitants must remove to a point ten miles from the coast; in other words, that "Cárthage must be destroyed." To such a revolting and infamous command the Carthagínians could not yield, and they resolved upon a desperate resistance.

Siege and Destruction of Cárthage (146 B.C.).—Never was there a more heroic defense than that made by Cárthage in this, her last struggle. She was without arms, without war ships, without allies. To make new weapons, the temples were turned into workshops; and it is said that the women cut off their long hair to be twisted into bowstrings. Supplies were collected for a long siege; the city became a camp. For three long years the brave Carthagínians resisted every attempt to take the city. They repelled the assault upon their walls. They were then cut off from all communication with the outside world by land, and they sought an egress by the sea. Their communication by water was then cut off by a great mole, or breakwater, built by the Rómans, and they cut a new outlet to the sea. They then secretly built fifty war ships, and attacked the Róman fleet. But all these heroic efforts simply put off the day of doom. At last, under Scípio Æmiliánus, the Rómans forced their way through the wall, and the city was taken street by street, and house by house. Cárthage became the prey of the Róman soldiers. Its temples were plundered; its inhabitants were carried away as captives; and by the command of the senate, the city itself was consigned to flames. The destruction of Cárthage took place in the same year (146 B.C.) in which Córinth was destroyed. The terrible punishment inflicted upon these two cities in Greece and África was an evidence of Rome's grim policy to be absolutely supreme everywhere.

Ruins of the Theater at Léptis Mágna in Rómanized África

África reduced to a Province.—Like Macedónia, África was now reduced to the form of a province. It comprised all the land which had hitherto been subject to Cárthage. Útica was made the new capital city, where the Róman governor was to reside. All the cities which had favored Cárthage were punished by the loss of their land, or the payment of tribute. The cities which had favored Rome were allowed to remain free. Numídia, on account of its fidelity to Rome, was continued as an independent ally. In this way the condition of every city and people was dependent upon the extent of its loyalty to Rome. After África was made a province, it soon became a Rómanized country. Its commerce passed into the hands of Róman merchants; the Róman manners and customs were introduced; and the Látin language became its language.

III. PACIFICATION OF THE PROVINCES

Condition of Spain.—While the Rómans were thus engaged in creating the new provinces of Macedónia and África, they were called upon to maintain their authority in the old provinces of Spain and Sícily. We remember that, after the second Púnic war, Spain was divided into two provinces, each under a Róman governor. But the Róman authority was not well established in Spain, except upon the eastern coast. The tribes in the interior and on the western coast were nearly always in a state of revolt. The most rebellious of these tribes were the Lusitánians in the west, in what is now Pórtugal; and the Celtibérians in the interior, south of the Ibérus River. In their efforts to subdue these barbarous peoples, the Rómans were themselves too often led to adopt the barbarous methods of deceit and treachery.

War with the Lusitánians.—How perfidious a Róman general could be, we may learn from the way in which Sulpícius Gálba waged war with the Lusitánians. After one Róman army had been defeated, Gálba persuaded this tribe to submit and promised to settle them upon fertile lands. When the Lusitánians came to him unarmed to receive their expected reward, they were surrounded and murdered by the troops of Gálba. But it is to the credit of Rome that Gálba was denounced for this treacherous act. Among the few men who escaped from the massacre of Gálba was a young shepherd by the name of Viriáthus. Under his brave leadership, the Lusitánians continued the war for nine years. Finally, Viriáthus was murdered by his own soldiers, who were bribed to do this treacherous act by the Róman general. With their leader lost, the Lusitánians were obliged to submit (138 B.C.).

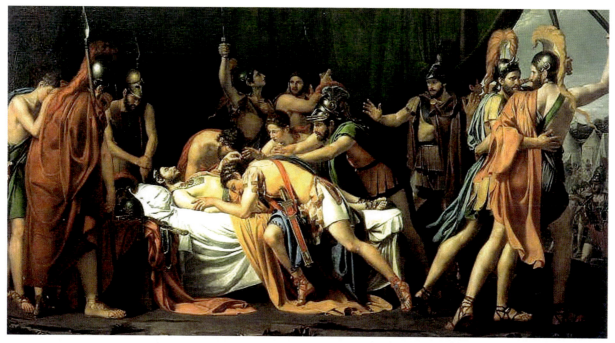

Death of Viriáthus (1806-1807), José de Madrazo (1781-1859), Museo del Prado, Madrid

The Númantine War.—The other troublesome tribe in Spain was the Celtibérians, who were even more warlike than the Lusitánians. At one time the Róman general was defeated and obliged to sign a treaty of peace, acknowledging the independence of the Spánish tribe. But the senate, repeating what it had done many years before after the battle of the Cáudine Forks, refused to ratify this treaty, and surrendered the Róman commander to the enemy. The "fiery war," as it was called, still continued and became at last centered about Numántia, the chief town of the Celtibérians. The defense of Numántia, like that of Cárthage, was heroic and desperate. Its fate was also like that of Cárthage. It was compelled to surrender (133 B.C.) to the same Scípio Æmiliánus. Its people were sold into slavery, and the town itself was blotted from the earth.

The Servile War in Sícily.—While Spain was being pacified, a more terrible war broke out in the province of Sícily. This was an insurrection of the slaves of the island. One of the worst results of the Róman conquest was the growth of the slave system. Immense numbers of the captives taken in war were thrown upon the market. One hundred and fifty thousand slaves had been sold by Æmílius Páullus; fifty thousand captives had been sent home from Cárthage. Ítaly and Sícily swarmed with a servile population. It was in Sícily that this system bore its first terrible fruit. Maltreated by their masters, the slaves rose in rebellion under a leader, called Eúnus, who defied the Róman power for three years. Nearly two hundred thousand insurgents gathered about his standard. Four Róman armies were defeated, and Rome herself was thrown into consternation. After the most desperate resistance, the rebellion was finally quelled and the island was pacified (132 B.C.).

Bequest of Pérgamum; Province of Ásia.—This long period of war and conquest, by which Rome finally obtained the proud position of mistress of the Mediterránean, was closed by the almost peaceful acquisition of a new province. The little kingdom of Pérgamum, in Ásia Minor, had maintained, for the most part, a friendly relation to Rome. When the last king, Áttalus III., died (133 B.C.), having no legal heirs, he bequeathed his kingdom to the Róman people. This newly acquired territory was organized as a province under the name of "Ásia." The smaller states of Ásia Mínor, and Égypt, Líbya, and Numídia, retained a subordinate relation as dependencies. The supreme authority of Rome, at home and abroad, was now firmly established.

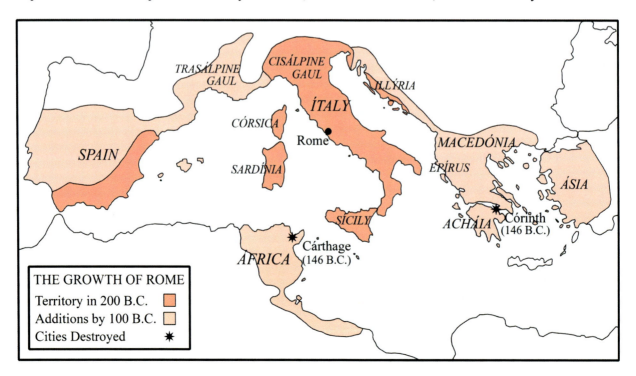

76

CHAPTER XVIII

ROME AS A WORLD POWER

The Róman Government, I.—Rome and the Provinces, II.—The New Civilization, III.

I. THE RÓMAN GOVERNMENT

Effects of the Conquests.—We have thus followed the career of Rome during the most heroic period of her history. We have traced the path of her armies from the time they crossed the Sicílian Strait until they were finally victorious in África, in Spain, in Greece, and in Ásia Mínor. We have seen new provinces brought under her authority, until she had become the greatest power of the world. We may well wonder what would be the effect of these conquests upon the character of the Róman people, upon their government, and upon their civilization. Many of these effects were no doubt very bad. By their conquests the Rómans came to be ambitious, to love power for its own sake, and to be oppressive to their conquered subjects. By plundering foreign countries, they also came to be avaricious, to love wealth more than honor, to indulge in luxury, and to despise the simplicity of their fathers. But still it was the conquests that made Rome the great power that she was. By bringing foreign nations under her sway, she was obliged to control them, and to create a system of law by which they could be governed. In spite of all its faults, her government was the most successful that had ever existed up to this time. It was the way in which Rome secured her conquests that showed the real character of the Róman people. The chief effect of the conquests was to transform Rome from the greatest *conquering* people of the world, to the greatest *governing* people of the world.

The New Nobility.—The oldest Róman government was, we remember, based upon the patrícian class. We have already seen how the separation between the patrícians and the plebéians was gradually broken down. The old patrícian aristocracy had passed away, and Rome had become, in theory, a democratic republic. Everyone who was enrolled in the thirty-five tribes was a full Róman citizen, and had a share in the government. But we must remember that not all the persons who were under the Róman authority were full Róman citizens. The inhabitants of the Látin colonies were not full Róman citizens. They could not hold office, and only under certain conditions could they vote. The Itálian allies were not citizens at all, and could neither vote nor hold office. And now the conquests had added millions of people to those who were not citizens. The Róman world was, in fact, governed by the comparatively few people who lived in and about the city of Rome. But even within this class of citizens at Rome, there had gradually grown up a smaller body of persons, who became the real holders of political power. This small body formed a new nobility, the *optimátes*. All who had held the office of cónsul, prǽtor, or cúrule ædile, that is, a "cúrule office," were regarded as nobles (*nóbiles*), and their families were distinguished by the right of setting up the ancestral images in their homes (*ius imáginis*). Any citizen might, it is true, be elected to the cúrule offices; but the noble families were able, by their wealth, to influence the elections, so as practically to retain these offices in their own hands.

The Greatness of the Senate.—The new nobility sought to govern the world through the senate. The senators were chosen by the cénsor, who was obliged to place upon his list, first of all, those who had held a cúrule office. On this account, the nobles had the first claim to a seat in the senate; and, consequently, they came to form the great body of its members. When a person was once chosen senator he remained a senator for life, unless disgraced for gross misconduct. In this way the nobles gained possession of the senate, which became, in fact, the most permanent and powerful branch of the Róman government. Although it was an aristocratic and exclusive body, it was made up of some of the most able men of Rome. Its members were men of distinction, of wealth, and generally of great political ability. Though often inspired by motives which were selfish, ambitious, and avaricious, it was still the greatest body of rulers that ever existed in the ancient world. It managed the finances of the state; controlled the erection of public works; directed the foreign policy; administered the provinces; determined largely the character of legislation, and was, in fact, the real sovereign of the Róman state.

The Weakness of the Assemblies.—With the increase of the power of the senate, the power of the popular assemblies declined. The old patrícian assembly of the cúries (*comítia curiáta*) had long since been reduced to a mere shadow. But the other two assemblies, that of the céntures and that of the tribes, still held an important place as legislative bodies. But there were two reasons why they declined in influence. The first reason was their unwieldy character. As they grew in size and could only say "yes" or "no" to the questions submitted to them, they lost their independent position. The second reason for their decline was the growing custom of first submitting to the senate the proposals which were to be passed upon by them. So that, as long as the senate was so influential in the state, the popular assemblies were weak and inefficient.

II. ROME AND THE PROVINCES

The Organization of the Provinces.—The most important feature of the new Róman government was the organization of the provinces. There were now eight: (1) Sícily, acquired as the result of the first Púnic war; (2) Sardínia and Córsica, obtained during the interval between the first and second Púnic wars; (3) Hither Spain and (4) Farther Spain, acquired in the second Púnic war; (5) Illýricum, reduced after the third Macedónian war; (6) Macedónia (to which Acháia was attached), reduced after the destruction of Córinth; (7) África, organized after the third Púnic war; and (8) Ásia, bequeathed by Áttalus III., the last king of Pérgamum.

The method of organizing these provinces was in some respects similar to that which had been adopted for governing the cities in Ítaly. Rome saw clearly that to control these newly conquered cities and communities, they must, like the cities of Ítaly, be isolated, that is, separated entirely from one another, so that they could not combine in any effort to resist her authority. Every city was made directly responsible to Rome. The great difference between the Itálian and the provincial towns was the fact that the chief burden of the Itálian town was to furnish military aid: soldiers and ships; while that of the provincial town was to furnish tribute: money and grain. Itálian land was also generally free from taxes, while provincial land was subject to tribute.

The Provincial Governor.—A province might be defined as a group of conquered cities, outside of Ítaly, under the control of a governor sent from Rome. At first these governors were prætors, who were elected by the people. Afterward they were propraetors or procónsuls, that is, persons who had already served as prætors or cónsuls at Rome. The governor held his office for one year; and during this time was the supreme military and civil ruler of the province. He was commander in chief of the army, and was expected to preserve his territory from internal disorder and from foreign invasion. He controlled the collection of the taxes, with the aid of the quæstor, who kept the accounts. He also administered justice between the provincials. Although the governor was responsible to the senate, the welfare or misery of the provincials depended largely upon his own disposition and will.

The Towns of the Province.—All the towns of the province were subject to Rome; but it was Rome's policy not to treat them all in exactly the same way. Like the cities of Ítaly, they were graded according to their merit. Some were favored, like Gádes and Áthens, and were treated as allied towns (*civitátes fœderátæ*); others, like Útica, were free from tribute (*immúnes*); but the great majority of them were considered as tributary (*stipendiáriæ*). But all these towns alike possessed local self-government, so far as this was consistent with the supremacy of Rome; that is, they retained their own laws, assemblies, and magistrates.

The Administration of Justice.—In civil matters, the citizens of every town were judged by their own magistrates. But when a dispute arose between citizens of different towns, it was the duty of the governor to judge between them. At the beginning of his term of office, he generally issued an edict, setting forth the rules upon which he would decide their differences. Each succeeding governor reissued the rules of his predecessor, with the changes which he saw fit to make. In this way justice was administered with great fairness throughout the provinces; and there grew up a great body of legal principles, called the "law of nations" (*ius géntium*), which formed an important part of the Róman law.

The Collection of Taxes.—The Róman revenue was mainly derived from the new provinces. But instead of raising these taxes directly through her own officers, Rome let out the business of collecting the revenue to a set of money dealers, called *publicáni*. These persons agreed to pay into the treasury a certain sum for the right of collecting taxes in a certain province. Whatever they collected above this sum, they appropriated to themselves. This rude mode of collecting taxes, called "farming" the revenues, was unworthy of a great state like Rome, and was the chief cause of the oppression of the provincials. The governors, it is true, had the power of protecting the people from being plundered. But as they themselves received no pay for their services, except what they could get out of the provinces, they were too busy in making their own fortunes to watch closely the methods of the tax-gatherers. Like every other conquering nation, the Rómans were tempted to benefit themselves at the expense of their subjects.

III. THE NEW CIVILIZATION

Foreign Influences; Héllenism at Rome.—When we think of the conquests of Rome, we usually think of the armies which she defeated, and the lands which she subdued. But these were not the only conquests which she made. She appropriated not only foreign lands, but also foreign ideas. While she was plundering foreign temples, she was obtaining new ideas of religion and art. The educated and civilized people whom she captured in war and of whom she made slaves, often became the teachers of her children and the writers of her books. In such ways as these Rome came under the influence of foreign ideas. The most powerful of these foreign influences was that of Greece. We might say that when Greece was conquered by Rome, Rome was civilized by Greece. These foreign influences were seen in her new ideas of religion and philosophy, in her literature, her art, and her manners.

The Róman Religion.—As Rome came into contact with other people, we can see how her religion was affected by foreign influences. The worship of the family remained much the same; but the religion of the state became considerably changed. It is said that the entire Greek Olýmpus was introduced into Ítaly. The Rómans adopted the Greek ideas and stories regarding the gods; and their worship became more showy and elaborate. Even some of the superstitious and fantastic rites of Ásia found their way into Rome. These changes did not improve the religion; they made it more corrupt. The Róman religion, by absorbing the various ideas of other people, became a world-wide and composite form of paganism. One of the redeeming features of the Róman religion was the worship of exalted qualities, like Honor and Virtue; for example, alongside of the temple to Júno, temples were also erected to Loyalty and Hope.

Róman Philosophy.—The more educated Rómans lost their interest in religion, and betook themselves to the study of Greek philosophy. They studied the nature of the gods and the moral duties of men. In this way the Greek ideas of philosophy found their way into Rome. Some of these ideas, like those of the Stóics, were elevating, and tended to preserve the simplicity and strength of the old Róman character. But other ideas, like those of the Epicuréans, seemed to justify a life of pleasure and luxury.

Mosaïc of Pláto's Academy at Pompéii

Róman Literature.—Before the Rómans came into contact with the Greeks, they cannot be said to have had anything which can properly be called a literature. They had certain crude verses and ballads; but it was the Greeks who first taught them how to write. It was not until the close of the first Púnic war, when the Greek influence became strong, that we begin to find the names of any Látin authors. The first author, Andronícus, who is said to have been a Greek slave, wrote a Látin poem in imitation of Hómer. Then came Nævius, who combined a Greek taste with a Róman spirit, and who wrote a poem on the first Púnic war; and after him, Énnius, who taught Greek to the Rómans, and wrote a great poem on the history of Rome, called the "Annals." The Greek influence is also seen in Pláutus and Térence, the greatest writers of Róman comedy; and in Fábius Píctor, who wrote a history of Rome, in the Greek language.

Róman Art.—As the Rómans were a practical people, their earliest art was shown in their buildings. From the Etrúscans they had learned to use the arch and to build strong and massive structures. But the more refined features of art they obtained from the Greeks. While the Rómans could never hope to acquire the pure æsthetic spirit of the Greeks, they were inspired with a passion for collecting Greek works of art, and for adorning their buildings with Greek ornaments. They imitated the Greek models and professed to admire the Greek taste; so that they came to be, in fact, the preservers of Greek art.

Róman Manners and Morals.—It is difficult for us to think of a nation of warriors as a nation of refined people. The brutalities of war seem inconsistent with the finer arts of living. But as the Rómans obtained wealth from their wars, they affected the refinement of their more cultivated neighbors. Some men, like Scípio Africánus, looked with favor upon the introduction of Greek ideas and manners; but others, like Cáto the Cénsor, were bitterly opposed to it. When the Rómans lost the simplicity of the earlier times, they came to indulge in luxuries and to be lovers of pomp and show. They loaded their tables with rich services of plate; they ransacked the land and the sea for delicacies with which to please their palates. Róman culture was often more artificial than real. The survival of the barbarous spirit of the Rómans in the midst of their professed refinement is seen in their amusements, especially the gladiatorial shows, in which men were forced to fight with wild beasts and with one another to entertain the people.

In conclusion, we may say that by their conquests the Rómans became a great and, in a certain sense, a civilized people, who appropriated and preserved many of the best elements of the ancient world; but who were yet selfish, ambitious, and avaricious, and who lacked the genuine taste and generous spirit which belong to the highest type of human culture.

CHAPTER XIX

THE TIMES OF THE GRÁCCHI

The Causes of Civil Strife, I.—The Reforms of Tibérius Grácchus, II.—The Reforms of Gáius Grácchus, III.

I. THE CAUSES OF CIVIL STRIFE

Character of the New Period.—If the period which we have just considered is the most heroic in Róman history, that which we are about to consider is one of the saddest, and yet one of the most interesting. It is one of the saddest, because it was a time when the Róman state was torn asunder by civil strifes, and the arms of the conquerors were turned against themselves. It is one of the most interesting, because it shows to us some of the greatest men that Rome ever produced, men whose names are a part of the world's history. Our attention will now be directed not so much to foreign wars as to political questions, to the struggle of parties, and the rivalry of party leaders. And as a result of it all, we shall see the republic gradually passing away, and giving place to the empire.

Divisions of the Róman People.—If we would understand this period of conflict, we should at the outset get a clear idea of the various classes of people in the Róman world. Let us briefly review these different grades of society.

First, there was the *senatorial order*, men who kept control of the higher offices, who furnished the members of the senate, and who really ruled the state. Next was the equestrian order, men who were called équites, or knights, on account of their great wealth, who formed the moneyed class, the capitalists of Rome, and who made their fortunes by all sorts of speculation, especially by gathering the taxes in the provinces. These two orders formed the aristocratic classes.

Below these was the great mass of the *city population*, the poor artisans and paupers, who formed a rabble and the materials of a mob, and who lived upon public charity and the bribes of office-seekers, and were amused by public shows given by the state or by rich citizens. Then came the poor *country farmers* living upon the Róman domain, the peasants, many of whom had been deprived of their lands by rich creditors or by the avaricious policy of the government. These two classes formed the mass of the poorer citizens of Rome.

Outside of the Róman domain proper (*áger Románus*) were the *Látin colonists*, who were settled upon conquered lands in Ítaly, who had practically no political rights, and who were very much in the same social condition as the Róman peasants. Besides these were the *Itálian allies*, who had been subdued by Rome in early times, and had been given none of the rights of citizenship. These two classes formed the subject population of Ítaly.

Now if we go outside of Ítaly we find the great body of *provincials*, some of them favored by being left free from taxation, but the mass of them subject to the Róman tribute; and all of them excluded from the rights and privileges of citizens.

Finally, if we go to the very bottom of the Róman population, we find the *slaves*, having none of the rights of citizens or of men. A part of them, the house slaves, were treated with some consideration; but the field slaves were treated wretchedly, chained in gangs by day and confined in dungeons by night.

Thus we have an aristocratic class, made up of the senators and équites; a poor citizen class, made up of the city rabble and the country farmers about Rome; and then a disfranchised class, made up of the Látins, the Itálians, and the provincials, besides the slaves.

Defects of the Róman Government.—When we look over these various classes of the Róman people, we must conclude that there were some radical defects in the Róman system of government. The great mass of the population were excluded from all political rights. The Látins, the Itálians, the provincials, and the slaves, as we have seen, had no share in the government. This seems quite contrary to the early policy of Rome. We remember that before she began her great conquests, Rome had started out with the policy of *incorporation*. She had taken in the Sábines on the Quírinal hill, the Lucéres on the Cǽlian, the plebéians of the city, and the rural tribes about Rome. But after that time she had abandoned this policy, and no longer brought her conquered subjects within the state. This was the first defect of the Róman system.

But even those people who were given the rights of citizens were not able to exercise these rights in an efficient way. Wherever a Róman citizen might be, he must go to Rome to vote or to take part in the making of the laws. But when the citizens of Rome met together in the Fórum, or on the Cámpus Mártius, they made a large and unwieldy body, which could not do any important political business. Rome never learned that a democratic government in a large state is impossible without *representation*; that is, the election by the people of a few leading men to protect their interests, and to make the laws for them. The giving up of the policy of incorporation and the absence of the principle of representation were the two great defects in the Róman political system.

The Decay of Patriotism.—We may not blame the Rómans for not discovering the value of representation, since this system may be regarded as a modern invention. But we must blame those who were the rulers of the state for their selfishness and their lack of true patriotism. There were, no doubt, some patriotic citizens at Rome who were devoted to the public welfare; but the majority of the men who governed the state were men devoted to their own interests more than to the interests of the country at large. The aristocratic classes sought to enrich themselves by the spoils of war and the spoils of office; while the rights and the welfare of the common citizens, the Itálians, and the provincials were too often forgotten or ignored.

The Growth of Large Estates.—One of the causes which led to the civil strife was the distress and misery of the people in different parts of Ítaly, resulting from the growth of large landed estates. Years before, the people had possessed their little farms, and were able to make a respectable living from them. Laws had been passed, especially the Licínian laws, to keep the public lands distributed in such a way as to benefit the poorer people. But it was more than two hundred years since the Licínian laws were passed; and they were now a dead letter. Many of the small farms had become absorbed into large estates held by rich landlords; and the class of small farmers had well-nigh disappeared. This change benefited one class of the people at the expense of the other. The Róman writer Plíny afterward saw the disastrous effects of this system, and said that it was the large estates which destroyed Ítaly.

The Evils of Slave Labor.—But this was not all. If the poor farmers, who had been deprived of their own fields, could have received good wages by working upon the estates of the rich landlords, they might still have had some means of living. But they were even deprived of this; because the estates were everywhere worked by slaves. So that slavery, as well as large estates, was a cause which helped to bring Ítaly to the brink of ruin.

II. THE REFORMS OF TIBÉRIUS GRÁCCHUS

Character of Tibérius Grácchus.—The first serious attempt to remedy the existing evils was made by Tibérius Semprónius Grácchus. He was the elder of two brothers who sacrificed their lives in efforts to benefit their fellow-citizens. Their mother was the noble-minded Cornélia, the daughter of the great Scípio Africánus, the type of the perfect mother, who regarded her boys as "jewels" more precious than gold, and who taught them to love truth, justice, and their country. Tibérius when a young man had served in the Spánish army under Scípio Æmiliánus, the

distinguished Róman who conquered Cárthage and Numántia. It is said that when Tibérius Grácchus passed through Etrúria, on his way to and from Spain, he was shocked to see the fertile fields cultivated by gangs of slaves, while thousands of free citizens were living in idleness and poverty. He was a man of refined nature and a deep sense of justice, and he determined to do what he could to remedy these evils.

Cornélia Presenting Her Children, the Grácchi, as Her Treasures (1785)
Angelica Kauffmann, Virginia Museum of Fine Arts, Richmond

His Agrarian Laws.—Tibérius Grácchus was elected tríbune and began his work of reform (133 B.C.). He believed that the wretched condition of the Róman people was due chiefly to the unequal division of the public land, and especially to the failure to enforce the Licínian laws. He therefore proposed to revive these laws; to limit the holding of public land to five hundred iúgera (about three hundred acres) for each person; to pay the present holders for any improvements they had made; and then to rent the land thus taken up to the poorer class of citizens. This seemed fair enough; for the state was the real owner of the public land, and could do what it wished with its own. But the rich landlords; who had held possession of this land for so many years, looked upon the measure as the same thing as taking away their own property. When it was now proposed to redistribute this land, there immediately arose a fierce conflict between the old senatorial party and the followers of Tibérius.

His Illegal Action.—Tibérius determined to pass his law in spite of the senate. The senate, on the other hand, was equally determined that the law should not be passed. Accordingly, the senators induced one of the tríbunes, whose name was M. Octávius, to put his "veto" upon the passage of the law. This act of Octávius was entirely legal, for he did what the law gave him the right to do. Tibérius, on the other hand, in order to outdo his opponent, had recourse to a highhanded measure. Instead of waiting a year for the election of new tríbunes who might be devoted to the people's cause, he called upon the people to deprive Octávius of his office. This was an illegal act, because there was no law which authorized such a proceeding. But the people did as Tibérius desired, and Octávius was deposed. The law of Tibérius was then passed in the assembly of the tribes, and three commissioners were chosen to carry it into effect.

This of course roused the indignation of the senators, who determined to prosecute Tibérius when his term of office had expired. Tibérius knew that as long as he held the office of tríbune his person would be sacred, and he could not be tried for his action; hence he announced himself as a candidate for reelection. This, too, was illegal, for the law forbade a reelection until after an interval of ten years.

Fall of Tibérius Grácchus.—The law of Tibérius and the method which he had used to pass it, increased the bitterness between the aristocratic party and the popular party who came to be known, respectively, as the *optimátes* and the *populáres*. The senators denounced Tibérius as a traitor; the people extolled him as a patriot. The day appointed for the election came. Two tribes had already voted for the reelection of Tibérius, when a band of senators appeared in the Fórum, headed by Scípio Nasíca, armed with sticks and clubs; and in the riot which ensued Tibérius Grácchus and three hundred of his followers were slain. This was the first blood shed in the civil wars of Rome. The killing of a tríbune by the senators was as much an illegal act as was the deposition of Octávius. Both parties had disregarded the law, and the revolution was begun.

The Grácchi, Jean-Baptiste Claude Eugène Guillaume (1822-1905), Musée d'Orsay, Paris

III. THE REFORMS OF GÁIUS GRÁCCHUS

The Rise of Gáius Grácchus.—After the death of Tibérius his law was for a time carried into execution. The commissioners proceeded with their work of redividing the land. But the people were for a time without a real leader. The cause of reform was then taken up by Gáius Grácchus, the brother of Tibérius, and the conflict was renewed. Gáius was in many respects an abler man than Tibérius. No more sincere and patriotic, he was yet a broader statesman and took a wider view of the situation. He did not confine his attention simply to relieving the poor citizens. He believed that to rescue Rome from her troubles, it was necessary to weaken the power of the senate, whose selfish and avaricious policy had brought on these troubles. He also believed that the Látins and the Itálians should be protected, as well as the poor Róman citizens.

His Efforts to Benefit the People.—When Gáius Grácchus obtained the position of tríbune (123 B.C.) his influence for a time was all-powerful. He was eloquent and persuasive, and

84

practically had the control of the government. From his various laws we may select those which were the most important, and which best show his general policy. First of all, he tried to help the people by a law which was really the most mischievous of all his measures. This was his famous "corn law." It was intended to benefit the poor population in the city, which was at that time troublesome and not easy to control. The law provided that any Róman citizen could receive grain from the public storehouses for a certain price less than its cost. But the number of the poor in the city was not decreased; the paupers now flocked to Rome from all parts of Ítaly to be fed at the public crib. This corn law became a permanent institution of Rome. We may judge of its evil effect when it is said that not many years afterward there were three hundred and twenty thousand citizens who were dependent upon the government for their food. Gáius may not have known what evil effect this law was destined to produce. At any rate, it insured his popularity with the lower classes. He then renewed the agrarian laws of his brother; and also provided for sending out colonies of poor citizens into different parts of Ítaly, and even into the provinces.

His Efforts to Weaken the Senate.—But Gáius believed that such measures as these would afford only temporary relief, as long as the senate retained its great power. It was, of course, impossible to overthrow the senate. But it was possible to take from it some of the powers which it possessed. From the senators had hitherto been selected the jurors (*iúdices*) before whom were tried cases of extortion and other crimes. By a law Gáius took away from the senate this right to furnish jurors in criminal cases, and gave it to the équites, that is, the wealthy class outside of the senate. This gave to the equites a more important political position, and drew them over to the support of Gáius, and thus tended to split the aristocratic classes in two. The senate was thus deprived not only of its right to furnish jurors, but also of the support of the wealthy men who had previously been friendly to it. This was a great triumph for the popular party; and Gáius looked forward to another victory.

His Effort to Enfranchise the Itálians.—When he was reelected to the tríbunate Gáius Grácchus came forward with his grand scheme of extending the Róman franchise to the people of Ítaly. This was the wisest of all his measures, but the one which cost him his popularity and influence. It aroused the jealousy of the poorer citizens, who did not wish to share their rights with foreigners. The senators took advantage of the unpopularity of Gáius, and now posed as the friends of the people. They induced one of the tríbunes, by the name of Drúsus, to play the part of the demagogue. Drúsus proposed to found twelve new colonies at once, each with three thousand Róman citizens, and thus to put all the reforms of Gáius Grácchus into the shade. The people were deceived by this stratagem, and the attempt of Gáius to enfranchise the Itálians was defeated.

His Failure and Death.—Gáius did not succeed, as he desired, in being elected tríbune for the third time. A great part of the people soon abandoned him, and the ascendency of the senate was again restored. It was not long before a new law was passed which prevented any further distribution of the public land (*lex Thória*). Gáius failed to bring about the reforms which he attempted; but he may be regarded as having accomplished three things which remained after his death: (1) the elevation of the equéstrian order; (2) the establishment of the Róman poor law, or the system of grain largesses; and (3) the extension of the colonial system to the provinces. He lost his life in a tumult in which three thousand citizens were slain (121 B.C.).

Thus in a similar way the two Grácchi, who had attempted to rescue the Róman people from the evils of a corrupt government, perished. Their efforts at agrarian reform did not produce any lasting effect; but they pointed out the dangers of the state, and drew the issues upon which their successors continued the conflict. Their career forms the first phase in the great civil conflict at Rome.

CHAPTER XX

THE TIMES OF MÁRIUS AND SÚLLA

The Rise of Márius, I.—The Social War and the Rise of Súlla, II.—The Civil War between Márius and Súlla, III. The Dictatorship of Súlla (82-79 B.C.), IV.

I. THE RISE OF MÁRIUS

New Phase of the Civil Strife.—The troubles under the Grácchi had grown out of the attempts of two patriotic men to reform the evils of the state. The shedding of Róman blood had been limited to riots in the city, and to fights between the factions of the different parties. We now come to the time when the political parties seek the aid of the army; when the civil strife becomes in reality a civil war, and the lives of citizens seem of small account compared with the success of this or that political leader. We must now consider what was the condition of Rome after the fall of the Grácchi; how Márius came to the front as the leader of the popular party; and how he was overthrown by Súlla as the leader of the aristocratic party.

Corrupt Rule of the Aristocracy.—After the fall of the Grácchi the rule of the aristocracy was restored, and the government became more corrupt than ever before. The senators were often incompetent, and they had no clearly defined policy. They seemed desirous only to retain power and to enrich themselves, while the real interests of the people were forgotten. The little farms which Tibérius Grácchus had tried to create were again swallowed up in large estates. The provincials were ground down with heavy taxes. The slaves were goaded into insurrection. The sea swarmed with pirates, and the frontiers were threatened by foreign enemies.

The Jugúrthine War and Márius (111-105 B.C.).—The attention of the senate was first directed to a war in África. This war has little interest, except to show how corrupt Rome was, and how it brought to the front a great soldier, who became for a time the leader of the people.

The war in África grew out of the attempt of Jugúrtha to make himself king of Numídia, which kingdom we remember was an ally of Rome. The senate sent commissioners to Numídia in order to settle the trouble; but the commissioners sold themselves to Jugúrtha as soon as they landed in África. The Róman people were incensed, and war was declared against Jugúrtha. The conduct of the war was placed in the hands of the cónsul, L. Calpúrnius Béstia, who on arriving in África accepted Jugúrtha's gold and made peace. The people were again indignant, and summoned Jugúrtha to Rome to testify against the cónsul. When Jugúrtha appeared before the assembly, and was about to make his statement, one of the tríbunes, who had also been bought by African gold, put a veto upon the proceedings; so that by the bribery of a tríbune it became impossible to punish the bribery of a cónsul. Jugúrtha remained in Rome until he caused one of his rivals to be murdered, when he was banished from the city. He expressed his private opinion of Rome when he called it "a venal city, ready to perish whenever it could find a purchaser."

The war in Numídia was continued under the new cónsul, Q. Cæcílius Metéllus, who selected as his lieutenant Gáius Márius, a rough soldier who had risen from the ranks, but who had a real genius for war. So great was the success of Márius that he was elected cónsul, and superseded Metéllus in the supreme command of the African army. Márius fulfilled all the expectations of the people; he defeated the enemy, and Jugúrtha was made a prisoner. A triumph was given to the conqueror, in which the captive king was led in chains; and Márius became the people's hero.

86

Jugúrtha's Capture (1772)
Print by Joaquin Ibarra (1725-1785)

Márius and the Címbric War (113-101 B.C.).—But a greater glory now awaited Márius. While he had been absent in África, Rome was threatened by a deluge of barbarians from the north. The Címbri and Téutones, fierce peoples from Gérmany, had pushed down into the southern part of Gaul, and had overrun the new province of Narbonénsis (established 120 B.C.). It seemed impossible to stay these savage invaders. Army after army was defeated. It is said that sixty thousand Rómans perished in one battle at Aráusio (107 B.C.) on the banks of the Rhône. The way seemed open to Ítaly, and all eyes turned to Márius as the only man who could save Rome. On the same day on which he received his triumph, Márius was reelected to the cónsulship, and assigned to his new command. This was contrary to law, to reelect an officer immediately after his first term; but the Rómans had come to believe that "in the midst of arms, the laws are silent."

Márius set to work to reorganize the Róman army. The army became no longer a raw body of citizens arranged according to wealth; but a trained body of soldiers drawn from all classes of society, and devoted to their commander. With the discretion of a true soldier Márius determined to be fully prepared before meeting his formidable foe. The Címbri turned aside for a time into Spain. Márius remained patiently on the Rhône, drilling his men and guarding the approaches to the Alps. As the time passed by, the people continued to trust him, and elected him as cónsul a third, and then a fourth time. At length the barbarians reappeared, ready for the invasion of Ítaly. One part, the Téutones, prepared to invade Ítaly from the west; while the other part, the Címbri, prepared to cross the Alps into the northwestern corner of Ítaly. Against the Téutones Márius posted his own army; and to meet the Címbri he dispatched his colleague, Q. Lutátius Cátulus. In the battle of Áquæ Séxtiæ he annihilated the host of the Téutones (102 B.C.); and the people elected him a fifth time to the cónsulship. Soon the Címbri crossed the Alps and drove Cátulus across the Po. Márius joined him, drove back the barbarians, and utterly routed them near Vercéllæ (101 B.C.). Ítaly was thus saved. For this twofold victory Rome gave to Márius a magnificent triumph, celebrated with double splendor. He was hailed as the savior of his Country, the second Camíllus, and the third Rómulus.

Márius as a Party Leader.—Márius was now at the height of his popularity. There had never before been a man in Rome who so far outshone his rivals. As he was a man of the common people, the leaders of the popular party saw that his great name would be a help to their cause.

The men who aspired to the leadership of the popular party since the death of the Grácchi were Saturnínus and Gláucia. To these men Márius now allied himself, and was elected to the cónsulship for the sixth time. This alliance formed a sort of political "ring," which professed to rule the state in the interest of the people; but which aroused a storm of opposition on the part of the senators. As in the days of the Grácchi, tumults arose, and the streets of Rome again became stained with blood. The senate called upon Márius, as cónsul, to put down the insurrection. Márius reluctantly complied; and in the conflict that followed, his colleagues, Saturnínus and Gláucia, were killed. Márius now fell into disrepute. Having allied himself to the popular leaders and afterward yielded to the senate, he lost the confidence of both. In spite of his greatness as a soldier, he proved his utter incapacity as a party leader. He soon retired from Rome in the hope of recovering his popularity, and of coming back when the tide should turn in his favor.

II. THE SOCIAL WAR AND THE RISE OF SÚLLA

Rome and the Itálian Allies.—With the failure of Márius, and the death of his colleagues, the senate once more recovered the reins of government. But the troubles still continued. The Itálian allies were now clamoring for their rights, and threatening war if their demands were not granted. We remember that when Rome had conquered Ítaly, she did not give the Itálian people the rights of citizenship. They were made subject allies, but received no share in the government. The Itálian allies had furnished soldiers for the Róman armies, and had helped to make Rome the mistress of the Mediterránean. They believed, therefore, that they were entitled to all the rights of Róman citizens; and some of the patriotic leaders of Rome believed so too. But it seemed as difficult to break down the distinction between Rómans and Itálians as it had been many years before to remove the barriers between the patrícians and the plebéians.

Attempt and Failure of Drúsus.—At this crisis there appeared its new reformer, the tríbune M. Lívius Drúsus, son of the Drúsus who opposed Gáius Grácchus. He was a well-disposed man, who seemed to believe that all the troubles of the state could be settled by a series of compromises. Of a noble nature, of pure motives, and of generous disposition, he tried to please everybody, and succeeded in pleasing nobody. First, to please the populace, he proposed to increase the largesses of grain; and to make payment easy by introducing a cheap copper coin which should pass for the same value as the previous silver one. Next, to reconcile the senators and the équites, he proposed to select the jurors (*iúdices*) from both classes, thus dividing the power between them. Finally, to meet the demands of the Itálians, he proposed to grant them what they asked for, the Róman franchise. It was one thing to propose these laws; it was quite another thing to pass them. As the last law was the most offensive, he began by uniting the équites and the people for the purpose of passing the first two laws. These were passed against the will of the senate, and amid scenes of great violence. The senate declared the laws of Drúsus null and void. Disregarding this act of the senate as having no legal force, he then proposed to submit to the assembly the law granting the franchise to the Itálians. But this law was as offensive to the people as the others had been to the senate. Denounced by the senate as a traitor and abandoned by the people, this large-hearted and unpractical reformer was at last murdered by an unknown assassin; and all his efforts came to nothing.

Revolt of the Itálian Allies (90 B.C.).—The death of Drúsus drove the Itálians to revolt. The war which followed is known in history as the "social war," or the war of the allies (*sócii*). It was, in fact, a war of secession. The purpose of the allies was now, not to obtain the Róman franchise, but to create a new Itálian nation, where all might be equal. They accordingly organized a new republic with the central government at Corfínium, a town in the Ápennines. The new state was modeled after the government at Rome, with a senate of five hundred members, two cónsuls, and other magistrates. Nearly all the peoples of central and southern Ítaly joined in this revolt.

Aquiléia 184

Cremóna 218
Placéntia 218
Mútina 183
Bonárda 189

Aríminum 268

Séna Gállica 283

Fírmum 264

Spolétium 240
Cósa 273
Nárnia 299
Népete 383
Sútrium 383
Carsíoli 298
Pýrgi 191
Fregénae 245
Róma
Alba 303
Velítrae 494
Signia 495
Sóra 303
Ardea 442
Sátricum 385
Sétia 382
Fragéllae 388
Antium 338
Cáles 334
Nórba 492
Circéii 393
Terracína 329
Sinuéssa 296

Nóvum Cástrum 283
Hátria 298

Aesérnia 263
Lucéria 314
Benevéntum 268
Venúsia 291

Brundísium 244

Páestum 273

Thúrii (Cópiae) 194

Cróton 194

Víbo Valéntia 194

	Roman Territory in 396 B.C.
	Roman Territory in 100 B.C.
	Latin Colonies in 100 B.C.
	Roman Allies in 100 B.C.
•	**Roman Colonies and Dates**

ADRIATIC SEA

TYRRHÉNIAN SEA

IÓNIAN SEA

ÍTALY BEFORE
THE SOCIAL WAR
(ca. 100 B.C.)

SÍCILY

ÁFRICA

Rome was now threatened with destruction, not by a foreign enemy like the Címbri and Téutones, but by her own subjects. The spirit of patriotism revived; and the parties ceased for a brief time from their quarrels. Even Márius returned to serve as a legate in the Róman army. A hundred thousand men took the field against an equal number raised by the allies. In the first year the war was unfavorable to Rome. In the second year (89 B.C.) new preparations were made and new commanders were appointed: Márius, on account of his age, was not continued in his command; while L. Cornélius Súlla, who was once a subordinate of Márius, was made chief commander in Campánia. Márius felt deeply this slight, and began to be envious of his younger rival. The great credit of bringing this war to a close was due to Pompéius Strábo (the father of Pómpey the Great) and Súlla. The first Itálian capital, Corfínium, was taken by Pompéius; and the second capital, Boviánum, was captured by Súlla (88 B.C.). The social war was thus ended; but it had been a great affliction to Ítaly. It is roughly estimated that three hundred thousand men, Rómans and Itálians, lost their lives in this struggle. The compensation of this loss was the incorporation of Ítaly with Rome.

The Enfranchisement of Ítaly.—Although Rome was victorious in the field, the Itálians obtained what they had demanded before the war began, that is, the rights of Róman citizenship. The Rómans granted the franchise (1) to all Látins and Itálians who had remained loyal during the war (*lex Iúlia*, 90 B.C.); and (2) to every Itálian who should be enrolled by the prǽtor within sixty days of the passage of the law (*lex Pláutia Papíria*, 89 B.C.). Every person to whom these provisions applied was now a Róman citizen. The policy of incorporation, which had been discontinued for so long a time, was thus revived. The distinction between Rómans, Látins, and Itálians was now broken down, at least so far as the Itálian peninsula was concerned. The greater part of Ítaly was joined to the *áger Románus*, and Ítaly and Rome became practically one nation.

Lúcius Cornélius Súlla (So-Called)
Glyptothek Museum, Munich

The Elevation of Súlla.—Another result of the social war, which had a great effect upon the destinies of Rome, was the rise of Súlla. War was not a new occupation for Súlla. In the campaign against Jugúrtha he had served as a lieutenant of Márius. In the Címbric war he had displayed great courage and ability. And now he had become the most conspicuous commander in the Itálian war. As a result of his brilliant exploits, he was elected to the cónsulship. The senate also recognized him as the ablest general of the time, when it now appointed him to conduct the war in the East against the great enemy of Rome, Mithridátes, king of Póntus.

III. THE CIVIL WAR BETWEEN MÁRIUS AND SÚLLA

The Jealousy of Márius.—Márius had watched with envy the growing fame of Súlla. Although old enough to retire from active life, he was mortified in not receiving the command of the Eastern army. When Súlla was now appointed to this command, Márius determined if possible to displace him, or to satisfy his revenge in some other way. From this time Márius, who once seemed to possess the elements of greatness, appears to us as a vindictive and foolish old man, deprived of reason and the sense of honor. To prove that he had not lost the vigor of youth, it is said that he used to appear in the Cámpus Mártius and exercise with the young soldiers in wrestling and boxing. The chief motive which now seemed to influence him was the hatred of Súlla and the Súllan party.

Gáius Márius (So-Called)
Glyptothek Museum, Munich

Márius rejoins the Popular Party.—To regain his influence with the people Márius once more entered politics, and joined himself to the popular leaders. The most prominent of these leaders was now the tríbune P. Sulpícius Rúfus. With the aid of this politician, Márius hoped to win back the favor of the people, to weaken the influence of the senate, which had supported Súlla, and then to displace Súlla himself. This program was set forth in what are called the "Sulpícian laws" (88 B.C.). By the aid of an armed force these laws were passed, and two messengers were sent to Súlla to command him to turn over his army to Márius. To displace a commander legally appointed by the senate was an act unheard of, even in this period of revolution.

Súlla appeals to the Army.—If Márius and Sulpícius supposed that Súlla would calmly submit to such an outrage, they mistook his character. Súlla had not yet left Ítaly. His légions were still encamped in Campánia. He appealed to them to support the honor and authority of their commander. They responded to his appeal, and Súlla at the head of his troops marched to Rome. For the first time the Róman légions fought in the streets of the capital, and a question of politics was settled by the army. Márius and Sulpícius were driven from the city, and Súlla for the time being was supreme. He called together the senate, and caused the leaders of the popular party to be declared outlaws. He then annulled the laws passed by Sulpícius, and gave the senate the power hereafter to approve or reject all laws before they should be submitted to the people. With the army at his back Súlla could do what he pleased. When he had placed the government securely in the hands of the senate, as he thought, he left Rome for the purpose of conducting the war against Mithridátes in the East.

The Flight of Márius.—Márius was now an exile, a fugitive from the country which he had once saved. The pathetic story of his flight and wanderings is graphically told by Plútarch. He says that Márius set sail from Óstia, and was forced by a storm to land at Circéii, where he wandered about in hunger and great suffering; that his courage was kept up by remembering that when a boy he had found an eagle's nest with seven young in it, which a soothsayer had interpreted as meaning that he would be cónsul seven times; that he was again taken on board a vessel and landed at Mintúrnæ, where he was captured and condemned to death; that the slave who was ordered to kill him dropped his sword as he heard the stern voice of his intended victim shouting, "Man, darest thou kill Gáius Márius?" that he was then released and wandered to Sícily, and then to África, where, a fallen hero, he sat amid the ruins of Cárthage; that at last he found a safe retreat in a little island off the Áfrican coast, and waited for vengeance and the time of his seventh cónsulship.

Márius at Mintúrnae (1786), Jean-Germain Drouais (1763-1788), Louvre Museum, Paris

Gáius Márius on the Ruins of Cárthage (1807)
John Vanderlyn (1775-1852)
Fine Arts Museum of San Francisco

Súlla and the Mithridátic War (88-84 B.C.).—While Márius was thus enduring the miseries of exile, Súlla was gathering fresh glories in the East. When Súlla landed in Greece he found the eastern provinces in a wretched state. Mithridátes, the king of Póntus, had extended his power over a large part of Ásia Mínor. He had overrun the Róman province of Ásia. He had induced the Greek cities on the coast, which had been brought under the Róman power, to revolt and join his cause. He had massacred over eighty thousand Itálians living on the Asiátic coast. He had also sent his armies into Greece and Macedónia, and many of the cities there, including Áthens, had declared in his favor. The Róman power in the East seemed well-nigh broken. It was at this time that Súlla showed his greatest ability as a soldier. He drove back the armies of Mithridátes, besieged Áthens and reduced it. He destroyed an army at Chæronéa (86 B.C.), and another at Orchómenus (85 B.C.). Within four years he reestablished the Róman power, and compelled Mithridátes to sign a treaty of peace. The defeated king agreed to give up all his conquests; to surrender eighty war vessels; and to pay 3000 talents. After imposing upon the disloyal cities of Ásia Minor the

92

immense fine of 20,000 talents, Súlla returned to Ítaly to find his own party overthrown, and himself an outlaw.

Cínna and the Márian Massacres.—During the absence of Súlla, Rome had passed through a reign of terror. The time had now come when parties sought to support themselves by slaughtering their opponents. The two cónsuls who were left in power when Súlla left Rome, were Cn. Octávius, a friend of Súlla, and L. Cornélius Cínna, a friend of Márius. Cínna, who was an extreme partisan, proposed to rescind the laws of Súlla and reenact those of Sulpícius. But the senate was vehemently opposed to any such scheme. When the assembly of the tribes met in the Fórum to vote upon this proposal of Cínna, Octávius carried the day in an armed conflict in which ten thousand citizens are said to have lost their lives. But the victory of Octávius was short. Cínna was, it is true, deprived of his office; but following the example of his enemy Súlla, he appealed to the army for support.

At the same time Márius returned from his exile to aid the cause of Cínna. Uniting their forces, Márius and Cínna then marched upon Rome. The city was taken. Márius saw that the time had now come to satisfy his vengeance for the wrongs which he thought had been done him. The gates of the city were closed, and the massacres began. The first victim was the cónsul Octávius, whose head was hung up in the Fórum. Then followed the leaders of the senatorial party. For five days Márius was furious, and revelled in blood. The friends of Súlla were everywhere cut down. The city was a scene of murder, plunder, and outrage. After this spasm of slaughter a reign of terror continued for several months. No man's life was safe if he was suspected by Márius. Márius and Cínna then declared themselves to be cónsuls. But Márius held this, his seventh cónsulship, but a few days, when he died, a great man who had crumbled into ruins. After the death of Márius, Cínna, the professed leader of the popular party, ruled with the absolute power of a despot. He declared himself cónsul each year, and named his own colleague. But he seemed to have no definite purpose, except to wipe out the work of Súlla, and to keep himself supreme. At last, hearing of the approach of Súlla, he led an army to prevent him from landing in Ítaly; but was killed in a mutiny of his own soldiers.

Súlla's War with the Márian Party.—Súlla landed in Ítaly (83 B.C.) with a victorious army of forty thousand men. He had restored the power of Rome against her enemies abroad; he now set to work to restore her authority against her enemies at home. He looked upon the popular party as a revolutionary faction, ruling with no sanction of law or justice. Its leaders since the death of Cínna were Cn. Papírius Cárbo, the younger Márius, and Q. Sertórius. The landing of Súlla in Ítaly without disbanding his army was the signal for civil war. Southern Ítaly declared in his favor, and many prominent men looked to him as the deliverer of Rome. The choicest of his new allies was the son of Pompéius Strábo, then a young man of twenty-three, but whose future fame, as Pómpey the Great, was destined to equal that of Súlla himself. Súlla marched to Campánia and routed the forces of one cónsul, while troops of the other cónsul deserted to him in a body. He then attacked the young Márius in Látium, defeated him, and shut him up in the town of Prænéste. Northern Ítaly was at the same time held in check by Pómpey. A desperate battle was fought at Clúsium, in Etrúria, in which Súlla and Pómpey defeated the army of Cárbo. At last an army of Sámnites which had joined the Márian cause was cut to pieces at the Cólline gate under the very walls of Rome. Súlla showed what might be expected of him when he ordered six thousand Sámnite prisoners to be massacred in cold blood.

The Súllan Proscriptions.—With Ítaly at his feet and a victorious army at his back, Súlla, the champion of the senate, was now the supreme ruler of Rome. Before entering upon the work of reconstructing the government, he determined first of all to complete the work of destroying his enemies. It is sometimes said that Súlla was not a man of vindictive nature. Let us see what he did. He first outlawed all civil and military officers who had taken part in the revolution against him, and offered a reward of two talents to the murderer of any of these men. He then posted a list (*proscríptio*) containing the names of those citizens whom he wished to have killed. He placed eighty names on the first list, two hundred and twenty more on the second, as many more on the third, and so on until nearly five thousand citizens had been put to death in Rome.

But these despotic acts were not confined to Rome; they extended to every city of Ítaly. "Neither temple, nor hospitable hearth, nor father's house," says Plútarch, "was free from murder." Súlla went to Prænéste, and having no time to examine each individual, had all the people brought to one spot to the number of twelve thousand, and ordered them to be massacred. His sense of justice was not satisfied by punishing the living. The infamous Cátiline had murdered his own brother before the war had closed, and he asked Súlla to proscribe him as though he were alive, which was done. The heads of the slain victims Súlla caused to be piled in the streets of Rome for public execration. The tomb of Márius himself was broken open and his ashes were scattered. Besides taking the lives of his fellow-citizens, Súlla confiscated the lands of Ítaly, swept away cities, and wasted whole districts. If the proscriptions of Súlla were not inspired by the mad fury of revenge which led to the Márian massacres, they were yet prompted by the merciless policy of a tyrant.

IV. THE DICTATORSHIP OF SÚLLA (82-79 B.C.)

The Office of Perpetual Dictator.—When Súlla had destroyed his enemies he turned to the work of reconstructing the government in the interests of the senate and the aristocracy. The first question with Súlla was, What office should he hold in order to accomplish all he wished to do? The Grácchi had exercised their great influence by being elected tríbunes. Márius had risen to power through his successive cónsulships. But the office neither of tríbune nor of cónsul was suited to the purposes of Súlla. He wished for absolute power, in fact, to hold the royal *impérium*. But since the fall of the Tárquins no man had ever dared assume the name of "king." Súlla was shrewd enough to see how he could exercise absolute power under another name than that of king. The dictator was, in fact, a sort of temporary king. To make this office perpetual would be practically to restore the royal power. Accordingly, Súlla had himself declared dictator to hold the office as long as he pleased. All his previous acts were then confirmed. He was given the full power of life and death, the power to confiscate property, to distribute lands, to create and destroy colonies, and to regulate the provinces.

Military Support of Súlla's Power.—Súlla believed that a ruler to be strong must always be ready to draw the sword. He therefore did not mean to lose his hold upon his veteran soldiers. When his twenty-three légions were disbanded, they were not scattered, but were settled in Ítaly as military colonies. Each légion formed the body of citizens in a certain town, the lands being confiscated and assigned to the soldiers. The légionaries were thus bound in gratitude to Súlla, and formed a devoted body of militia upon which he felt that he could rely. By means of these colonies, Súlla placed his power upon a military basis.

Restoration of the Senate.—It was one of Súlla's chief purposes to restore the senate to its former position as the chief ruling body. In the first place, he filled it up with three hundred new members, elected by the *comítia tribúta* from the équites. The senatorial list was no longer to be made out by the cénsor, but everyone who had been quæstor was now legally qualified to be a senator. In the next place, the jurors (*iúdices*) in criminal trials were henceforth to be taken from the senate, and not from the equéstrian order. But as the new senators were from this order, the two classes became reconciled; and Súlla succeeded in doing what Drúsus had failed to accomplish. But more than all, no laws could hereafter be passed by the assembly of the tribes until first approved by the senate.

Weakening of the Assembly.—Súlla saw that the revolutionary acts of the last fifty years had been chiefly the work of the *comítia tribúta* under the leadership of the tríbunes. The other assembly, that of the cénturies, had, it is true, equal power to make laws. But the assembly of the tribes was more democratic, and the making of laws had gradually passed into the hands of that body. Súlla took away from the tribes the legislative power, and gave to the senate the authority to propose all laws to be submitted to the cénturies. The tendency of this change was to limit the assemblies to the mere business of electing the officers, the lower officers being elected by the tribes, and the higher officers by the cénturies. To keep control of the elections Súlla enfranchised ten thousand slaves, and gave them the right to vote; these creatures of Súlla were known as "Cornélii," or Súlla's freedmen.

Changes in the Magistrates.—In Súlla's mind the most revolutionary and dangerous office in the government was that of the tríbune. This officer hitherto could practically control the state. He had had the chief control of legislation; and also by his veto he could stop the wheels of government. Súlla changed all this. He limited the power of the tríbune to simple "intercession," that is, the protection of a citizen from an act of official injustice. He also provided that no tríbune could be elected to the cúrule offices. The other officers were also looked after. The cónsuls and prǽtors must henceforth devote themselves to their civil duties in the city; and then as procónsuls and proprǽtors they might afterward be assigned by the senate to the governorship of the provinces. Again, no one could be cónsul until he had been prǽtor, nor prǽtor until he had been quǽstor; and the old law was enforced, that no one could hold the same office the second time until after an interval of ten years.

Reform of the Judicial System.—The most permanent part of Súlla's reforms was the creation of a regular system of criminal courts. He organized permanent commissions (*quǽstiónes perpétuǽ*) for the trial of different kinds of crimes. Every criminal case was thus tried before a regular court, composed of a presiding judge, or prǽtor, and a body of jurymen, called *iúdices*. We must remember that whenever the word *iúdices* is used in the political history of this period it refers to these jurors in criminal cases, who were first chosen from the senate, then from the équites, and now under Súlla from the senate again. The organization of regular criminal courts by Súlla was the wisest and most valuable part of his legislation.

Súlla's Abdication and Death.—After a reign of three years (82-79 B.C.), and after having placed the government securely in the hands of the senate, as he supposed, Súlla resigned the dictatorship. He retired to his country house at Putéoli on the Bay of Náples. He spent the few remaining months of his life in writing his memoirs, which have unfortunately been lost. He hastened his end by dissipation, and died the next year (78 B.C.). The senate decreed him a public funeral, the most splendid that Rome had ever seen. His body was burned in the Cámpus Mártius. Upon the monument which was erected to his memory were inscribed these words: "No friend ever did him a kindness, and no enemy a wrong, without being fully repaid."

Súlla was a man of blood and iron. Cool and calculating, definite in his purpose, and unscrupulous in his methods, he was invincible in war and in peace. But the great part of the work which he seemed to accomplish so thoroughly did not long survive him. His great foreign enemy, Mithridátes, soon renewed his wars with Rome. His boasted constitution fell in the next political conflict. The career of Súlla, like that of the Grácchi and of Márius, marks a stage in the decline of the republic and the establishment of the empire.

CHAPTER XXI

THE TIMES OF PÓMPEY AND CÆSAR

The Rise of Pómpey, I.—The Growing Influence of Cǽsar, II.—Civil War between Pómpey and Cǽsar, III.
The Rule of Július Cǽsar, IV.

I. THE RISE OF PÓMPEY

Failures of the Súllan Party.—When Súlla resigned his power and placed the government in the hands of his party, he no doubt thought that he had secured the state from any further disturbance. He had destroyed all opposition, he fancied, by wiping out the Márian party. But as soon as he died, the remnants of this party began to reappear on every side. With the restoration of the senate's power there also returned all the old evils of the senatorial rule. The aristocratic party was still a selfish faction ruling for its own interests, and with little regard for the welfare of the people. The separation between the rich and the poor became more marked than ever. Luxury and dissipation were the passion of one class, and poverty and distress the condition of the other. The feebleness of the new government was evident from the start, and Súlla was scarcely dead when symptoms of reaction began to appear.

The Revolt of Lépidus (77 B.C.).—The first attempt to overthrow the work of Súlla was made by the cónsul M. Æmílius Lépidus, a vain and petulant man, who aspired to be chief of the popular party. Lépidus proposed to restore to the tríbunes the full power which Súlla had diminished, and then to rescind the whole Súllan constitution. But his colleague, Q. Lutátius Cátulus, had no sympathy with his schemes and opposed him at every step. To prevent a new civil war the senate bound the two cónsuls by an oath not to take up arms. But Lépidus disregarded this oath, raised an army, and marched on Rome. He was soon defeated by Cátulus with the aid of Cn. Pompéius. It is well for us to notice that Pómpey by this act came into greater prominence in politics as a supporter of the senate and the Súllan party.

The Sertórian War and Pómpey (80-72 B.C.).—A much more formidable attempt at revolution was made by Q. Sertórius, who was one of the friends of Márius, and who had escaped to Spain during the Súllan proscriptions. Sertórius was a man of noble character, brave, prudent, generous, and withal a very able soldier. The native tribes of Spain were chafing under the Róman governors; and Spain itself had become the retreat of many Márian refugees. Sertórius, therefore, formed the plan of delivering Spain from the power of Rome, and setting up an independent republic. He won the devotion and loyalty of the Spánish provincials, whom he placed on an equality with his Róman subjects. He organized the cities after the Itálian model. He encouraged the natives to adopt the arts of civilization. He formed a school at Ósca, where the young men were instructed in Látin and Greek. He also defeated the Róman légions under Q. Cæcílius Metéllus Píus, who had been sent against him.

The Róman senate was firmly convinced that something must be done to save the Spánish province. Pómpey was therefore appointed procónsul in Spain, although he had never been cónsul or held any other civil office. Sertórius showed what kind of general he was when he defeated the young Pómpey in the first battle, and might have destroyed his army if Metéllus had not come to his assistance. But fortune at last frowned upon Sertórius and favored Pómpey. Sertórius, in a fit of wrath, caused the boys in the school at Ósca to be put to death. This cruel act aroused the indignation of the Spánish subjects. It was not long before he himself was murdered by one of his lieutenants. With Sertórius out of the way, Pómpey obtained an easy victory; and Spain was reduced to submission.

War of the Gladiators, and Crássus (73-71 B.C.).—Before the war with Sertórius was ended, the senate was called upon to meet a far greater danger at home. In order to prepare the gladiators for their bloody contests in the arena, training schools had been established in different parts of Ítaly. At Cápua, in one of these so-called schools (which were rather prisons), was confined a brave Thrácian, Spártacus. With no desire to be "butchered to make a Róman holiday," Spártacus incited his companions to revolt. Seventy of them fled to the crater of Vesúvius and made it a stronghold. Reinforced by other slaves and outlaws of all descriptions, they grew into a motley mass of one hundred thousand desperate men. They ravaged the fields and plundered the cities, until all Ítaly seemed at their mercy. Four Róman armies were defeated in succession. With Pómpey still absent in Spain, the senate sought some other leader to crush this fearful insurrection. The command fell to M. Crássus, who finally defeated Spártacus and his army. A remnant of five thousand men fled to the north, hoping to escape into Gaul; but they fell in with Pómpey, who was just returning from Spain, and were destroyed. By this stroke of luck, Pómpey had the assurance to claim that in addition to closing the war in Spain, he had also finished the war with the gladiators.

First Cónsulship of Pómpey and Crássus (70 B.C.).—With their victorious légions, Pómpey and Crássus now returned to the capital and claimed the cónsulship. Neither of these men had any great ability as a politician. But Crássus, on account of his wealth, had influence with the capitalists; and Pómpey, on account of his military successes, was becoming a sort of popular hero, as Márius had been before him. The popular party was now beginning to gather up its scattered forces, and to make its influence felt. With this party, therefore, as offering the greater prospect of success, the two soldiers formed a coalition, and were elected cónsuls.

The chief event of the cónsulship of Pómpey and Crássus was the complete overthrow of the Súllan constitution. The old power was given back to the tríbunes. The legislative power was restored to the assembly, which now could pass laws without the approval of the senate. The exclusive right to furnish jurors in criminal cases was taken away from the senate; and henceforth the jurors (*iúdices*) were to be chosen, one third from the senate, one third from the équites, and one third from the wealthy men below the rank of the équites (the so-called *tribúni ærárii*). Also, the power of the cénsors to revise the list of the senators, which Súlla had abolished, was restored; and as a result of this, sixty-four senators were expelled from the senate. By these measures the Súllan regime was practically destroyed, and the supremacy of the senate taken away. This was a great triumph for the popular party. After the close of his cónsulship, Pómpey, with affected modesty, retired to private life.

Pómpey and the War with the Pirates.—But Pómpey was soon needed to rescue Rome from still another danger. Since the decline of the Róman navy the sea had become infested with pirates. These robbers made their home in Crete and Cilícia, from which they made their depredations. They had practically the control of the whole Mediterránean, and preyed upon the commerce of the world. They plundered the cities of nearly every coast. They even cut off the grain supplies of Rome, so that Ítaly was threatened with a famine. To meet this emergency a law was passed (*lex Gabínia*, 61 B.C.) giving to Pómpey for three years supreme control over the Mediterránean Sea and its coasts for fifty miles inland. He was given five hundred ships and as many soldiers as he might wish. The public treasuries and all the resources of the provinces were placed at his disposal.

97

Such extraordinary power had never before been given to any man, except Súlla. But Pómpey fully satisfied the expectations of the people. Within ninety days from the time he set sail, he had cleared the whole Mediterránean Sea of its pirates. He had captured three thousand vessels, slain ten thousand of the enemy, and taken twenty thousand prisoners. Cícero said in his rhetorical way that "Pómpey had made his preparations for the war at the end of the winter, began it in the early spring, and finished it in the middle of the summer." Pómpey remained in the East to settle affairs in Cilícia, and perhaps to win fresh laurels as a soldier.

Bust of Pómpey (Gnǽus Pompéius Mágnus)
Ny Carlsberg Glyptotek, Copenhagen

Pómpey and the Conquest of the East.—The splendid success of Pómpey against the pirates led his friends to believe that he was the only man who could bring to a close the long and tedious war against Mithridátes. Since the death of Súlla the king of Póntus had continued to be a menace to Rome. The campaigns in the East had been conducted by L. Licínius Lucúllus, who was a really able general, but who was charged with prolonging the war in order to enrich himself. There was some ground, too, for this charge: for, as it was afterward well said of him, "he transplanted the luxury of Ásia to Rome." Lucúllus had already gained several victories over Mithridátes; but the war still lingered. A law was then passed at Rome (*lex Manília*, 66 B.C.) displacing Lucúllus and giving to Pómpey supreme control over all the Róman dominions in the East. Armed with this extensive authority, Pómpey began the conquest of the East. He soon succeeded in defeating Mithridátes, and in driving him from his kingdom. He then invaded Sýria and took possession of that kingdom. He next entered Judéa, and after a severe struggle succeeded in capturing Jerúsalem (63 B.C.). All the eastern coasts of the Mediterránean were now subject to Pómpey. Out of the conquered countries he formed four new provinces: (1) Bithýnia with Póntus; (2) Sýria; (3) Cilícia; and (4) Crete. When he returned to Ítaly he had the most successful and brilliant record that any Róman general had ever achieved.

II. THE GROWING INFLUENCE OF CÆSAR

Rome during the Absence of Pómpey.—During the absence of Pómpey in the East (67-61 B.C.) the politics of the capital were mainly in the hands of three men: Márcus Pórcius Cáto, Márcus Túllius Cícero, and Gáius Július Cæsar. Cáto was the grandson of Cáto the Cénsor; and like his great ancestor he was a man of firmness and of the strictest integrity. He was by nature a conservative, and came to be regarded as the leader of the aristocratic party. He contended for the power of the senate as it existed in the days of old. But lacking the highest qualities of a statesman, he could not prevent the inroads which were being made upon the constitution.

Bust of Gáius Július Cæsar, Musée Arles Antique

On the other hand, Július Cǽsar was coming to the front as the leader of the popular party. Though born of patrícian stock, he was related by family ties to Márius and Cínna, the old leaders of the people. He was wise enough to see that the cause of the people was in the ascendancy. He aroused the sympathies of the Itálians by favoring the extension of the Róman franchise to cities beyond the Po. He appealed to the populace by the splendor of the games which he gave as cúrule ǽdile. He allied himself to Cróssus, whose great wealth and average ability he could use to good advantage.

Between these two party leaders stood Cícero, who, in spite of his vanity, was a man of great intellect and of excellent administrative ability; but being a moderate man, he was liable to be misjudged by both parties. He was also what was called a "new man" (*nóvus hómo*), that is, the first of his family to obtain the senatorial rank. Cícero was made cónsul, and rose to the highest distinction during the absence of Pómpey.

Cícero and the Catilínian Conspiracy.—If Cícero had done nothing else, he would have been entitled to the gratitude of his country for two acts, the impeachment of Vérres and the defeat of Cátiline. Cícero stood for law and order, and generally for constitutional government. By his impeachment of Vérres, the corrupt governor of Sícily, he brought to light, as had never been done before, the infamous methods employed in the administration of the provinces. He not only brought to light this corruption; he also brought to justice one of the greatest offenders. Then by the defeat of Cátiline during his cónsulship Cícero saved Rome from the execution of a most infamous plot.

Cícero Denounces Cátiline (1882-1888), Fresco by Cesare Maccari (1840-1919), Villa Madama, Italy

Cátiline was a man of great influence with a certain class, and had already become quite a politician. He had been a partisan of Súlla; had held the office of prǽtor; and had twice been defeated for the cónsulship. But if one half of the accounts of him are true, he was a man of most abandoned and depraved character. When Cáto threatened to prosecute him, he said that if a fire were kindled against him he would put it out, not with water, but by a general ruin. Ruined himself in fortune, he gathered about him the ruined classes: insolvent debtors, desperate adventurers, and the rabble of Rome. It is said that his plot involved the purpose to kill the cónsuls, massacre the senators, and to burn the city of Rome. The plot was discovered by Cícero, and was foiled. Cícero delivered in the senate an oration against Cátiline, who was present and attempted to reply; but his voice was drowned with the cries of "Traitor," and he fled from the senate to his camp in Etrúria. Here a desperate battle ensued; and Cátiline was defeated and slain, with three thousand of his followers (62 B.C.). Five of his fellow-conspirators were condemned to death by the senate; and Cícero put the judgment into execution. This act afterward exposed Cícero to the charge of executing Róman citizens without a proper trial. But the people hailed Cícero as the savior of Rome, the Father of his Country.

It was charged that Cæsar was implicated in the plot of Cátiline; but this charge was answered when Cícero declared that Cæsar had done all that a good citizen could do to crush it. The great success of Cícero gave to the senate and the moderate party a temporary advantage. But the senate under the leadership of Cáto and Lucúllus had not the skill to retain this advantage.

The First Triúmvirate: Pómpey, Cæsar, and Crássus (60 B.C.).—Pómpey soon returned to Ítaly from his victories in the East (61 B.C.). Like Márius returning from the Címbric war, he was given a magnificent triumph. But like Súlla returning from the East, he was feared by those in power, lest he might use his victorious army to overthrow the existing government, and reign in its stead. To allay all suspicion, Pómpey disbanded his army as soon as it touched the soil of Ítaly; and he hoped that his great services would give him the proud position of the first citizen of Rome. But in this he was disappointed. By disbanding his army, he had given up the source of his influence. Still, he hoped that the senate would at least confirm his arrangements in the East and reward his veterans by grants of land. In this, too, he was disappointed. Yielding to the influence of Lucúllus, who had been deposed from the command in the East, the senate refused either to confirm his acts, or to reward his soldiers. Pómpey had thus a serious grievance against the senate.

But this grievance of Pómpey might not have been very dangerous, if the senate had not also offended Cæsar. Cæsar was rapidly gaining power and influence. He had held the offices of military tríbune, quǽstor, ædile, póntifex máximus, and prǽtor. Then as proprǽtor he had been sent to Spain, where he laid the basis of his military fame. On his return from Spain the senate thwarted him in his desire to have a triumph. In other ways Cæsar was embarrassed by the senate. But he was beginning to feel his power, and was not the man to put up with petty annoyances. He accordingly entered into a coalition with Pómpey, to which Crássus was also admitted. This coalition, or self-constituted league, is known as the "first triúmvirate." It was formed for the purpose of opposing the senatorial party, and of advancing the personal designs of its members. By the terms of this compact Pómpey was to have his acts confirmed and his veterans rewarded; Crássus was to have an opportunity to increase his fortune; and Cæsar was to have the cónsulship, and afterward a command in Gaul. Pómpey was ostensibly at the head of the league, but Cæsar was its ruling spirit.

The Cónsulship of Cæsar (59 B.C.).—The first fruit of the new alliance was the election of Cæsar to the cónsulship. On his election Cæsar went faithfully to work to fulfill his obligations to Pómpey, and to strengthen his hold upon the people. He obtained, in the first place, the passage of an agrarian law which provided for the veterans of Pómpey, and which also gave estates in Campánia to the needy citizens of Rome. In the next place, he secured a law confirming all the acts of Pómpey in the East. Finally, he obtained the passage of a law which pleased and conciliated the équites. The tax collectors had made a high offer for the privilege of collecting the taxes of Ásia, and afterward concluded that they had made a bad bargain.

Accordingly, Cæsar took their part, and succeeded in remitting one third of what they had agreed to give.

These laws were bitterly opposed by the senators, but without success. Pómpey was now satisfied; the people were pleased; and the capitalists were reconciled. The senate under its bad management was thus outgeneraled by Cæsar; and it lost the temporary advantage it had gained during the cónsulship of Cícero. So completely did Július Cæsar overshadow his weak colleague, Bíbulus, who was a partisan of the senate, that this term of office was humorously called the cónsulship of Július and Cæsar. At the close of his cónsulship Cæsar obtained the government of Cisálpine Gaul and Illýricum, to which was added Transálpine Gaul (Narbonénsis). This power was granted for five years. Cæsar was thus furnished with an opportunity for the exercise of his military talents, and the building up of a powerful army devoted to his cause.

Clódius and the Banishment of Cícero.—Before Cæsar departed for his provinces, he was careful to see that his interests would be looked after during his absence. He chose as his agent P. Clódius, an unscrupulous politician whose personal character was not above reproach, but whose hostility to the senate could be depended upon. To Clódius, who held the position of tríbune, was given the task, first, of keeping hold of the populace; and, next, of getting out of the way as best he could the two most influential men in the senate, Cícero and Cáto.

The first part of this task he easily accomplished by passing a law that grain should hereafter be distributed to the Róman people free of all expense.

To carry out the second part of his task was not so easy: to remove from the senate its chief leaders. Cáto was disposed of, however, by a law annexing Cýprus to the Róman dominion, and appointing him as its governor. Cícero was also got rid of by a law which Clódius succeeded in passing, and which provided that any magistrate who had put a Róman citizen to death without a trial should be banished. Cícero knew that this act was intended for him, and that it referred to his execution of the Catilínian conspirators. After vainly attempting to enlist sympathy in his own behalf, Cícero retired to Greece (58 B.C.) and devoted himself to literary pursuits. With their leaders thus removed, the senate was for a time paralyzed.

Renewal of the Triúmvirate at Lúcca (56 B.C.).—When Cæsar had departed from Rome to undertake his work in Gaul, Clódius began to feel his own importance and to rule with a high hand. The policy of this able and depraved demagogue was evidently to govern Rome with the aid of the mob. He paraded the streets with armed bands, and used his political influence to please the rabble. Pómpey as well as the senate became disgusted with the regime of Clódius. They united their influence, and obtained the recall of Cícero from exile. At the same time Cáto returned from his absence in Cýprus. On the return of the old senatorial leaders, it looked as though the senate would once more regain its power, and the triúmvirate would go to pieces.

But the watchful eye of Cæsar detected these symptoms of discontent, and a conference of the leaders took place at Lúcca, a town in northern Ítaly, where a new arrangement was brought about. Cæsar was now to be given an additional term of five years in Gaul, and to be elected cónsul at the end of that time; Pómpey and Crássus were to receive the cónsulship; and at the close of their term of office Pómpey was to have the provinces of Spain and África, and the money-loving Crássus was to receive the rich province of Sýria. In this way they would divide the world among them. The terms of the agreement were apparently satisfactory to the parties concerned. Cæsar now felt that matters at Rome were safe, at least until he could complete his work in Gaul and fortify his own power with a devoted and invincible army.

101

Cæsar and his Province.—It is not easy for us to say exactly what was in the mind of Cæsar when he selected Gaul for his province. It was at this time the most forbidding part of the Róman territory. It was the home of barbarians, with no wealth like that of Ásia, and few relics of a former civilization like those of Spain and África. But there were three or four things, no doubt, that Cæsar saw clearly.

In the first place, he saw that the power which should hereafter rule the Róman state must be a military power. Súlla had succeeded by the help of his army, and Pómpey had failed by giving up his army. If he himself should ever establish his own power, it must be by the aid of a strong military force. In the next place, he saw that no other province afforded the same political opportunities as those which Gaul presented. It is true that the distant province of Sýria might open a way for the conquest of Párthia, and for attaining the glories of another Alexánder. But Sýria was too far removed from Róman politics; and Cæsar's first ambition was political power, and not military glory. Again, he saw that the conquest of Gaul was necessary for the protection of the Róman state. The invasions of the northern barbarians—the Gauls, the Címbri and the Téutones—had twice already threatened Rome with destruction. By its conquest Gaul might be made a barrier against barbarism. Moreover, he saw that Rome was in need of new and fertile lands for colonization. Ítaly was overcrowded. The most patriotic men had seen the need of extra-Itálian colonies. Gáius Grácchus had sought an outlet in África. He himself had advocated settlements in the valley of the Po. What Ítaly needed most, after a stable government, was an outlet for her surplus population. His own ambition and the highest interests of his country Cæsar believed to be at one. By conquering Gaul he would be fighting not for Pómpey or the senate, but for himself and Rome.

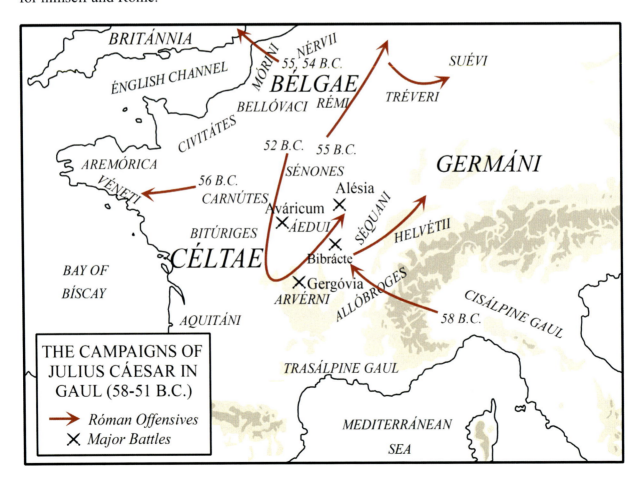

The Conquest of Gaul (58-51 B.C.).—The provinces over which Cæsar was placed at first included Cisálpine Gaul, that is, the valley of the Po; Illýricum, that is, the strip of territory across the Adriátic Sea; and Narbonénsis, that is, a small part of Transálpine Gaul lying about the mouth of the Rhône. Within eight years he brought under his power all the territory bounded by the Pýrenees, the Alps, the Rhine, and the Atlántic Ocean, or about what corresponds to the modern countries of France, Bélgium, and the Nétherlands.

He at first conquered the Helvétii, a tribe lying on the outskirts of his own province of Narbonénsis. He then met and drove back a great invasion of Gérmans, who, under a prince called Ariovístus, had crossed the Rhine, and threatened to overrun the whole of Gaul. He then pushed into the northern parts of Gaul, and conquered the Nérvii and the neighboring tribes. He overcame the Véneti on the Atlántic coast, and conquered Aquitánia. He also made two invasions into Brítain (55, 54 B.C.), crossed the Rhine into Gérmany, and revealed to the Róman soldiers countries they had never seen before. After once subduing the various tribes of Gaul, he was finally called upon to suppress a general insurrection, led by a powerful leader called Vercingétorix. The conquest of Gaul was then completed.

Vercingétorix Throws his Arms at the Feet of Július Cæsar (1899), Lionel-Noël Royer (1852-1926)
Crozatier Museum, Le Puy-en-Velay, France

A large part of the population had been either slain in war or reduced to slavery. The new territory was pacified by bestowing honors upon the Gállic chiefs, and self-government upon the surviving tribes. The Róman légions were distributed through the territory; but Cæsar established no military colonies like those of Súlla. The Róman arts and manners were encouraged; and Gaul was brought within the pale of civilization.

Dissolution of the Triúmvirate.—While Cǽsar was absent in Gaul, the ties which bound the three leaders together were becoming weaker and weaker. The position of Crássus tended somewhat, as long as he was alive, to allay the growing suspicion between the two great rivals. But after Crássus departed for the East to take control of his province in Sýria, he invaded Párthia, was badly defeated, lost the Róman standards, and was himself killed (53 B.C.). The death of Crássus practically dissolved the triúmvirate; or we might rather say, it reduced the triúmvirate to a duúmvirate. But the relation between the two leaders was now no longer one of friendly support, but one of mutual distrust.

The Sole Cónsulship of Pómpey (52 B.C.)—The growing estrangement between Pómpey and Cǽsar was increased when the senate appointed Pómpey "sole cónsul." This was not intended as an affront to Cǽsar, but was evidently demanded to meet a real emergency. The city was distracted by continual street fights between the armed bands of Clódius, the demagogue, and those of T. Ánnius Mílo, who professed to be defending the cause of the senate. In one of these broils Clódius was killed. His excited followers made his death the occasion of riotous proceedings. His body was burned in the Fórum by the wild mob, and the senate house was destroyed by fire. In the anarchy which followed, the senate felt obliged to confer some extraordinary power upon Pómpey. On the proposal of Cáto, he was appointed "cónsul without a colleague." Under this unusual title Pómpey restored order to the state, and was looked upon as "the savior of society." He became more and more closely bound to the cause of the senate; and the senate recognized its obligations to him by prolonging his command in Spain for five years.

The Rupture between Pómpey and Cǽsar.—It was a part of the agreement made at the conference of Lúcca, we remember, that Cǽsar was to receive the cónsulship at the close of his command in Gaul. He naturally wished to retain the control of his army until he had been elected to his new office. The senate was determined that he should not, but should present himself at Rome as a private citizen before his election. Cǽsar well knew that he would be helpless as a private citizen in the presence of the enemies who were seeking to destroy him. Cáto had already declared that he would prosecute him as soon as he ceased to be procónsul in Gaul. Cǽsar promised, however, to give up his province and his army, if Pómpey would do the same; but Pómpey refused. The senate then called upon Cǽsar to give up two of his légions on the plea that they were needed in the Párthian war. The légions were given up; but instead of being sent to the East they were stationed in Campánia. Upon further demands, Cǽsar agreed to give up eight légions of his army, if he were allowed to retain two légions in Cisálpine Gaul until the time of his election. This the senate refused; and demanded that he must give up his province and his whole army by a certain day, or be declared a public enemy. The senate had offered him humiliation or war. He chose war, and crossed the Rúbicon (49 B.C.), the stream which separated his province of Cisálpine Gaul from Ítaly.

Campaigns in Ítaly, Spain, and Greece.—The contest was now reduced to a struggle between the two greatest soldiers which Rome had ever produced. Cǽsar knew the value of time; at the instant when he decided upon war, he invaded Ítaly with a single légion. Pómpey, unprepared for such a sudden move and not relying upon the two légions which the senate had taken from Cǽsar, was obliged to withdraw to Brundísium. Besieged in this place by Cǽsar, he skillfully withdrew his forces to Greece, and left Cǽsar master of Ítaly.

Cǽsar was now between two hostile forces, the army in Spain under Pómpey's lieutenants, and the army in Greece under Pómpey himself. He must now defeat these armies separately before they could be united against him. As he had no fleet with which to follow Pómpey into Greece, he decided at once to attack the army in Spain. He dispatched his Gállic légions across the Pýrenees, while he secured himself at Rome. He entered the city, and dispelled the fear that there might be repeated the horrors of the first civil war. He showed that he was neither a Márius nor a Súlla. Rejoining his légions in Spain, he soon defeated Pómpey's lieutenants. When he returned to Rome he found that he had been proclaimed dictator. He resigned this title and accepted the office of cónsul.

In the beginning of the next year (48 B.C.), with the few ships that he had collected, he transported his troops from Brundísium across the Adriátic to meet the army of Pómpey. In the first conflict, at Dyrráchium, he was defeated. He then retreated across the peninsula in the direction of Pharsálus in order to draw Pómpey away from his supplies on the seacoast. The two generals met at Pharsálus (48 B.C.), when Cǽsar with about twenty thousand men completely defeated the army of Pómpey, which numbered more than forty thousand. Pómpey fled to Égypt, where he was treacherously murdered. Cǽsar had now accomplished the first part of his work, by taking possession of Ítaly and defeating the two armies of Pómpey in Spain and Greece. He had established his title to supremacy. Especial honors were paid to him at Rome. He was made cónsul for five years, tríbune for life, and dictator for one year.

Campaigns in Égypt, Ásia, África, and Spain.—Cǽsar now entered upon the second part of his work, that of pacifying the provinces. While in Égypt, be became fascinated by the charms of Cleopátra, and settled a dispute in which she was involved. That country was disturbed by a civil war between this princess and her brother Ptólemy. Each claimed the right to the throne. Cǽsar defeated the forces of Ptólemy and assigned the throne to Cleopátra, under the protection of two Róman légions. On his way back to Ítaly he passed through Ásia Mínor. Here he found Phárnaces, the son of the great Mithridátes, stirring up a revolt in Póntus. At the battle of Zéla (47 B.C.) he destroyed the armies of this prince, and restored the Asiátic provinces, recording his speedy victory in the famous words, *"Véni, vídi, víci."*

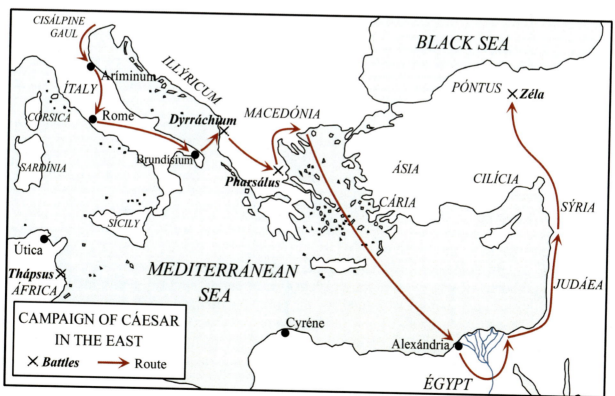

The armies of Cæsar had now swept over all the provinces of Rome, except África. Here the Pompéian leaders, assisted by the king of Numídia, determined to make a last stand against the conqueror. Their forces were under Cáto, who held Útica, and Metéllus Scípio, who commanded in the field. After subduing a mutiny of his tenth légion by a single word, calling the men "citizens," instead of "fellow-soldiers," Cæsar invaded África. The battle of Thápsus (46 B.C.) destroyed the last hope of the Pompéian party. The republican forces were defeated; and Cáto, the chief of the senatorial party, committed suicide at Útica. In this war Numídia was conquered and attached to the province of África. All resistance to Cæsar's power was now at an end, except a brief revolt in Spain, led by the sons of Pómpey, which was soon put down, the enemy being crushed (45 B.C.) at the battle of Múnda.

IV. THE RULE OF JÚLIUS CÆSAR

Cæsar's Triumphs and Titles.—When Cæsar returned to Rome after the battle of Thápsus, he came not as the servant of the senate, but as master of the world. He crowned his victories by four splendid triumphs, one for Gaul, one for Égypt, one for Póntus, and one for Numídia. He made no reference to the civil war; and no citizens were led among his captives. His victory was attended by no massacres, no proscriptions, no confiscations. He was as generous in peace as he had been relentless in war. Cæsar was great enough to forgive his enemies. A general amnesty was proclaimed; and friend and foe were treated alike. We may see the kind of power which he exercised by the titles which he received. He was cónsul, dictator, controller of public morals (*præféctus mórum*), tríbune, póntifex máximus, and chief of the senate (*prínceps senátus*). He thus gathered up in his own person the powers which had been scattered among the various republican officers. The name of imperátor with which the soldiers had been accustomed to salute a victorious general, was now made an official title, and prefixed to his name. In Cæsar was thus embodied the one-man power which had been growing up during the civil wars. He was in fact the first Róman emperor.

Cæsar's Political Reforms.—Cæsar held his great power only for a short time. But the reforms which he made are enough to show us his policy, and to enable us to judge of him as a statesman. The first need of Rome was a stable government based on the interest of the whole people. The senate had failed to secure such a government; and so had the popular assemblies led by the tríbunes. Cæsar believed that the only government suited to Rome was a democratic monarchy, a government in which the supreme power should be held permanently by a single man, and exercised, not for the benefit of himself or any single class, but for the benefit of the whole state. Let us see how his changes accomplished this end.

In the first place, the senate was changed to meet this view. It had hitherto been a comparatively small body, drawn from a single class and ruling for its own interests. Cæsar increased the number to nine hundred members, and filled it up with representative men of all classes, not simply nobles, but also *ignóbiles*: Spániards, Gauls, military officers, sons of freedmen, and others. It was to be not a legislative body but an advisory body, to inform the monarch of the condition and wants of Ítaly and the provinces. In the next place, he extended the Róman franchise to the inhabitants beyond the Po, and to many cities in the provinces, especially in Transálpine Gaul and Spain. All his political changes tended to break down the distinction between nobles and commons, between Itálians and the provincials, and to make of all the people of the empire one nation.

Cæsar's Economic Reforms.—The next great need of Rome was the improvement of the condition of the lower classes. Cæsar well knew that the condition of the people could not be changed in a day; but he believed that the government ought not to encourage pauperism by helping those who ought to help themselves. There were three hundred and twenty thousand persons at Rome to whom grain was distributed. He reduced this number to one hundred and fifty thousand, or more than one half. He provided means of employment for the idle, by constructing new buildings in the city, and other public works; and also by enforcing the law that one third of the labor employed on landed estates should be free labor. As the land of Ítaly was so completely occupied, he encouraged the establishment, in the provinces, of agricultural colonies which would not only tend to relieve the farmer class, but to Rómanize the empire. He relieved the debtor class by a bankruptcy law which permitted the insolvent debtor to escape imprisonment by turning over his property to his creditors. In such ways as these, while not pretending to abolish poverty, he afforded better means for the poorer classes to obtain a living.

His Reform of the Provincial System.—The despotism of the Róman republic was nowhere more severe and unjust than in the provinces. This was due to two things: the arbitrary authority of the governor and the wretched system of farming the taxes. The governor ruled the province, not for the benefit of the provincials, but for the benefit of himself. It is said that the procónsul hoped to make three fortunes out of his province: one to pay his debts, one to bribe the jury if he were brought to trial, and one to keep himself. The tax collector also looked upon the property of the province as a harvest to be divided between the Róman treasury and himself. Cǽsar put a check upon this system of robbery. The governor was now made a responsible agent of the emperor; and the collection of taxes was placed under a more rigid supervision. The provincials found in Cǽsar a protector; because his policy involved the welfare of all his subjects.

His Other Reforms and Projects.—The most noted of Cǽsar's other changes was the reform of the calendar, which has remained as he left it, with slight change, down to the present day. He also intended to codify the Róman law; to provide for the founding of public libraries; to improve the architecture of the city; to drain the Póntine Marshes for the improvement of the public health; to cut a channel through the Ísthmus of Córinth; and to extend the empire to its natural limits, the Euphrátes, the Dánube, and the Rhine. These projects show the comprehensive mind of Cǽsar. That they would have been carried out in great part, if he had lived, we can scarcely doubt, when we consider his wonderful executive genius and the works he actually accomplished in the short time in which he held his power.

The Assassination of Cǽsar.—If Cǽsar failed, it was because he did not adjust himself sufficiently to the conservative spirit of the time. There were still living at Rome men who were blindly attached to the old republican forms. To them the reforms of Cǽsar looked like a work of destruction, rather than a work of creation. They saw in his projects a scheme for reviving the kingship. It was said that when Cǽsar was offered a crown he looked at it wistfully; and that he had selected his nephew Octávius as his royal heir.

The men who hated Cǽsar, and who conspired to kill him, were men who had themselves received special favors from him. The leading conspirators, M. Brútus and C. Cássius, had both served in Pómpey's army, and had been pardoned by Cǽsar and promoted to offices under his government. Joined by some fifty other conspirators, these men formed a plot to kill Cǽsar in the senate house. The story of his assassination has been told by Plútarch and made immortal by Shákespeare. When the appointed day came, the Ides of March (March 15, 44 B.C.), Cǽsar was struck down by the daggers of his treacherous friends, and he fell at the foot of Pómpey's statue. It has been said that the murder of Cǽsar was the most senseless act that the Rómans ever committed. His death deprived Rome of the greatest man she ever produced. But the work of the conspirators did not destroy the work of Cǽsar.

The Death of Cǽsar (1798), Vincenzo Camuccini (1771-1844), Galleria Nazionale d'Arte Moderna, Rome

CHAPTER XXII

THE TIMES OF ÁNTONY AND OCTÁVIUS

I. THE RISE OF ÁNTONY AND OCTÁVIUS

Rome after the Death of Cæsar.—The men who murdered Cæsar considered themselves as liberators of the republic. Whatever may have been their motives, they seem to have taken little thought as to how Rome would be governed after they had killed their tyrant. If they thought that the senate would take up the powers it had lost, and successfully rule the republic, they were grievously mistaken. The only leading man of the senate who had survived the last civil war was Cícero; but Cícero with all his learning and eloquence could not take the place of Cæsar. What Rome needed was what the liberators had taken from her, a master mind of broad views and of great executive power. We need not be surprised that the death of Cæsar was followed by confusion and dismay. No one knew which way to look or what to expect. Soon there appeared new actors upon the scene, men struggling for the supreme power in the state: M. Antónius (Ántony), the friend of Cæsar and his fellow-cónsul; C. Octávius, his adopted son and heir; M. Æmílius Lépidus, his master of horse; Séxtus Pompéius, his previous enemy and the son of his greatest rival; while Cícero still raised his voice in defense of what he regarded as his country's freedom.

The Supremacy of Ántony.—The first to take advantage of the confusion which followed Cæsar's death was Márcus Antónius. With the aid of Lépidus he got possession of Cæsar's will and other papers, and seized his treasury. He influenced the senate to confirm all of Cæsar's acts, and obtained permission to speak at his public funeral. He made a strong appeal to the populace to avenge the death of their great friend; and read the will of Cæsar, which left his palace and gardens to the people, and a legacy to every citizen. Excited to fury by the eloquence of Ántony, the people seized firebrands from the burning funeral pile, and rushed through the streets swearing vengeance to the so-called liberators. The liberators were obliged to flee from the city; and Ántony was for the time supreme. As the senate had confirmed Cæsar's acts, and as Ántony

had Cæsar's papers, which were supposed to contain these acts, he assumed the role of Cæsar's executor and did what he pleased. The chief liberators hastened to the provinces to which they had previously been assigned by Cæsar: Cássius to Sýria, Márcus Brútus to Macedónia, and Décimus Brútus to Cisálpine Gaul.

Mark Ántony on Denárius (42 B.C.)

The Rise of Octávius.—Antony's dream of power was soon disturbed by the appearance of the young Octávius, Cæsar's grand-nephew and adopted son. Although a young man, only nineteen, he was a born politician, and soon became Ántony's greatest rival. He assumed his adopted name, Gáius Július Cæsar Octaviánus, and claimed his inheritance and the treasures which had fallen into Ántony's hands. But Ántony said that these were public moneys, and that they had been spent in the interests of the Róman state.

Octávius now for the first time showed that adroit skill for which he was always distinguished. Ántony had raised the false hopes of the people by reading Cæsar's will, which promised a legacy to every citizen. The people had heard the will; but they had not yet received the promised legacies. To humiliate Ántony and to insure his own popularity, the young Octávius sold his own estates, borrowed money of his friends, and paid the legacies which Cæsar had promised to the people. By this act Octávius displaced Ántony as the people's friend. The young heir grew so rapidly in popular favor that his influence was sought both by Cícero, who represented the senate, and by Ántony, who represented himself.

Cícero's Attack upon Ántony.—Cícero thought that everything should be done to weaken the power of Ántony, and to prevent any possible coalition between him and the young Octávius. The hostility between Cícero and Ántony grew to be bitter and relentless; and they were pitted against each other on the floor of the senate. But in a war of words Ántony was no match for Cícero. By a series of famous speeches known as the "Philíppics," the popularity of Ántony was crushed; and he retired from Rome to seek for victory upon other fields. He claimed Cisálpine Gaul as his province. But this province was still held by Décimus Brútus, one of the liberators to whom the senate looked for military support.

When Ántony attempted to gain possession of this territory, Cícero thought he saw an opportunity to use Octávius in the interests of the senate. Accordingly Ántony was declared a public enemy; Octávius was made a senator with the rank of a cónsul, and was authorized to conduct the war against Ántony. In this war, the so-called war of Mútina (44-43 B.C.), Octávius was successful. As a reward for his victory he demanded of the senate that he receive a triumph and the cónsulship. Cícero had intended Décimus Brútus for this office, and the request of Octávius was refused. But the young heir, then twenty years of age, following the example of Cæsar, enforced his claims with the sword; he took possession of the city, and obtained his election to the cónsulship. Octávius thus became the ruling man in Rome.

Bust of Márcus Túllius Cícero, Musei Capitolini, Rome

The Second Triúmvirate: Ántony, Octávius, and Lépidus (43 B.C.).—Cícero's attempt to defeat Ántony by the aid of Octávius was not a successful piece of diplomacy. It resulted not only in alienating the young heir; but worse than that, it brought about the very coalition which Cícero was trying to prevent. Octávius had broken with the senate, and had obtained a complete victory. But he was not yet ready to break with Ántony, who was supported by Lépidus, especially as the two chief liberators, Brútus and Cássius, were still in control of the eastern provinces. If he had had the military genius of Cæsar, he might have destroyed all their armies in detail. But the young Octávius was not inclined to overrate his military abilities. He saw that it would be for his interest to make friends with Ántony and Lépidus. A coalition was therefore formed between the three leaders, usually called the "second triúmvirate." They agreed to divide the western provinces among themselves, and then to make a new division after they had driven Brútus and Cássius from the eastern provinces.

The Proscriptions; Murder of Cícero.—No government could be more despotic than that of the three masters who now governed Rome. They assumed the cónsular power for five years, with the right of appointing all magistrates. Their decrees were to have the force of law without the sanction of either the senate or the people. It is to the eternal disgrace of these men who professed to espouse the cause of Cǽsar, that they abandoned the humane policy of their great exemplar, and turned to the infamous policy of Márius and Súlla. Ántony especially desired a proscription, as he was surrounded by thousands of personal enemies, chief among whom was Cícero, the author of the "Philíppics." Octávius was reconciled to the horrible work as a matter of policy; and Lépidus acquiesced in it as a matter of indifference. It is said that three hundred senators and two thousand équites were outlawed, and their property confiscated. The triúmvirs justified their atrocious acts as a retaliation for the murder of Cǽsar. Many of the proscribed escaped from Ítaly and found a refuge with Brútus and Cássius in the East. But a large number of persons were slain.

The Vengeance of Fúlvia (1888), Francisco Maura y Montaner (1857-1931), Prado National Museum

The world will always feel a painful interest in these black days, because it was then that Cícero lost his life. When the old man was warned of his danger, and urged to flee, he replied, "Let me die in my fatherland which I have so often saved." He was slain, and his head was sent to Ántony, whose wife, Fúlvia, is said to have pierced the lifeless tongue with a needle, in revenge for the words it had uttered against her husband. Thus perished the greatest orator of Rome. Cícero has been accused of timidity; but he remained at his post, the last defender of the republic. He has been charged with vacillation; but he lived in days when no man knew which way to turn for help. He failed as a politician, because he continually bungled in the fine arts of intrigue. He failed as a statesman, because he persisted in defending a lost cause. He appealed to reason, when the highest arbiter was the sword. But with all his faults, Cícero was, next to Cáto, the most upright man of his time; and his influence has been, next to that of Cǽsar, the most enduring. To practical politics he contributed little; but his numerous writings have exercised a wonderful influence in the intellectual and moral education of the world.

War against the Liberators; Battle of Philíppi (42 B.C.).—Having murdered their enemies at home, the triúmvirs were now prepared to crush their enemies abroad. There were three of these enemies whom they were obliged to meet, Brútus and Cássius, who had united their forces in the East; and Séxtus Pompéius, who had got possession of the island of Sícily, and had under his command a powerful fleet. While Lépidus remained at Rome, Ántony and Octávius invaded Greece with an army of one hundred and twenty thousand men. Against them the two liberators, Brútus and Cássius, collected an army of eighty thousand men. The hostile forces met near Philíppi (42 B.C.), a town in Macedónia on the northern coast of the Ægéan Sea. Octávius was opposed to Brútus, and Ántony to Cássius. Octávius was driven back by Brútus, while Ántony, more fortunate, drove back the wing commanded by Cássius. As Cássius saw his flying légions, he thought that all was lost, and stabbed himself with the same dagger, it is said, with which he struck Cæsar. This left Brútus in sole command of the opposing army; but he also was defeated

in a second battle, and, following the example of Cássius, committed suicide. The double battle at Philíppi decided the fate of the republic. As Cícero was its last political champion, Brútus and Cássius were its last military defenders; and with their death we may say that the republic was at an end.

EID•MAR ("Ides of March") Denárius (42 B.C.)
Brútus with Daggers, Píleus (Cap of Freedmen)

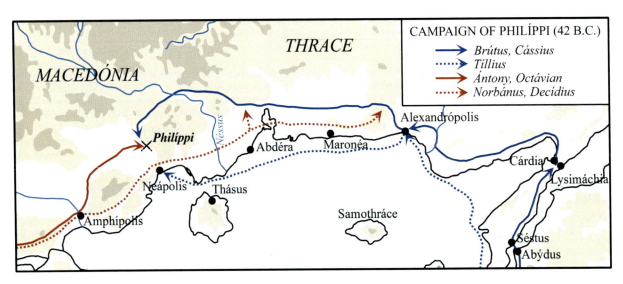

II. CIVIL WAR BETWEEN ÁNTONY AND OCTÁVIUS

New Division of the Provinces.—With the republic overthrown, it now remained to be seen who should be the master of the new empire, Ántony or Octávius. Lépidus, although ambitious, was too weak and vacillating to be dangerous. The triúmvirs were growing to be envious of each other; but they contrived to smother their jealousy, and made a new division of the empire. Ántony was now to have the East, and Octávius the West. It was a question what to do with Lépidus, as he was accused of giving aid to the only remaining enemy of the triúmvirs, that is, Séxtus Pompéius. If he could prove himself innocent of the charge, he was to be given the small province of África. The real work of the triúmvirate was to be done by Ántony and Octávius. Ántony was to take control of the eastern provinces, and to push the Róman conquests if possible into Párthia. Octávius was to preserve the peace of Ítaly and the western provinces, and to destroy the fleet of Séxtus Pompéius, which was seriously interfering with Róman commerce

Octávius in the West.—Octávius proceeded to secure his position in the West by means of force and craft. He first put down an insurrection incited by the partisans of Ántony. The young conqueror won the affections of the people, and tried to show them that peace and prosperity could come only through his influence. The next thing was to dispose of Séxtus Pompéius and his hostile fleet. With the help of his friend and able general, Agríppa, and with the aid of a hundred ships lent him by Ántony, Octávius destroyed the forces of Pompéius. The defeated general fled to the East, and was killed by the soldiers of Ántony.

Octávius was then called upon to deal with a treacherous friend. This was the weak and ambitious Lépidus, who with twenty légions thought that he could defeat Octávius and become the chief man of Rome. But Octávius did not think the emergency grave enough to declare war. He defeated Lépidus without a battle. Unarmed and almost unattended he entered his rival's camp, and made an eloquent appeal to the soldiers. The whole army of Lépidus deserted to Octávius. Lépidus was deposed from his position as triúmvir, but was generously allowed to retain the office of póntifex máximus on condition of remaining quiet. By the use of force and diplomacy Octávius thus baffled all his foes in the West, and he and Ántony were now the undisputed rulers of the Róman world.

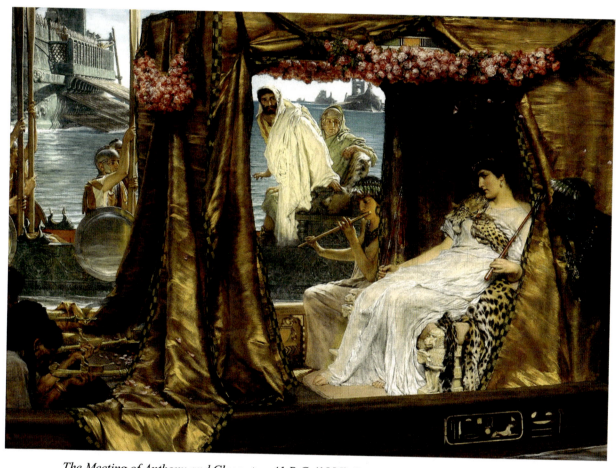

The Meeting of Anthony and Cleopatra, 41 B.C. (1885), Lawrence Alma-Tadema (1836-1912)

Ántony in the East.—While everything in the West was turning in favor of Octávius, all things in the East were also contributing to his success. But this was due not so much to his own skill as to the weakness and folly of Ántony. Octávius had tried to cement the league of the triumvirs by giving his sister Octávia to Ántony in marriage. But Ántony soon grew tired of Octávia, and became fascinated by Cleopátra, the "Serpent of the Nile." His time was divided between campaigns in Párthia and dissipations in Égypt. His Párthian wars turned out to be failures; and his Égyptian entanglements resulted in his ruin. He aspired to the position of an Oriéntal monarch. He divided the Róman provinces with Cleopátra, who was called "the queen of kings." The Róman people were shocked when he desired his disgraceful acts to be confirmed by the senate. They could not help contrasting this weak and infatuated slave of Cleopátra with their

113

own Octávius, the strong and prudent governor of the West. While Octávius was growing in popularity, Ántony was thus becoming more and more an object of detestation.

Bust of Cleopátra (1st Century B.C.), Altes Museum, Berlin

Rupture between Ántony and Octávius.—The strong feeling at Rome against Ántony, Octávius was able to use to his own advantage. But he wished it to appear that he was following, and not directing, the will of the people. He therefore made no attempt to force an issue with Ántony, but bided his time. The people suspected Ántony of treasonable designs, as they saw his military preparations, which might be used to enthrone himself as king of the East, or to install Cleopátra as queen of Rome.

All doubt as to Ántony's real character and purpose was settled when his will was found and published. In it he had made the sons of Cleopátra his heirs, and ordered his own body to be buried at Alexándria beside that of the Egýptian queen. This was looked upon as an insult to the majesty of Rome. The citizens were aroused. They demanded that war be declared against the hated triúmvir. Octávius suggested that it would be more wise to declare war against Cleopátra than against Ántony and the deluded citizens who had espoused his cause. Thus what was really a civil war between Octávius and Ántony assumed the appearance of a foreign war between Rome and Egýpt. But Ántony well understood against whom the war was directed; and he replied by publicly divorcing Octávia, and accepting his real position as the public enemy of Rome.

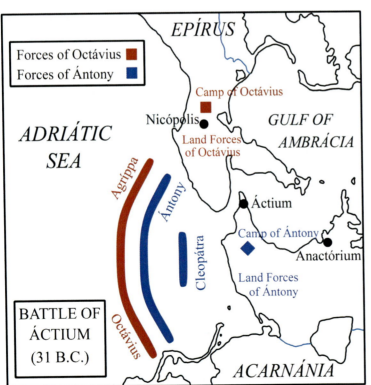

Defeat of Ántony; Battle of Áctium (31 B.C.).—When war was declared, Antony and Cleopátra united their forces against Rome. Antony gathered together an immense army of eighty thousand men, and occupied the western coasts of Greece, where he could either threaten Ítaly or resist the approach of Octávius. His main army was posted at Áctium, south of the strait leading into the Gulf of Ambrácia. His fleet of five hundred heavy ships was for the most part moored within the gulf. Octávius, with the aid of his trusted general Agríppa, succeeded in transporting an army of fifty thousand men to the coast of Epírus, and took up a position north of the strait and opposite the land forces of Ántony. His fleet of two hundred and fifty light galleys was stationed outside of the strait to await the approach of the enemy's vessels. Ántony, on the advice of his ablest officers, desired that the battle should be waged with the land forces. But Cleopátra, proud of her navy, insisted that it should be fought on the sea. The contest was therefore decided by a naval battle. As the fleet of

114

Ántony emerged from the strait, it was immediately attacked by Octávius and Agríppa. But scarcely had the battle begun when Cleopátra with her squadron withdrew from the line, and was quickly followed by Ántony. Their sailors fought on until their fleet was destroyed. The battle at Áctium closed the political career of Ántony, and left Octávius the sole master of the Róman world. The date of this battle may be taken to mark the beginning of the empire.

The Triumph of Octávius.—Before returning to Rome Octávius restored order to the eastern provinces, and followed the fugitives to Égypt. The arts by which Cleopátra had fascinated Cæsar and enslaved Ántony, she tried to use upon her new Róman guest. But Octávius did not fall into the tempter's snare. The Egýptian queen found in the Róman sovereign a nature as crafty as her own. Octávius kept his thoughts upon the prosperity and honor of Rome, and no allurements could draw him away from his high mission. Ántony, defeated and ruined, committed suicide; and Cleopátra followed his example rather than be led a captive in a Róman triumph. Together this wretched pair were laid in the mausoleum of the Ptólemies. Égypt was annexed as a province of the new empire (30 B.C.). Octávius returned to Rome (29 B.C.), where he was given the honors of a triple triumph—for Dalmátia (where he had gained some previous victories), for Áctium, and for Égypt. The temple of Jánus was now closed for the first time since the second Púnic war; and the Rómans, tired of war and of civil strife, looked upon the triumph of Octávius as the dawn of a new era of peace and prosperity.

III. REVIEW OF THE PERIOD OF THE CIVIL WARS

Progress of Rome.—As we look back over the period which we have just completed, we may ask the question whether Rome had made any progress since the days of her great conquests. More than a hundred years had passed away since the beginning of the commotions under the Grácchi. During this time we have seen the long conflict between the senate and the people; we have seen the republic gradually declining and giving way to the empire. But we must not suppose that the fall of the republic was the fall of Rome. The so-called republic of Rome was a government neither by the people nor for the people. It had become the government of a selfish aristocracy, ruling for its own interests. Whether the new empire which was now established was better than the old republic which had fallen, remains to be seen. But there are many things in which we can see that Rome was making some real progress.

Appearance of Great Men.—The first thing that we notice is the fact that during this period of conflict Rome produced some of the greatest men of her history. It is in the times of stress and storm that great men are brought to the front; and it was the fierce struggles of this period which developed some of the foremost men of the ancient world, men like the two Grácchi, Márius, Súlla, Cáto, Cícero, and Július Cæsar. Whatever we may think of their opinions, of the methods which they used, or of the results which they accomplished, we cannot regard them as ordinary men.

Extension of the Franchise.—Another evidence of the progress of Rome was the extension of the rights of citizenship, and the bringing into the state of many who had hitherto been excluded. At the beginning of this period only the inhabitants of a comparatively small part of the Itálian peninsula were citizens of Rome. The franchise was restricted chiefly to those who dwelt upon the lands in the vicinity of the capital. But during the civil wars the rights of citizenship had been extended to all parts of Ítaly and to many cities in Gaul and Spain.

Improvement in the Róman Law.—We have already seen the improvement which Súlla made in the organization of the criminal courts for the trial of public crimes. But there were also improvements made in the civil law, by which the private rights of individuals were better protected. Not only were the rights of citizens made more secure, but the rights of foreigners were also more carefully guarded. Before the social war, the rights of all foreigners in Ítaly were protected by a special prǽtor (*prǽtor peregrínus*); and after that war all Itálians became equal before the law. There was also a tendency to give all foreigners in the provinces rights equal to those of citizens, so far as these rights related to persons and property.

Progress in Architecture.—That the Rómans were improving in their culture and taste is shown by the new and splendid buildings which were erected during this period. While some public buildings were destroyed by the riots in the city, they were replaced by finer and more durable structures. Many new temples were built: temples to Hércules, to Minérva, to Fortune, to Concord, to Honor and Virtue. There were new basílicas, or halls of justice, the most notable being the Basílica Júlia, which was commenced by Július Cǽsar. A new forum, the Fórum Júlii, was also laid out by Cǽsar, and a new theater was constructed by Pómpey. The great national temple of Júpiter Capitolínus, which was burned during the civil war of Márius and Súlla, was restored with great magnificence by Súlla, who adorned it with the columns of the temple of the Olýmpian Zeus brought from Áthens. It was during this period that the triumphal arches were first erected, and became a distinctive feature of Róman architecture.

Advancement in Literature.—The most important evidence of the progress of the Rómans during the period of the civil wars is seen in their literature. It was at this time that Rome began to produce writers whose names belong to the literature of the world. Cǽsar wrote his "Commentaries on the Gállic War," which is a fine specimen of clear historical narrative. Sállust wrote a history of the Jugúrthine War and an account of the conspiracy of Cátiline, which give us graphic and vigorous descriptions of these events. Lucrétius wrote a great poem "On the Nature of Things," which expounds the Epicuréan theory of the universe, and reveals powers of description and imagination rarely equaled by any other poet, ancient or modern. Catúllus wrote lyric poems of exquisite grace and beauty. Cícero was the most learned and prolific writer of the age; his orations, letters, rhetorical and philosophical essays furnish the best models of classic style, and have given him a place among the great prose writers of the world.

Decay of Religion and Morals.—While the Rómans, during this period, showed many evidences of progress in their laws, their art, and their literature, they were evidently declining in their religious and moral sense. Their religion was diluted more and more with Oriéntal superstitions and degrading ceremonies. In their moral life they were suffering from the effects of their conquests, which had brought wealth and the passion for luxury and display. Ambition and avarice tended to corrupt the life of the Róman people. The only remedy for this condition of religious and moral decay was found in the philosophy of the Greeks, which, however, appealed only to the more educated classes.

CHAPTER XXIII

THE REIGN OF AUGÚSTUS (31 B.C. - A.D. 14)

The New Imperial Government, I.—Augústus and the Róman World, II.—The Age of Augústus, III.

I. THE NEW IMPERIAL GOVERNMENT

Beginning of the Empire.—We have taken the date of the battle of Áctium (31 B.C.) to mark the beginning of the empire, because Octávius then became the sole and undisputed master of the Róman world. But it is not so important for us to fix upon a particular date for the beginning of the empire, as it is to see that some form of imperialism had come to be a necessity. During the whole period of the civil wars we have seen the gradual growth of the one-man power. We have seen it in the tríbunate under the Grácchi; in the successive cónsulships of Márius; in the perpetual dictatorship of Súlla; in the sole cónsulship of Pómpey; in the absolute rule of Július Cǽsar. The name of "king" the Rómans hated, because it brought to mind the memory of the last Tárquin. But the principle of monarchy they could not get rid of, because they had found no efficient form of government to take its place. The aristocratic government under the senate had proved corrupt, inefficient, and disastrous to the people. A popular government without representation had shown itself unwieldy, and had become a prey to demagogues. There was nothing left for the Rómans to do except to establish some form of monarchy which would not suggest the hated name of king.

Príma Pórta Augústus, Museo Chiaramonti, Vatican

The Policy of Augústus.—There was no other man so well fitted to put the new monarchy into an attractive form as Octávius, whom we may now call by his official title of Augústus. We have been accustomed to think of this man as merely a shrewd politician. But when we contrast the distracted condition of Rome during the last hundred years with the peace and prosperity which he brought with him, we shall be inclined to look upon him as a wise and successful statesman. His whole policy was a policy of conciliation. He wished to wipe out the hatreds of the civil war. He regarded himself as the chief of no party, but as the head of the whole state. He tried to reconcile the conservative and the progressive men of his time. All the cherished forms of the republic he therefore preserved; and he exercised his powers under titles which were not hateful to the senate or the people.

The Titles and Powers of Augústus.—Soon after returning to Rome, Augústus resigned the powers which he had hitherto exercised, giving "back the commonwealth into the hands of the senate and the people" (27 B.C.). The first

117

official title which he then received was the surname *Augústus*, bestowed by the senate in recognition of his dignity and his services to the state, He then received the procónsular power (*impérium proconsuláre*) over all the frontier provinces, or those which required the presence of an army. He had also conferred upon himself the tribunícian power *tribunícia potéstas*, by which he became the protector of the people. He moreover was made póntifex máximus, and received the title of *Páter Pátriæ*. Although Augústus did not receive the permanent titles of cónsul and cénsor, he occasionally assumed, or had temporarily assigned to himself, the duties of these offices. He still retained the title of *Imperátor*, which gave him the command of the army. But the title which Augústus chose to indicate his real position was that of *Prínceps Civitátis*, or "the first citizen of the state," The new "prince" thus desired himself to be looked upon as a magistrate rather than a monarch, a citizen who had received a trust rather than a ruler governing in his own name.

Augústus and the Senate.—Augústus showed his conciliatory policy in fixing the position which the senate was to assume in the new government. He did not adopt fully the plan either of Súlla or of Július Cæsar; but reconciled as far as possible their different ideas. He restored to the senate the dignity which it had in the time of Súlla. He did this by excluding the provincials and freedmen whom Cæsar had introduced into it, and by reducing its number from nine hundred to six hundred members. But still he did not confer upon it the great legislative power which Súlla intended it should have; he rather made it a kind of advisory-body, according to Cæsar's idea. In theory the senate was to assist the emperor in matters of legislation; but in fact it was simply to approve the proposals which he submitted to it.

The Assemblies of the People.—Augústus did not formally take away from the popular assemblies their legislative power, but occasionally submitted to them laws for their approval. This was, however, hardly more than a discreet concession to custom. The people in their present unwieldy assemblies, the emperor did not regard as able to decide upon important matters of state. Their duties were therefore practically restricted to the election of the magistrates, whose names he usually presented to them.

The Republican Magistrates.—In accordance with his general policy Augústus did not interfere with the old republican offices, but allowed them to remain as undisturbed as possible. The cónsuls, prætors, quæstors, and other officers continued to be elected just as they had been before. But the emperor did not generally use these magistrates to carry out the details of his administration. This was performed by other officers appointed by himself. The position of the old republican magistrates was rather one of honor than one of executive responsibility.

The Army.—While the emperor knew that his power must have some military support, he was careful not to make the army a burden to the people. He therefore reduced the number of légions from fifty to twenty-five. As each légion contained not more than six thousand men, the whole army did not exceed one hundred and fifty thousand soldiers. These légions were distributed through the frontier provinces; the inner provinces and Ítaly were thus not burdened by the quartering of troops. To support the imperial authority at home, and to maintain public order, Augústus organized a body of nine thousand men called the "prætórian guard," which force was stationed at different points outside of Rome.

II. AUGÚSTUS AND THE RÓMAN WORLD

Rome, Ítaly, and the Provinces.—We can get some further idea of the policy of Augústus by looking at the way in which he governed the different parts of the Róman world. The whole empire may be regarded as made up of three parts: Rome, Ítaly, and the provinces. We are now to look at the improvements which he made in these three spheres of administration.

The Administration of Rome.—We have read enough of the distracted condition of the Róman city during the last hundred years to see the need of some improvement. Augústus met this need by creating certain new officers to keep the city under better control. In the first place, he established a city police under the charge of a chief (*præféctus úrbi*), to preserve order and prevent the scenes of violence which had been of such frequent occurrence. In the next place, he created a fire and detective department under the charge of another chief (*præféctus vígilum*), to have jurisdiction over all incendiaries, burglars, and other night-prowlers. He then placed the grain supply under a regular officer (*præféctus annónæ*) who was to superintend the transport of grain from Égypt, and was held responsible for its proper distribution. Moreover, he broke up the "secret clubs" which had been hotbeds of disorder, and substituted in their place more orderly societies under the supervision of the government. For administrative purposes the city was divided into fourteen districts, or wards. By these arrangements, life and property became more secure, and the populace became more orderly and law-abiding.

The Administration of Ítaly.—Ítaly was now extended to the Alps, the province of Cisálpine Gaul having lately been joined to the peninsula. The whole of Ítaly was divided by Augústus into eleven "regions," or administrative districts. In order to maintain the splendid system of roads which had been constructed during the republican period, the emperor appointed a superintendent of highways (*curátor viárum*) to keep them in repair. He also established a post system by which the different parts of the peninsula could be kept in communication with one another. He suppressed brigandage by establishing military patrols in the dangerous districts. It was his policy to encourage everywhere the growth of a healthy and vigorous municipal life. To relieve the poverty of Ítaly he continued the plan of Július Cæsar in sending out colonies into the provinces, where there were better opportunities to make a living.

The Administration of the Provinces.—During the reign of Augústus the number of provinces was increased by taking in the outlying territory south of the Rhine and the Dánube. The new frontier provinces were Rhǽtia, Nóricum, Pannónia, and Mœsia. The provinces were not only increased in number, but were thoroughly reorganized. They were first divided into two groups: the *senatorial*, or those which remained under the control of the senate; and the *imperial*, or those which passed under the control of the emperor. The latter were generally on the frontiers, and required the presence of an army and a military governor. The governors of the imperial provinces were lieutenants (*legáti*) of the emperor. Appointed by him, and strictly responsible to him, they were no longer permitted to prey upon their subjects, but were obliged to rule in the name of the emperor, and for the welfare of the people. The senatorial provinces, on the other hand, were still under the control of procónsuls and proprǽtors appointed by the senate. But the condition of these provinces was also greatly improved. The establishment of the new government thus proved to be a great benefit to the provincials. Their property became more secure, their commerce revived, their cities prospered, and their lives were made more tolerable.

The Finances of the Empire.—With the division of the provinces, the administration of the finances was also divided between the senate and the emperor. The revenues of the senatorial provinces went into the treasury of the senate, or the *ærárium*; while those of the imperial provinces passed into the treasury of the emperor, or the *fiscus*. The old wretched system of farming the revenues, which had disgraced the republic and impoverished the provincials, was gradually abandoned. The collection of the taxes in the senatorial as well as the imperial provinces was placed in the charge of imperial officers. It was not long before the cities themselves were allowed to raise by their own officers the taxes due to the Róman government.

119

Augústus also laid the foundation of a sound financial system by making careful estimates of the revenues and expenditures of the state; and by raising and expending the public money in the most economical and least burdensome manner.

Várus's Battle (1909)
Otto Albert Koch (1866-1920)

The Frontiers of the Empire.— By the wars of Augústus, the boundaries of the empire were extended to the Rhine and the Dánube (including the Álpine region) on the north, to the Atlántic Ocean on the west, to the desert of África on the south, and nearly to the Euphrátes on the east. The only two great frontier nations which threatened to disturb the peace of Rome were the Párthians on the east and the Gérmans on the north. The Párthians still retained the standards lost by Crássus; but Augústus by his skillful diplomacy was able to recover them without a battle. He abandoned, however, all design of conquering that Eastern people. But his eyes looked longingly to the country of the Gérmans. He invaded their territory; and after a temporary success his general, Várus, was slain and three Róman légions were utterly destroyed by the great Gérman chieftain Armínius at the famous battle of the Téutoberg forest (A.D. 9). The frontiers remained for many years where they were fixed by Augústus; and he advised his successors to govern well the territory which he left to them rather than to increase its limits.

III. THE AGE OF AUGÚSTUS

The Advisers of Augústus.—The remarkable prosperity that attended the reign of Augústus has caused this age to be called by his name. The glory of this period is largely due to the wise policy of Augústus himself; but in his work he was greatly assisted by two men, whose names are closely linked to his own. These men were Agríppa and Mæcénas.

Agríppa had been from boyhood one of the most intimate friends of Augústus, and during the trying times of the later republic had constantly aided him by his counsel and his sword. The victories of Augústus before and after he came to power were largely due to this able general. By his artistic ability Agríppa also contributed much to the architectural splendor of Rome.

The man who shared with Agríppa the favor and confidence of Augústus was Mæcénas, a wise statesman and patron of literature. It was by the advice of Mæcénas that many of the important reforms of Augústus were adopted and carried out. But the greatest honor is due to Mæcénas for encouraging those men whose writings made this period one of the "golden ages" of the world's literature. It was chiefly the encouragement given to architecture and literature which made the reign of Augústus an epoch in civilization.

Encouragement to Architecture.—It is said that Augústus boasted that he "found Rome of brick and left it of marble." He restored many of the temples and other buildings which had either fallen into decay or been destroyed during the riots of the civil war. On the Pálatine hill he began the construction of the great imperial palace, which became the magnificent home of the Cǽsars. He built a new temple of Vésta, where the sacred fire of the city was kept burning. He erected a new temple to Apóllo, to which was attached a library of Greek and Látin authors; also temples to Júpiter Tónans and to the Divine Július. One of the noblest and most useful of the public works of the emperor was the new Fórum of Augústus, near the old Róman Fórum and the Fórum of Július. In this new Fórum was erected the temple of Mars the Avenger (*Mars Últor*), which Augústus built to commemorate the war by which he had avenged the death of Cǽsar. We must not forget to notice the massive Pántheon, the temple of all the gods, which is today the best preserved monument of the Augústan period. This was built by Agríppa, in the early part of Augústus's reign (27 B.C.), but was altered by the emperor Hádrian.

Left: Model of the Temple of Mars Últor (1930's), Italo Gismondi
Right: *Vírgil Reading the 'Ænéid' to Augústus and Octávia* (1787)
Jean-Joseph Taillasson (1745-1809), National Gallery, England

Patronage of Literature.—But more splendid and enduring than these temples of marble were the works of literature which this age produced. At this time was written Vérgil's "Ænéid," which is one of the greatest epic poems of the world. It was then that the "Odes" of Hórace were composed, the race and rhythm of which are unsurpassed. Then, too, were written the élegies of Tibúllus, Propértius, and Óvid. Greatest among the prose writers of this time was Lívy, whose "pictured pages" tell of the miraculous origin of Rome, and her great achievements in war and in peace. During this time also flourished certain Greek writers whose works are famous. Dionýsius of Halicarnássus wrote a book on the antiquities of Rome, and tried to reconcile his countrymen to the Róman sway. Strábo, the geographer, described the subject lands of Rome in the Augústan age. The whole literature of this period was inspired with a growing spirit of patriotism, and an appreciation of Rome as the great ruler of the world.

Religious and Social Reforms.—With his encouragement of art and literature Augústus also tried to improve the religious and moral condition of the people. The old religion was falling into decay. With the restoration of the old temples, he hoped to bring the people back to the worship of the ancient gods. The worship of Júno, which had been neglected, was restored, and assigned to the care of his wife, Lívia, as the representative of the matrons of Rome. Augústus tried to purify the Róman religion by discouraging the introduction of the foreign deities whose worship

was corrupt. He believed that even a great Róman had better be worshiped than the degenerate gods and goddesses of Sýria and Égypt; and so the Divine Július was added to the number of the Róman gods. He did not favor the Jéwish religion; and Christiánity had not yet been preached at Rome. With the attempt to restore the old Róman religion, he also wished to revive the old morality and simple life of the past. He himself disdained luxurious living and foreign fashions. He tried to improve the lax customs which prevailed in respect to marriage and divorce, and to restrain the vices which were destroying the population of Rome. But it is difficult to say whether these laudable attempts of Augústus produced any real results upon either the religious or the moral life of the Róman people.

Death and Character of Augústus.—Augústus lived to the age of seventy-five; and his reign covered a period of forty-five years. During this time he had been performing "the difficult part of ruling without appearing to rule, of being at once the autocrat of the civilized world and the first citizen of a free commonwealth." His last words are said to have been, "Have I not played my part well?" But it is not necessary for us to suppose that Augústus was a mere actor. The part which he had to perform in restoring peace to the world was a great and difficult task. In the midst of conflicting views which had distracted the republic for a century, he was called upon to perform a work of reconciliation. And it is doubtful whether any political leader ever performed such a work with greater success. When he became the supreme ruler of Rome he was fully equal to the place, and brought order out of confusion. He was content with the substance of power and indifferent to its form. Not so great as Július Cǽsar, he was yet more successful. He was one of the greatest examples of what we may call the "conservative reformer," a man who accomplishes the work of regeneration without destroying existing institutions.

Top: Res Géstæ Dívi Augústi ("Deeds of the Divine Augústus")

Bottom: Genius of Cǽsar Augústus from Otricoli

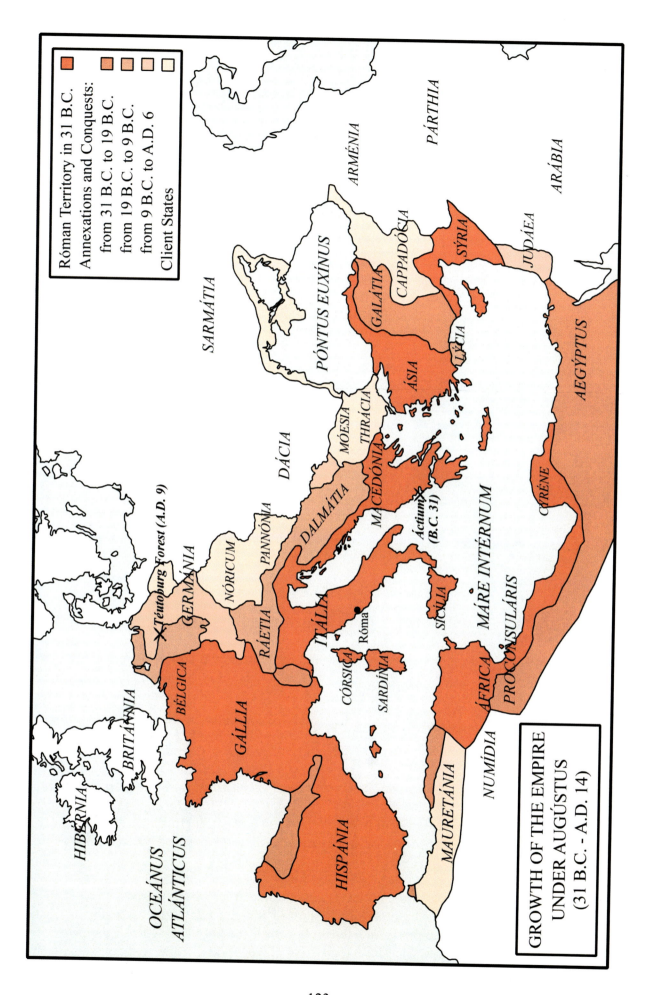

Róman Territory in 31 B.C.
Annexations and Conquests:
from 31 B.C. to 19 B.C.
from 19 B.C. to 9 B.C.
from 9 B.C. to A.D. 6
Client States

HIBÉRNIA

OCEÁNUS
ATLÁNTICUS

BRITÁNNIA

✕ Téutoburg Forest (A.D. 9)

GERMÁNIA

BÉLGICA

GÁLLIA

HISPÁNIA

NÓRICUM

RÁETIA

PANNÓNIA

DÁCIA

SARMÁTIA

DALMÁTIA

MÓESIA

THRÁCIA

PÓNTUS EUXÍNUS

ARMÉNIA

PÁRTHIA

ARÁBIA

GALÁTIA

CAPPADÓCIA

ÁSIA

LÝCIA

SÝRIA

JUDÁEA

AEGÝPTUS

ITÁLIA

Áctium ✕
(B.C. 31)

MACEDÓNIA

• Róma

CÓRSICA

SARDÍNIA

SICÍLIA

MÁRE INTÉRNUM

CYRÉNE

MAURETÁNIA

NUMÍDIA

ÁFRICA
PROCONSULÁRIS

GROWTH OF THE EMPIRE
UNDER AUGÚSTUS
(31 B.C. - A.D. 14)

CHAPTER XXIV

THE JÚLIAN EMPERORS: TIBÉRIUS TO NÉRO

The Reign of Tibérius (A.D. 14-37), I.—The Reign of Calígula (A.D. 37-41), II.
The Reign of Cláudius (A.D. 41-54), III.—The Reign of Néro (A.D. 54-68), III.

I. THE REIGN OF TIBÉRIUS (A.D. 14-37)

The Character of Tibérius.—The system established by Augústus was put to a severe test by the character of the men who immediately followed him. The emperors who made up the Júlian line were often tyrannical, vicious, and a disgrace to Rome. That the empire was able to survive at all is, perhaps, another proof of the thoroughness of the work done by the first emperor. Of the

four Júlian emperors who succeeded Augústus, Tibérius was perhaps the ablest. He had already shown his ability as a general; and having been adopted by Augústus and associated with him in the government, he was prepared to carry out the policy already laid down. But in his personal character he presented a strong contrast to his predecessor. Instead of being generous and conciliatory, he was cruel and tyrannical to those with whom he was brought into personal relations. But we must distinguish between the way in which he treated his enemies and the way in which he ruled the empire. He had a certain sense of duty, and tried to maintain the authority which devolved upon him. If he could not accomplish this by the winning ways of Augústus, he could do it by more severe methods.

Bust of Tibérius (ca. A.D. 4-14), Brítish Museum, London

Campaigns of Germánicus.—The first duty which fell to Tibérius was to gain the support of the army. The légions on the Rhine and the Dánube were at first not disposed to accept his authority. Those on the Dánube were soon subdued by Drúsus, the son of Tibérius, who took advantage of an eclipse of the moon to appeal to the superstitious dread of the soldiers. The légions on the Rhine were more determined, and desired to place their favorite general, Germánicus (a nephew of Tibérius), on the throne in place of Tibérius. But Germánicus, loyal to his chief, resisted this first attempt of the army to enthrone an emperor. To turn their minds from thoughts of treason, he planned the invasion and conquest of Gérmany. Three successful campaigns were made across the Rhine. A portion of the Gérman territory was occupied, and the lost standards of Várus were recovered. These campaigns in Gérmany were cut short by Tibérius, who recalled Germánicus from the Rhine, and sent him to the East to oppose the Párthians. Whether this act was inspired by envy or by wisdom on the part of Tibérius, we cannot say. After a brief and unsuccessful career in the East, Germánicus died, whether as the result of natural causes or as the result of foul play, we are also at a loss to determine.

Despotic Measures of Tibérius.—While Tibérius pursued in many respects the policy of Augústus, he adopted certain measures which showed that he had little sympathy with the "disguises of monarchy." In the first place, he extinguished the political rights of the people by taking away from the assemblies what little legislative power had been left to them; and also by transferring to the senate the election of the regular magistrates. The popular assemblies were thus reduced to a mere shadow.

In the next place, he gave a new meaning to the law of treason (*lex maiestátis*). This law had hitherto referred only to actual crimes against the state. Now it was made to include any words or conduct, looks or gestures, which could be interpreted as hostile to the emperor. This is what we call "constructive treason"; and at Rome, as in any other country where it has been tolerated, it became an instrument of despotism. Again, in order to punish his enemies, Tibérius encouraged the practice of "delátion"; that is, he offered rewards to all persons who would give information regarding offenders. There thus sprang up at Rome a class of informers (*delatóres*), who acted as professional spies, or inquisitors, to detect the enemies of the emperor.

Finally, we may mention another change made by Tibérius. This was the bringing together of the prætórian cohorts into one camp near Rome, to protect the person of the emperor and thus to secure more strongly his power.

The Influence of Sejánus.—The removal of the prætórian camp to Rome was done at the suggestion of Sejánus, a wily and unscrupulous officer, who had obtained command of these cohorts. As Tibérius was suspicious of everyone else he selected Sejánus as his trusted adviser. Sejánus was to Tibérius what Agríppa or Mæcénas had been to Augústus. But unlike those imperial friends, Sejánus was desirous of power and was treacherous to his master. To secure his position, Sejánus caused the murder of Drúsus, the son of Tibérius. He even induced the emperor himself to retire from Rome to the island of Cápreæ in the Bay of Náples, and to leave him in control of the government. The schemes and crimes of Sejánus formed a large part of this despotic reign. When his treason was discovered by Tibérius, he was deposed from his place and strangled in prison. The fall of Sejánus was followed by the prosecution of his fellow-conspirators, or those who were suspected of plotting against the emperor. Although these prosecutions were made under the forms of law, the law was the *lex maiestátis*; and the methods of its execution produced a reign of terror at Rome.

Prosperity of the Provinces.—The cruel tyranny of Tibérius was restricted mainly to the city of Rome, and to those persons whom he suspected as his personal enemies. The provinces were relieved from this suspicion, and hence they continued to be prosperous as they had been under Augústus. Indeed, Tibérius seemed to be especially anxious regarding their welfare. Like Augústus he tried to protect them from unjust government and oppressive taxation. His favorite maxim is said to have been, "A good shepherd should shear his flock, and not flay them." While he prosecuted his own enemies, he also brought to justice the provincial governors who were guilty of extortion. It is said that while he was hated at Rome, he was loved in the provinces. When many cities of Ásia were destroyed by an earthquake, he sent to them relief in the form of money and remitted their taxes for five years. When he died, his faults were exaggerated by the Róman historians, and his virtues were extolled by the provincials.

II. THE REIGN OF CALÍGULA (A.D. 37-41)

The Early Promise of Calígula.—Tibérius had made no provision for a successor. Hence the choice lay entirely with the senate, which selected a favorite of the army. This was Gáius Cæsar, the son of the famous general, Germánicus. He was familiarly called by the soldiers "Calígula," by which name he is generally known. He was joyfully welcomed by the people, and gave promise of a successful reign. He declared his intention of devoting himself to the public welfare. But the high hopes which he raised at his accession were soon dashed to the ground,

125

when it was discovered that the empire was in the hands of a man who had lost his reason. The brief career of Calígula may be of interest as showing the vagaries of a diseased and unbalanced mind; but they have no special political importance, except as proving that the empire could survive even with a mad prince on the throne.

His Insanity and Extravagances.—Calígula was subject in childhood to epileptic fits, and his mind was evidently diseased. When he was placed in the high position of emperor his brain was turned and he revealed all the grotesque symptoms of insanity. He believed himself a god. He wasted the money of the treasury in senseless projects. He built a bridge from the Pálatine hill, where he resided, to the Cápitoline, that he might be "next door neighbor to Júpiter." To lead his army over the sea he constructed a bridge three miles long over the Gulf of Báiæ, a part of the Bay of Náples, and conducted his soldiers over it in a triumphal procession. He professed to lead an expedition against Británia; and when he had collected his soldiers on the seashore as if for embarkation, he suddenly issued an order to them to gather the shells from the beach and carry them to Rome as "the spoils of the ocean." The senate was directed to deposit these spoils among the treasures of the Cápitol. It is said that he nominated his horse for cónsul. In order to exceed the luxuries of Lucúllus, he expended an astronomical amount on a single meal. He threatened to set up his own image in the temple at Jerúsalem and to compel the Jews to worship it. Numerous other stories of a similar kind are told of this delirious man, stories which are more suited to illustrate a treatise on insanity than to burden the pages of history.

Bust of Calígula, Getty Museum, Los Angeles

Significance of his Reign.—The reign of Calígula, which was fortunately limited to the brief space of four years, shows to us the perils inherent in a despotic form of government that permitted a madman to rule the civilized world. The Róman Empire had no provision by which any prince could be held responsible, either to law or to reason. A cruel tyrant could revel in blood, or a maniac could indulge in the wildest excesses without restraint. The only limit to such a despotism was assassination; and by this severe method the reign of Calígula was brought to an end.

III. THE REIGN OF CLÁUDIUS (A.D. 41-54)

His Elevation by the Prætórians.—Cláudius was the first emperor proclaimed by the army. The murder of Calígula had been provoked by an insult given to an officer of the prætórian guard. When the senate hesitated to choose a successor, the prætórians, accidentally finding Cláudius in the palace, and recognizing him as the brother of Germánicus, assumed the right to name him as emperor. The senate was obliged to submit; and for a long time after this the prætórians continued to exercise the right of naming the prince. Cláudius is usually represented as a weak imbecile; but his reign stands out in refreshing contrast to the cruel tyranny of Tibérius and the wild extravagances of Calígula.

The Emperor's Household.—Cláudius was naturally weak and timid, and came under the influence of the members of his household: his wives and freedmen. The intrigues and crimes of his wife Messalína, and of his niece Agrippína, whom he married after the death of Messalína, were a scandal to Róman society. So far as he was influenced by these abandoned women, his reign was a disgrace. But the same can scarcely be said of the freedmen of his household:

Narcíssus, his secretary; Pállas, the keeper of accounts; and Polýbius, the director of his studies. These men were educated Greeks and he benefitted from their advice.

His Public Works.—Cláudius followed the example of Augústus in the execution of works of public utility. He constructed the Cláudian áqueduct, which brought water to the city from a distance of forty-five miles. For the purpose of giving Rome a good harbor where the grain supplies from Égypt might be landed, he built the *Pórtus Románus* at the mouth of the Tíber near Óstia. To improve the agriculture of the Mársians, he constructed a great tunnel to drain the Fúcine Lake, a work which required the labor of thirty thousand men for eleven years. He celebrated the completion of this work by a mimic naval battle on the waters of the lake.

Top: Bas-Relief of Members of the Prætórian Guard (A.D. 51-52), Louvre Museum, Paris

Middle: *Proclaiming Cláudius Emperor* (1867) Sir Lawrence Alma-Tadema (1836-1912)

Bottom: *Cláudian Áqueduct* (at Porta Maggiore) Colored Aquatint with Etching (1820), Matthew Dubourg

The Conquest of Southern Brítain.—But the most important event of the reign of Cláudius was the invasion and partial conquest of Brítain. Since the invasion of Július Cæsar a hundred years before, the Rómans had taken little interest in this island. With the aid of his lieutenants, Áulus Pláutius and Vespásian, Cláudius now effected a permanent landing in Brítain. He was opposed by the famous Céltic chief Caráctacus, but succeeded in subduing the southern part of the island. Brítain was thus opened to the benefits of Róman civilization.

His Care of the Provinces.—It is to the credit of Cláudius that he was greatly interested in the condition of the provinces. He spent much time in regulating the affairs of the East. The kingdom of Thrace was changed into a province, and governed by a Róman procurator. Lýcia, in Ásia Mínor, also was made a province, as well as Mauretánia in África. One of the most important changes which he made was the restoration of the kingdom of the Jews to Hérod Agríppa. This he did out of respect for this people, and to allay the bad feeling which had been stirred up during the previous reign. But

Cláudius especially showed his interest in the provinces by extending to them the rights of Róman citizenship. The *civitas* was granted to a large part of Gaul, thus carrying out the policy which had been begun by Július Cæsar. If we except the scandals of the court, the reign of Cláudius may be regarded as inspired by prudence and a wise regard for the welfare of his subjects.

IV. THE REIGN OF NÉRO (A.D. 54-68)

The "Quinquénnium Nerónis."—Néro was the grandson of Germánicus and a descendant of Augústus. He was proclaimed by the prætórians and accepted by the senate. He had been educated by the great philosopher Séneca; and his interests had been looked after by Búrrhus, the able captain of the prætórian guards. His accession was hailed with gladness. He assured the senate that he would not interfere with its powers. The first five years of his reign, which are known as the *Quinquénnium Nerónis*, were marked by a wise and beneficent administration. During this time he yielded to the advice and influence of Séneca and Búrrhus, who practically controlled the affairs of the empire and restrained the young prince from exercising his power to the detriment of the state. Under their influence delátion was forbidden, the taxes were reduced, and the authority of the senate was respected.

Tyranny and Crimes of Néro.—But Néro's worst foes were those of his own household, especially his unscrupulous and ambitious mother, Agrippína. The intrigues of this woman to displace Néro and to elevate Británnicus, the son of Cláudius, led to Néro's first domestic tragedy, the poisoning of Británnicus. He afterward yielded himself to the influence of the infamous Poppæa Sabína, the most beautiful and the wickedest woman of Rome. At her suggestion, he murdered first his mother, and then his wife. He discarded the counsels of Séneca and Búrrhus, and accepted those of Tigellínus, a man of the worst character. Then followed a career of wickedness, extortion, atrocious cruelty, which it is not necessary to describe, but which has made his name a synonym for all that is vicious in human nature, and despicable in a ruler.

Bust of the Emperor Néro

The Suicide of Séneca (1871), Manuel Dominguez Sanchez, Museo del Prado

Burning and Rebuilding of the City.—In the tenth year of his reign occurred a great fire which destroyed a large part of the city of Rome. It is said that out of the fourteen regions, six were reduced to ashes. Many ancient temples and public buildings were consumed, such as the temple of Júpiter Státor ascribed to Rómulus, and the temples of Vésta and Diána, which dated from the time of the kings. The reports which have come to us of the conduct of Néro during this great disaster are very diverse. Some represent him as gloating over the destruction of the city

128

and repeating his own poem on the "Sack of Troy." Other reports declare that he never showed himself in a more favorable light, exerting himself to put out the flames, opening the public buildings and the imperial palace for the shelter of the homeless, and relieving the suffering by reducing the price of grain. But it is charged that if he performed these charities, it was to relieve himself of the suspicion of having caused the conflagration. Whatever may be the truth as to his conduct, the burning of Rome resulted in rebuilding the city on a more magnificent scale. The narrow streets were widened, and more splendid buildings were erected. The vanity of the emperor was shown in the building of an enormous and meretricious palace, called the "golden house of Néro," and also in the erection of a colossal statue of himself near the Pálatine hill. To meet the expenses of these structures the provinces were obliged to contribute; and the cities and temples of Greece were plundered of their works of art to furnish the new buildings.

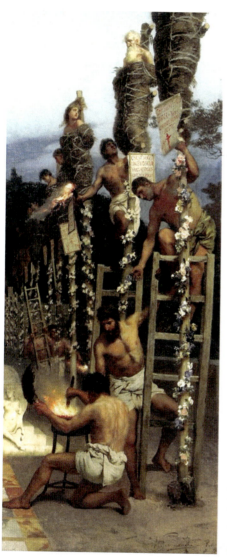

Leading Light of Christiánity. Néro's Torches (1876)
Henryk Siemiradski (1843-1902), National Museum, Krakow, Poland

First Persecution of the Christians.—In order to shield himself from the suspicion of firing the city, Néro accused the Christians and made them the victims of his cruelty. Nothing can give us a more vivid idea of this first persecution than the account of the Róman historian Tácitus, which is of great interest to us because it contains the first reference found in any pagan author to Christ and his followers. This passage shows not only the cruelty of Néro and the terrible sufferings of the early Christian martyrs, but also the pagan prejudice against the new religion. Tácitus says: "In order to drown the rumor, Néro shifted the guilt on persons hated for their abominations and known as Christians, and punished them with exquisite tortures. Christ, from whom they derive their name, had been punished under Tibérius by the procurátor Póntius Pílate. Checked for a time, this pernicious religion broke out again not only in Judéa but in Rome. Those who confessed their creed were first arrested; and then by their information a large number were convicted, not so much on the charge of burning the city, as of hating the human race. In their deaths they were made the subjects of sport; for they were covered with the skins of wild beasts, worried to death by dogs, nailed to crosses, burned to serve for torches in the night. Néro offered his own gardens for this spectacle. The people were moved with pity for the sufferers; for it was felt that they were suffering to gratify Néro's cruelty, not from considerations for the public welfare."

General Condition of the Empire.—In spite of such enormous crimes as those practiced by Néro, the larger part of the empire was beyond the circle of his immediate influence, and remained undisturbed. While the palace and the city presented scenes of intrigue and bloodshed, the world in general was tranquil and even prosperous. Except the occasional extortion by which the princes sought to defray the expenses of their debaucheries, Ítaly and the provinces were reaping the fruits of the reforms of Július Cǽsar and Augústus. During this early period, the empire was better than the emperor. Men tolerated the excesses and vices of the palace, on the ground that a bad ruler was better than anarchy.

CHAPTER XXV

THE FLÁVIAN EMPERORS: VESPÁSIAN TO DOMÍTIAN

The Disputed Succession, I.—The Reign of Vespásian (A.D. 69-79), II.—The Reign of Títus (A.D. 79-81), III. Life and Manners of the Rómans, IV.—The Reign of Domítian (A.D. 81-96), V.

I. THE DISPUTED SUCCESSION

Extinction of the Júlian Line.—With the death of Néro, the imperial line which traced its descent from Július Cǽsar and Augústus became extinct. We are now about to discover one of the great defects of the empire as established by Augústus. With all his prudence, Augústus had failed to provide a definite law of succession. In theory the appointment of a successor depended upon the choice of the senate, with which he was supposed to share his power. But in fact it depended quite as much upon the army, upon which his power rested for support. Whether the appointment was made by the senate or by the army, the choice had hitherto always fallen upon some member of the Júlian family. But with the extinction of the Júlian line, the imperial office was open to anyone.

The War of Succession.—Under such circumstances we could hardly expect anything else than a contest for the throne. Not only the prætórian guards, but the légions in the field, claimed the right to name the successor. The rival claims of different armies to place their favorite generals on the throne led to a brief period of civil war, the first to break the long peace established by Augústus.

Gálba (A.D. 68-69).—At the time of Néro's death, the Spánish légions had already selected their commander, Gálba, for the position of emperor. Advancing upon Rome, this general was accepted by the prætórians and approved by the senate. He was a man of high birth, and with a good military record. But his career was a brief one. The légions on the Rhine revolted against him. The prætórians were discontented with his severity and small donations: He soon found a rival in Ótho, the husband of the infamous Poppǽa Sabína who had disgraced the reign of Néro. Ótho enlisted the support of the prætórians, and Gálba was murdered to give place to his rival.

Ótho (A.D. 69).—The brief space of three months, during which Ótho was emperor, cannot be called a reign, but only an attempt to reign. On his accession the new aspirant to the throne found his right immediately disputed by the légions of Spain and Gaul, which proclaimed Vitéllius. The armies of these two rivals met in northern Ítaly, and fortune declared in favor of Vitéllius.

Vitéllius (A.D. 69).—No sooner had Vitéllius begun to revel in the luxuries of the palace, than the standard of revolt was again raised, this time by the légions of the East in favor of their able and popular commander, Vespásian. The events of the previous contest were now repeated; and on the same battlefield in northern Ítaly where Ótho's army had been defeated by that of Vitéllius, the forces of Vitéllius were now defeated by those of Vespásian. Afterward a severe and bloody contest took place in the streets of Rome, and Vespásian made his position secure.

The only significance of these three so-called reigns, and the civil wars which attended them, is the fact that they showed the great danger to which the empire was exposed by having no regular law of succession.

Beginning of a New Era.—The accession of Vespásian was the beginning of a new era for Rome. Indeed, the next century may be regarded as the most prosperous in her whole history. The ideals of Július Cæsar and Augústus seemed to be realized. The hundred and eleven years which elapsed from the beginning of Vespásian's reign to the death of Márcus Aurélius, have been called the happiest in the history of mankind. The new emperor belonged to the Flávian family, which furnished three rulers, Vespásian, Títus, and Domítian. Vespásian was an able and efficient prince. He rescued Rome from the bankrupt condition into which it had been plunged by his predecessors. He retrenched the expenses of the court and set the example of moderation. He appointed good governors for the provinces, and extended the Látin right, that is, the *commércium*, to the people of Spain.

Róman Civilization in Gaul.—The first duty of Vespásian was to suppress a revolt in Gaul which, under Cláudius Civílis, threatened to deprive Rome of that province. After three defeats Civílis was obliged to give up his ambitious scheme, and Gaul again was pacified. Nowhere in the West, outside of Ítaly, did the civilization of Rome take a firmer hold. Gaul became the seat of Róman colonies; its cities were united by Róman roads; and the Róman language, literature, law, manners, and art found there a congenial home. The ruins which we find today in France, of the ancient buildings, baths, aqueducts and amphitheaters, show how completely the province of Gaul was Rómanized.

Pont du Gard at Nimes, France
Portion of an Aqueduct in Róman Gaul

Depiction of the Spoils of Jerúsalem
Arch of Títus in the Róman Fórum

Destruction of Jerúsalem (A.D. 70).—The most unfortunate event in the reign of Vespásian was the revolt of the Jews, which finally resulted in the destruction of Jerúsalem. There had been many changes in the government of Judéa since its first conquest by Pómpey. Some of these changes had been made to reconcile the Jews to the Róman sway. But there had been many things to awaken the opposition of the people; for example, the unreasonable prejudice against them at Rome, the insane attempt of Calígula to place his statue in their temple, as well as the harsh government of Néro. At last the Jews were provoked into a general rebellion. Vespásian was conducting the war against them when he was proclaimed emperor by his légions. The war was then left in the hands of his son Títus, who, in spite of desperate resistance, captured and destroyed the sacred city. The Jews were left without a national home; and Judéa became a separate province of the empire. The representation of the golden candlestick cut upon the arch of Títus is a striking memorial of this unfortunate war.

The Siege and Destruction of Jerúsalem by the Rómans Under the Command of Títus, A.D. 70 (1850),
David Roberts (1796-1864)

Mountain Fortress of Masáda Defended by Jéwish Zealots and Besieged by Lúcius Flávius Sílva in A.D. 72
(Showing Róman Ramp Constructed to Fortress, Wall of Circumvallation, and Légionary Camp at Right)

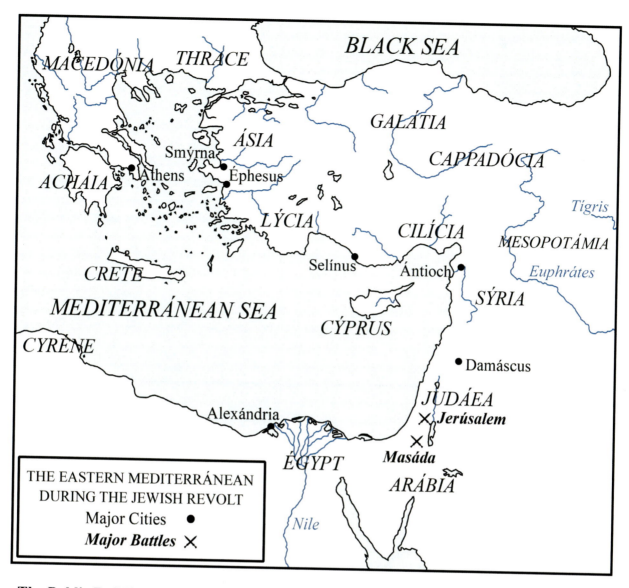

THE EASTERN MEDITERRÁNEAN
DURING THE JEWISH REVOLT
Major Cities   ●
Major Battles ✕

The Public Buildings.—By the strictest economy Vespásian was able to replenish the treasury; and by the means thus obtained he spent large sums upon the public buildings of Rome. He restored the Cápitoline temple, which had been destroyed during the late civil war. He laid out a new Fórum which bore his name. He built a temple to Peace, the goddess whom he delighted to

honor. But the most memorable of his works was the Flávian Amphitheater, or as it is sometimes called, the Colosséum. This stupendous building occupied about six acres of ground, and was capable of seating nearly fifty thousand spectators. The sports which took place in this great structure were the most popular of all the Róman amusements.

Exterior of the Flávian Amphitheater (ca. 1880-1900)

Remains of the Interior of the Flávian Amphitheater Showing Rooms Under the Arena

Mosaïc of Róman Chariot Team

Amusements of the Rómans.—The chief public amusements of the Rómans were those which took place in the circus, the theater, and the amphitheater. The greatest circus of Rome was the Círcus Máximus. It was an enclosure about two thousand feet long and six hundred feet wide. Within it were arranged seats for different classes of citizens, a separate box being reserved for the imperial family. The games consisted chiefly of chariot races. The excitement was due to the reckless and dangerous driving of the charioteers, each striving to win by upsetting his competitors. There were also athletic sports; running, leaping, boxing, wrestling, throwing the quoit, and hurling the javelin. Sometimes sham battles and sea fights took place.

The Rómans were not very much addicted to the theater, there being only three principal structures of this kind at Rome, those of Pómpey, Marcéllus, and Bálbus. The theater was derived from the Greeks and was built in the form of a semicircle, the seats being apportioned, as in the case of the circus, to different classes of persons. The shows consisted largely of dramatic exhibitions, of mimes, pantomimes, and dancing. It is said that the poems of Óvid were acted in pantomime.

The most popular and characteristic amusements of the Rómans were the sports of the amphitheater. This building was in the form of a double theater, forming an entire circle or ellipse. Such structures were built in different cities of the empire, but none equaled the colossal building of Vespásian. The sports of the amphitheater were chiefly gladiatórial shows and the combats of wild beasts. The amusements of the Rómans were largely sensational, and appealed to the tastes of the populace. Their influence was almost always bad, and tended to degrade the morals of the people.

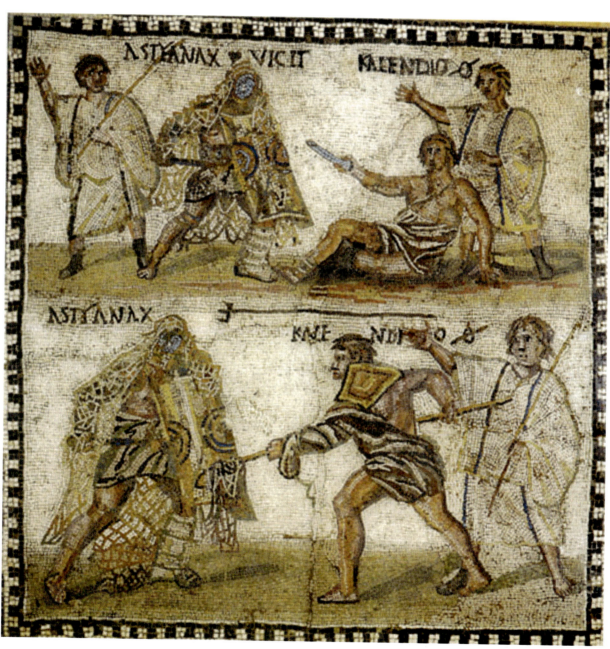

Mosaïc Depicting Gladiatorial Combat
Astýanax (Secútor) vs. Kaléndio (Retiárius / Net Fighter)

135

III. THE REIGN OF TÍTUS (A.D. 79-81)

"Delight of Mankind."—Vespásian had prepared for his death by associating with the government his son, Títus; so the change to the new reign was attended by no war of succession or other disturbance. The great aim of Títus was to make himself loved by the people. He was lavish in the giving of public shows. He dedicated the great amphitheater built by his father with a magnificent naval spectacle. He ruled with so much kindness and moderation that he became the most popular of the emperors, and was called the "Delight of Mankind." It is related that one evening he remembered that he had bestowed no gift upon any one, and in regret exclaimed to his friends, "I have lost a day."

Denárius of Emperor Títus

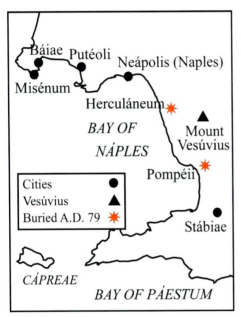

Destruction of Herculáneum and Pompéii.—But the reign of Títus, delightful as it was, was marked by two great calamities. One was a great fire which consumed the new temple of the Cápitoline Júpiter, which his father had just erected; and which also injured the Pántheon, the baths of Agríppa, and the theaters of Pómpey and Marcéllus. But the greatest calamity of this reign was due to the terrible eruption of Mt. Vesúvius, which destroyed the two cities of Herculáneum and Pompéii, situated on the Bay of Náples. The Rómans had never suspected that this mountain was a volcano, although a few years before it had been shaken by an earthquake. The scenes which attended this eruption are described by the younger Plíny, whose uncle, the elder Plíny, lost his life while investigating the causes of the eruption. The buried city of Pompéii has been exhumed, and its relics reveal in a vivid way the private life and customs of the Róman people.

IV. LIFE AND MANNERS OF THE RÓMANS

Houses of the Rómans.—The uncovered ruins of Pompéii show to us a great many houses, from the most simple to the elaborate "House of Pánsa" or "House of the Véttii." The ordinary house (*dómus*) consisted of front and rear parts connected by a central area, or court. The front part contained the entrance hall (*vestíbulum*); the large reception room (*átrium*); and the private room of the master (*tablínum*), which contained the archives of the family. The large central court was surrounded by columns (*peristýlum*). The rear part contained the more private apartments - the dining room (*triclínium*), where the members of the family took their meals reclining on couches; the kitchen (*culína*); and the bathroom (*bálneum*). The Rómans had no stoves like ours, and rarely did they have any chimneys. The house was warmed by portable furnaces (*fóculi*), like fire pans, in which coal or charcoal was burned, the smoke escaping through the doors or an open place in the roof; sometimes hot air was introduced by pipes from below. The rooms were lighted either by candles (*candélæ*) made of tallow or wax; or by oil lamps (*lucérnæ*) made of terra cotta, or of bronze, worked sometimes into exquisite designs.

Reconstructed House of the Véttii, Ruins of Pompéii

Meals.—There were usually three daily meals: the breakfast (*ientáculum*), soon after rising; the luncheon, or midday meal (*prándium*); and the chief meal, or dinner (*céna*), in the afternoon. The food of the poorer classes consisted of a kind of porridge, or breakfast

food (*farína*), made of a coarse species of wheat (*far*), together with ordinary vegetables, such as turnips and onions, with milk and olives. The wealthy classes vied with one another in procuring the rarest delicacies from Ítaly and other parts of the world.

Fresco from Ruins of Pompéii Depicting Fruit

Dress.—The characteristic dress of the men was the *tóga*, a loose garment thrown about the person in ample folds, and covering a closer garment called the tunic (*túnica*). The Rómans wore sandals on the feet, but generally no covering for the head. The dress of a Róman matron consisted of three parts: the close-fitting *túnica*; the *stóla*, a gown reaching to the feet; and the *pálla*, a shawl large enough to cover the whole figure. The ladies took great pains in arranging the hair, and possessed a fondness for ornaments: necklaces, bracelets, earrings, and costly jewels.

Róman Woman, ca. A.D. 100
Glyptothek Museum, Munich

137

Writing Materials.—For writing the Rómans used different materials: first, the tablet (*tábula*), or a thin piece of board covered with wax, which was written upon with a sharp iron pencil (*stýlus*); next, a kind of paper (*chárta*) made from the plant called *papýrus*; and, finally, parchment (*membrána*) made from the skins of animals. The paper and parchment were written upon with a pen made of reed sharpened with a penknife, and ink made of a mixture of lampblack. When a book (*líber*) was written, the different pieces of paper or parchment were pasted together in a long sheet and rolled upon a round stick. When collected in a library (*bibliothéca*), the rolls were arranged upon shelves or in boxes.

Fresco of a Young Woman Holding a Stýlus and Wax Tablets (ca. A.D. 50), Herculáneum

Employments.— The Employments of the Rómans comprised many of the chief occupations and trades with which we are familiar today, including professional, commercial, mechanical, and agricultural pursuits. To the learned professions belonged the priest, the lawyer, the physician, and the teacher. The commercial classes included the merchant, the banker, the broker, the contractor, to whom may also be added the tax gatherer of earlier times. The mechanical trades comprised a great variety of occupations, such as the making of glass, earthenware, bread, cloth, wearing apparel, articles of wood, leather, iron, bronze, silver, and gold. The artisans were often organized into societies or guilds (*collégia*) for their mutual benefit; these guilds were very ancient, their origin being ascribed to Núma. The agriculturists of Rome comprised the large landowners, who were regarded as a highly respectable class, and the small proprietors, the free laborers, and the slaves, the last mentioned forming a great part of the tillers of the soil. In general, the Róman who claimed to be respectable disdained all manual labor, and resigned such labor into the hands of slaves and freedmen.

Marriage.—The marriage customs comprised, first, the ceremony of betrothal (*sponsália*), which included the formal consent of the bride's father, and an announcement in the form of a festival or the presentation of the betrothal ring; secondly, the marriage ceremony, which might be either a religious ceremony, in which a consecrated cake was eaten in the presence of the priest (*confarreátio*), or a secular ceremony, in which the. father gave away his daughter by the forms of a legal sale (*coémptio*). In the time of the empire it was customary for persons to be married without these ceremonies, by their simple consent, During this time, also, divorces became common and the general morals of society became corrupt.

Teréntius Néo and his Wife
Fresco from Pompéii

138

Life in the Towns.—The towns of the empire were in their general appearance reflections of the capital city on the Tíber. Each town had its forum, its temples, its courthouse (*basílica*) and its places of entertainment, Its government seemed to be copied after the old city government of Rome. It had its magistrates, chief among whom were two men (*duúmviri*), something like the old cónsuls. It had its municipal council or senate (*cúria*), controlled by a municipal aristocracy (*curiáles*). Its people delighted in the same kind of shows and amusements that we have seen at Rome. At Pompéii we find in the *graffiti*, or writings left upon the walls of buildings, some remarkable evidences of the ordinary life of the townsmen. Some of these writings hardly rise above the dignity of mere scribblings. They are most numerous upon the buildings in those places frequented by the crowds. There we find advertisements of public shows, memoranda of sales, cookery receipts, personal lampoons, love effusions, and hundreds of similar records of the common life of this ancient people. If we should attempt to draw a distinction among the various towns of the empire, we might observe that the people of the Western towns became more Rómanized than those of the Eastern towns. The Látin language prevailed in the West, and the Greek language in the East. But still the Látin was used as the official language in the East as well as in the West; and, on the other hand, the knowledge of the Greek was a mark of culture in the West as in the East.

V. THE REIGN OF DOMÍTIAN (A.D. 81-96)

Exceptional Tyranny of Domítian.—The happy period begun by Vespásian and Títus was interrupted by the exceptional tyranny of Domítian, the younger brother of Títus. Domítian seemed to take for his models Tibérius and Néro. He ignored the senate and the forms of the constitution. He revived the practice of delátion, and was guilty of confiscations and extortions. He teased and irritated all classes, He persecuted the Jews and the Christians. Like Tibérius, he was suspicious, and lived in perpetual fear of assassination. His fears were realized; a conspiracy was organized against him, and he was murdered by a freedman of the palace.

Agrícola in Britain.—The chief event of importance in the reign of Domítian was the extension of the Róman power in Brítain. Agrícola had already been appointed governor of Britain by Vespásian; but it was not until this time that his arms were crowned with marked success. The limits of the province were now pushed to the north, and a new field was opened for the advance of civilization. Brítain became dotted with Róman cities, united by great military roads. As in Gaul, the Róman law and customs found a home, although they did not obtain so enduring an influence as in the continental provinces.

Bust of Domítian (ca. A.D. 90), Cápitoline Museum, Rome

The Silver Age of Róman Literature.—The period of Róman literature which followed the age of Augústus is often called "the Silver Age." The despotic rule of the Júlian emperors had not been favorable to literature. Only two names of that period stand out with prominence, those of Séneca, the Stóic philosopher, and Lúcan, who wrote an epic poem describing the civil war between Pómpey and Cæsar. Under the Flávians occurred a revival of letters, which continued under the subsequent emperors. Among the most noted writers who flourished at this time were Júvenal, the satirist; Tácitus, the historian; Suetónius, the biographer of the "Twelve Cæsars"; Mártial, the epigrammatist; Quintílian, the rhetorician; and Plíny the Younger, the writer of epistles. Although the writings of the Silver Age do not equal those of the age of Augústus in grace of style, they show quite as much vigor and originality.

CHAPTER XXVI

THE FIVE GOOD EMPERORS: NÉRVA TO MÁRCUS AURÉLIUS

The Reign of Nérva (A.D. 96-98), I.—The Reign of Trájan (A.D. 98-117), II.
The Reign of Hádrian (A.D. 117-138), III.—The Reign of Antonínus Píus (A.D. 138-161), IV.
The Reign of Márcus Aurélius (A.D. 161-180), V.

I. THE REIGN OF NÉRVA (A.D. 96-98)

Prosperity of the Empire.—With the death of Domítian the empire came back into the hands of wise and beneficent rulers. The "five good emperors," as they are usually called, were Nérva, Trájan, and Hádrian (who were related to one another only by adoption), and the two Ántonines, Antonínus Píus and Márcus Aurélius. The period of general prosperity which began under Vespásian continued under these emperors. It is during this time that we are able to see Róman civilization at its best, its highest stage of development. Nérva was chosen neither by the prætórians nor by the légions, but by the senate. Within the brief time that he sat upon the throne, he could do little except to remedy the wrongs of his predecessor. He forbade the practice of delátion, recalled the exiles of Domítian, relieved the people from some oppressive taxes and was tolerant to the Chrístians. His wise and just reign is praised by all ancient writers. In order to prevent any trouble at his death, he adopted Trájan as his successor and gave him a share in the government.

Nérva's Attempt to relieve the Poor.—One of the characteristic features of Nérva's short reign was his attempt to relieve the poor. In the first place, he bought up large lots of land from the wealthy landlords, and let them out to the needy citizens. It is noteworthy that he submitted this law to the assembly of the people. In the next place, he showed his great interest in the cause of public education. He set apart a certain fund, the interest of which was used to educate the children of poor parents. This interest in providing for the care and education of the poorer classes was continued by his successors.

Bust of the Emperor Nérva, Tívoli

Róman Education.—Education among the Rómans, though not usually endowed by the state, was very general and was highly appreciated. Its main features were derived from the Greeks. It was intended to develop all the mental powers, and to train a man for public life. Children, both boys and girls, began to attend school at six or seven years of age. The elementary studies were reading, writing, and arithmetic. The children were tempted to learn the alphabet by playing with pieces of ivory with the letters marked upon them. They were taught writing by a copy, set upon their tablets; and arithmetic by means of the calculating board (*ábacu*s) and counters (*cálculi*). The higher education comprised what were called the liberal arts (*ártes liberáles*), including the Látin and Greek languages, composition and oratory, and mental and moral philosophy. An important part of education consisted in public recitals and declamations, which were intended to train young men for the forum, and which were often held in the temples. The state sometimes patronized education, as we have already seen in the case of Nérva. Hádrian afterward instituted a public school in a building called the Athenǽum. Public fees were sometimes paid to the instructors (*professóres*) in addition to the fees of the pupils.

II. THE REIGN OF TRÁJAN (A.D. 98-117)

The Greatness of Trájan.—After Július Cǽsar and Augústus, Trájan may be called, in many respects, the greatest of the Róman sovereigns. Adopted by Nérva, he was accepted by the senate. He made himself popular with the army and with the great body of the people. He was a Spániard by birth; and the fact that he was the first emperor who was not a native of Ítaly, shows that the distinction between Rómans and provincials was passing away. He was a brave general, a wise statesman, and a successful administrator. He continued the efforts of Nérva to remedy the evils which the early despotism had brought upon Rome. To the people he restored the elective power; to the senate, liberty of speech and of action; to the magistrates, their former authority. He abolished the law of treason (*lex maiestátis*), and assumed his proper place as the chief magistrate of the empire. He was a generous patron of literature and of art. He also desired

to relieve the condition of the poor. It is said that five thousand children received from him their daily allowance of food. So highly was Trájan esteemed by the Rómans that to his other imperial titles was added that of "Óptimus" (the Best).

Bust of Trájan with Civic Crown, Glyptothek, Munich

The Conquests of Trájan.—Since the death of Augústus there had been made no important additions to the Róman territory, except Brítain. But under Trájan the Rómans became once more a conquering people. The new emperor carried his conquests across the Dánube and acquired the province of Dácia. He then extended his arms into Ásia, and brought into subjection Arménia, Mesopotámia, and Assýria, as the result of a short war with the Párthians. Under Trájan the boundaries of the empire reached their greatest extent.

A List of the Chief Róman Provinces with the Dates of Their Acquisition or Organization

I. Európéan Provinces:

Western:
Spain (205-19 B.C.)
Gaul (120-17 B.C.)
Brítain (A.D. 43-84)

Central:
Rhǽtia et Vindelícia (15 B.C.)
Nóricum (15 B.C.)
Pannónia (A.D. 10)

II. African Provinces:

África proper (146 B.C.)
Cyrenäïca and Crete (74, 63 B.C.)
Numídia (46 B.C.)
Égypt (30 B.C.)
Mauretánia (A.D. 42)

IV. Island Provinces:

Sícily (241 B.C.)
Sardínia et Córsica (238 B.C.)
Cýprus (58 B.C.)

III. Asiátic Provinces:

In Ásia Mínor:
Ásia proper (133 B.C.)
Bithýnia and Póntus (74, 65 B.C.)
Cilícia (67 B.C.)
Galátia (25 B.C.)
Pamphýlia et Lýcia (25 B.C., A.D. 43)
Cappadócia (A.D. 17).

In Southwestern Ásia:
Sýria (64 B.C.)
Judéa (63 B.C. - A.D. 70)
Arábia Petrǽa (A.D. 105).
Arménia (A.D. 114)
Mesopotámia (A.D. 115)
Assýria (A.D. 115)

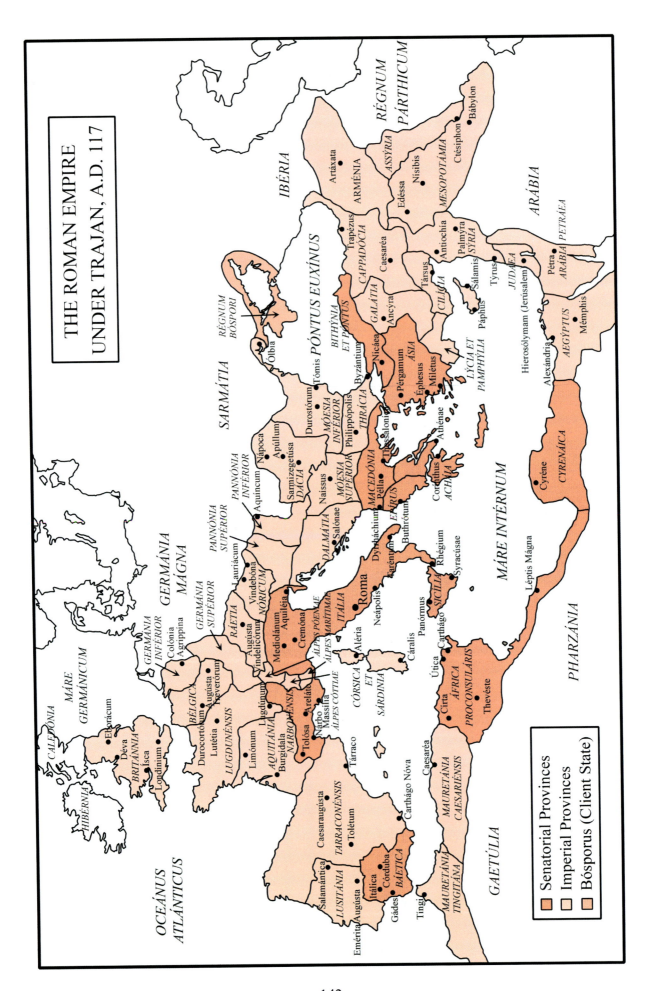

THE ROMAN EMPIRE
UNDER TRAJAN, A.D. 117

OCEÁNUS
ATLÁNTICUS

CALEDÓNIA

HIBÉRNIA

BRITÁNNIA
Eborácum
Déva
Ísca
Londinium

MÁRE
GERMÁNICUM

GERMÁNIA
INFÉRIOR
Colónia
Agrippína

BÉLGICA
Durocortórum
Augusta
Treverórum
Lutétia

LUGDUNÉNSIS
Limónum
Burgídala

AQUITÁNIA
Lugdúnum

NARBONÉNSIS
Tolósa
Narbo
Massília
Arelátte

GERMÁNIA
SUPÉRIOR
Augusta
Vindelicórum

RAETIA

NÓRICUM
Vindebóna

GERMÁNIA
MÁGNA

Lauriácum

PANNÓNIA
SUPÉRIOR
Aquincum

PANNÓNIA
INFÉRIOR

SARMÁTIA

RÉGNUM
BÓSPORI

Olbia

IBÉRIA

RÉGNUM
PÁRTHICUM

Artáxata

ARMÉNIA

ASSÝRIA
Edéssa
Nisibis

Ctésiphon
Bábylon

MESOPOTÁMIA

ARÁBIA

Palmyra
ARÁBIA PETRÁEA
Pétra

Caesaraugústa
Tolétum

TARRACONÉNSIS
Tárraco

Carthágo Nóva

Salamántica

LUSITÁNIA
Emérita
Augusta
Gádes
Itálica
Córduba
BÁETICA

Tingi

MAURETÁNIA
TINGITÁNA

Caesaréa

MAURETÁNIA
CAESARIÉNSIS

GAETÚLIA

CÓRSICA
ET
SÁRDINIA
Cáralis

Alériá

Úticа
Cirta
Carthágo

ÁFRICA
PROCONSULÁRIS
Thevéste

Panórmus
SICÍLIA
Syracusae
Rhégium

Léptis Mágna

MÁRE INTÉRNUM

PHARZÁNIA

Mediolánum
Aquiléia
Cremóna

ALPES POENAE
ITÁLIA
ALPES MARÍTIMAE
ALPES CÓTTIAE

Roma

Neápolis
Tárentum
Brundísium

DALMÁTIA
Salónae

Naissus
DACIA
Sarmizegetusa
Nápoca
Apúllum

MÓESIA
SUPÉRIOR

MÓESIA
INFÉRIOR
Durostórum
Tómis

PÓNTUS EUXÍNUS

Trapézus

CAPPADÓCIA
Caesaréa

Melitene

ARMÉNIA

SÝRIA
Antiochia
Tarsus

CILÍCIA

Philippópolis
THRÁCIA
Byzántium
BITHÝNIA
ET PONTUS
Ancýra

GALÁTIA
Nicáea
Pérgamum
ÁSIA
Éphesus
Milétus

LÝCIA ET
PAMPHÝLIA
Páphus
Salamis

Hierosólymam (Jerúsalem)
JUDÁEA
Týrus

AEGÝPTUS
Alexándria
Mémphis

CYRENÁICA
Cyréne

ACHÁIA
Coríntus
Athénae
Thessaloníca

MACEDÓNIA
Pélla

EPÍRUS
Dyrrháchium
Buthrótum

Rhégium

■ Senatorial Provinces
□ Imperial Provinces
■ Bósporus (Client State)

His Public Works and Buildings.—Rome and Ítaly and the provinces all received the benefit of his wise administration; and the empire reached its highest point of material grandeur. Roads were constructed for the aid of the provincials. He restored the harbors of Ítaly, and improved the water supply of Rome. He built two new baths, one of which was for the exclusive use of women. The greatest monument of Trájan was the new Fórum, in which a splendid column was erected to commemorate his victories.

Trájan's River Voyage and Disembarkment (Casts of Relief from Trájan's Column) (1896)
Photograph of Conrad Cichorius (1863-1932)

Remains of the Fórum of Trájan and Column of Trájan

143

Róman Art.—During this period Róman art reached its highest development. The art of the Rómans, as we have before noticed, was modeled in great part after that of the Greeks. While lacking the fine sense of beauty which the Greeks possessed, the Rómans yet expressed in a remarkable degree the ideas of massive strength and of imposing dignity. In their sculpture and painting they were least original, reproducing the figures of Greek deities, like those of Vénus and Apóllo, and Greek mythological scenes, as shown in the wall paintings at Pompéii. Róman sculpture is seen to good advantage in the statues and busts of the emperors, and in such reliefs as those on the arch of Títus and the column of Trájan.

But it was in architecture that the Rómans excelled; and by their splendid works they have taken rank among the world's greatest builders. We have already seen the progress made during the later Republic and under Augústus. With Trájan, Rome became a city of magnificent public buildings. The architectural center of the city was the Róman Fórum, with the additional Fórums of Július, Augústus, Vespásian, Nérva, and Trájan. Surrounding these were the temples, the basílicas or halls of justice, porticoes, and other public buildings. The most conspicuous buildings which would attract the eyes of one standing in the Fórum were the splendid temples of Júpiter and Júno upon the Cápitoline hill. While it is true that the Rómans obtained their chief ideas of architectural beauty from the Greeks, it is a question whether Áthens, even in the time of Péricles, could have presented such a scene of imposing grandeur as did Rome in the time of Trájan and Hádrian, with its forums, temples, aqueducts, basílicas, palaces, porticoes, amphitheaters, theaters, circuses, baths, columns, triumphal arches, and tombs.

Left to Right: Temple of Cástor and Póllux, Temple of Vésta, Temples of Sáturn and Vespásian

III. THE REIGN OF HÁDRIAN (A.D. 117-138)

The Statesmanship of Hádrian.—At the death of Trájan, his adopted son Hádrian was proclaimed by the prætórian guards. But Hádrian did not regard this as a constitutional act; and he requested to be formally elected by the senate. In some respects he was similar to Trájan, with the same generous spirit and desire for the welfare of the people, and with the same wish to add to the architectural splendor of Rome. He was, like Trájan, a friend of literature and a patron of the fine arts, But he differed from Trájan in not thinking that the greatness of Rome depended upon military glory. He believed that the army should be maintained; but that foreign conquest was less important than the prosperity of his subjects. In his political ideas and administrative ability he was a type of the true statesman. He is said to have been a man of wider acquirements and greater general capacity than any previous ruler since Július Cæsar. He was in the best sense liberal and cosmopolitan. He was tolerant of the Chrístians, and put himself in sympathy with the various races and creeds which made up the empire. Against the Jews only, who rose in revolt during his reign, did he show a spirit of unreasonable severity.

Bust of the Emperor Hádrian, Glyptothek, Munich

His Abandonment of Trájan's Conquests.—Hádrian did not believe that the mission of Rome was to conquer the world, but to civilize her own subjects. He therefore voluntarily gave up the extensive conquests of Trájan in the East, the provinces of Arménia, Mesopotámia, and Assýria. He declared that the Eastern policy of Trájan was a great mistake. He openly professed to cling to the policy of Augústus, which was to improve the empire rather than to enlarge it.

The Imperial Council.—Another evidence of the statesmanship of Hádrian is seen in the fact that he was willing to take advice. While he is said to have shown on some occasions an exceptional irritability of temper, he is represented as a man distinguished on the whole by an a ability rarely equaled by the Róman princes. He paid great deference to the senate; and the body of imperial counselors (*consílium príncipis*), which had been occasionally consulted by the previous emperors, became from his time a permanent institution. The emperor was not now the victim of unworthy advisers, as in the time of Tibérius, but was surrounded by men noted for their learning and wisdom. These men were often trained lawyers, who were skilled in the rules of justice.

The Perpetual Edict of Sálvius Juliánus.—Perhaps the most important event in the reign of Hádrian was his compilation of the best part of the Róman law. Since the XII. Tables there had been no collection of legal rules. That ancient code was framed upon the customs of a primitive people. It did not represent the actual law by which justice was now administered. A new and better law had grown up in the courts of the prǽtors and of the provincial governors. It had been expressed in the edicts of these magistrates; but it had now become voluminous and scattered. Hádrian delegated to one of his jurists, Sálvius Juliánus, the task of collecting this law into a concise form, so that it could be used for the better administration of justice throughout the empire. This collection was called the Perpetual Edict (*Edíctum Perpétuum*).

The Pántheon of Agríppa as Redesigned by Hádrian (Left: Exterior Portico, Right: Interior of Dome)

145

The Visitation of the Provinces.—Hádrian showed a stronger sympathy with the provinces than any of his predecessors, and under his reign the provincials attained a high degree of prosperity and happiness. He conducted himself as a true sovereign and friend of his people. To become acquainted with their condition and to remedy their evils, he spent a large part of his time in visiting the provinces. Of his long reign of twenty-one years, he spent more than two thirds outside of Ítaly. He made his temporary residence in the chief cities of the empire, in York, in Áthens, in Ántioch, and in Alexándria, where he was continually looking after the interests of his subjects. In the provinces, as at Rome, he constructed many magnificent public works; and won for himself a renown equal, if not superior, to that of Trájan as a great builder. Rome was decorated with the temple of Vénus and Róma, and the splendid mausoleum which today bears the name of the Castle of St. Ángelo. Hádrian also built strong fortifications to protect the frontiers, one of these connecting the head waters of the Rhine and the Dánube, and another built on the northern boundary of Brítain.

Hádrian's Wall Near Housesteads
in Northern Brítain

Mausoléum of Hádrian (Castle of St. Ángelo)

Life in the Provinces: Travel, Correspondence, Commerce.— The general organization of the provinces remained with few changes. There were still the two classes, the senatorial, governed by the procónsuls and proprǽtors, and the imperial, governed by the *legáti*, or the emperor's lieutenants. The improvement which took place under the empire in the condition of the provinces was due to the longer term of office given the governors, the more economic management of the finances, and the abolition of the system of farming the revenues.

The good influence of such emperors as Hádrian is seen in the new spirit which inspired the life of the provincials. The people were no longer the prey of the taxgatherer, as in the times of the later republic. They could therefore use their wealth to improve and beautify their own cities. The growing public spirit is seen in the new buildings and works, everywhere erected, not only by the city governments, but by the generous contributions of private citizens. The relations between the people of different provinces were also becoming closer by the improvement of the means of communication. The roads were now extended throughout the empire, and were used not merely for the transportation of armies, but for travel and correspondence. The people thus became better acquainted with one another. Many of the highways were used as post-roads, over which letters might be sent by means of private runners or government couriers.

The different provinces of the empire were also brought into closer communication by means of the increasing commerce, which furnished one of the most honored pursuits of the Róman citizen. The provinces encircled the Méditerránean Sea, which was now the greatest highway of the empire. The sea was traversed by merchant ships exchanging the products of various lands. The provinces of the empire were thus joined together in one great commercial community.

IV. THE REIGN OF ANTONÍNUS PÍUS (A.D. 138-161)

The Virtues of Antonínus.—If we desired to find in Róman history a more noble character than that of Hádrian, we should perhaps find it in his adopted son and successor, Antonínus, surnamed Píus. The description given of him by his son, Márcus Aurélius, is worthy to be read by the young people of all times. "In my father," he says, "I saw mildness of manners, firmness of resolution, contempt of vain glory. He knew when to rest as well as to labor. He taught me to forbear from all improper indulgences, to conduct myself as an equal among equals, to lay on my friends no burden of servility. From him I learned to be resigned to every fortune and to bear myself calmly and serenely; to rise superior to vulgar applause, and to despise vulgar criticism; to worship divinity without superstition and to serve mankind without ambition. He was ever prudent and moderate; he looked to his duty only, and not to the opinions that might be formed of him. Such was the character of his life and manners: nothing harsh, nothing excessive, nothing rude, nothing which showed roughness and violence."

The "Reign without Events."—The reign of Antonínus, although a long one of twenty-three years, is known in history as the uneventful reign. Since much that is usually called "eventful" in history is made up of wars, tumults, calamities, and discords, it is to the greatest credit of Antonínus that his reign is called uneventful. We read of no conquests, no insurrections, no proscriptions, no extortions, no cruelty. His reign is an illustration of the maxim, "Happy is the people which has no history." Although not so great a statesman as Hádrian, he yet maintained the empire in a state of peace and prosperity. He managed the finances with skill and economy. He was kind to his subjects; and interfered to prevent the persecution of the Christians at Áthens and Thessalonica.

Bust of Antonínus Píus, Glyptothek Museum, Munich

His Influence upon Law and Legislation.—If we should seek for the most distinguishing feature of his reign, we should doubtless find it in the field of law. His high sense of justice brought him into close relation with the great jurists of the age, who were now beginning to make their influence felt. With them he believed that the spirit of the law was more important than the letter. One of his maxims was this: "While the forms of the law must not be lightly altered, they must be interpreted so as to meet the demands of justice." He laid down the important principle that everyone should be regarded as innocent until proved guilty. He mitigated the evils of slavery, and declared that a man had no more right to kill his own slave than the slave of another. It was about the close of his reign that the great elementary treatise on the Róman law, called the "Institutes" of Gáius, appeared.

Róman Jurisprudence.—Some one has said that the greatest bequests of antiquity to the modern world were Christiánity, Greek philosophy, and the Róman law. We should study the history of Rome to little purpose if we failed to take account of this, the highest product of her civilization. It is not to her amphitheaters, her circuses, her triumphal arches, or to her sacred temples that we must look in order to see the most distinctive and enduring features of Róman life. We must look rather to her basílicas, that is, her courthouses where the principles of justice were administered to her citizens and her subjects in the forms of law.

The Government and Administration.—It was during the period of the Ántonines that the imperial government reached its highest development. This government was, in fact, the most remarkable example that the world has ever seen of what we may call a "paternal autocracy," that is government in the hands of a single ruler, but exercised solely for the benefit of the people. In this respect the ideals of Július and Augústus seem to have been completely realized. The emperor was looked upon as the embodiment of the state, the personification of law, and the promoter of justice, equality, and domestic peace. Every department of the administration was under his control. He had the selection of the officials to carry into execution his will. The character of such a government the Rómans well expressed in their maxim, "What is pleasing to the prince has the force of law."

V. THE REIGN OF MÁRCUS AURÉLIUS (A.D. 161-180)

Denárius of Márcus Aurélius

Philosopher on the Throne.—Márcus Aurélius was the adopted son of Antonínus Píus, and came to the throne at his father's death. The new emperor was first of all a philosopher. He had studied in the school of the Stóics, and was himself the highest embodiment of their principles. He was wise, brave, just, and temperate. The history of the pagan world presents no higher example of uprightness and manhood. In whatever he did he acted from a pure sense of duty. But his character as a man was no doubt greater than his ability as a statesman. So far as we know, Márcus Aurélius never shrank from a known duty, private or public; but it is not so clear that his sense of personal duty was always in harmony with the best interests of the empire.

Misfortunes of his Reign.—In judging of this great man we must not forget that his reign was a time of great misfortunes. Rome was afflicted by a deadly plague and famine, the most terrible in her history. From the East it spread over the provinces, carrying with it death and desolation. One writer affirms, with perhaps some exaggeration, that half the population of the empire perished. The fierce barbarians of the north were also trying to break through the frontiers, and threatening to overrun the provinces. But Márcus Aurélius met all these dangers and difficulties with courage and patience.

His Persecution of the Chrístians.—The most striking example of the fact that the emperor's sense of duty was not always in harmony with the highest welfare of the people is shown in his persecution of the Chrístians. The new religion had found its way throughout the eastern and western provinces. It was at first received by the common people in the cities. As it was despised by many, it was the occasion of bitter opposition and often of popular tumults. The secret meetings of the Chrístians had given rise to scandalous stories about their practices. They were also regarded as responsible in some way for the calamities inflicted by the gods upon the people. Since the time of Néro, the policy of the rulers toward the new sect had varied. But the

best of the emperors had hitherto been cautious like Trájan, or tolerant like Hádrian, or openly friendly like Antonínus. But Márcus Aurélius sincerely believed that the Christians were the cause of the popular tumults, and that the new sect was dangerous to the public peace. He therefore issued an order that those who denied their faith should be let alone, but those who confessed should be put to death. The most charitable judgment which can be passed upon this act is that it was the result of a great mistake made by the emperor regarding the character of the Christians and their part in disturbing the peace of society.

Bas-Relief of Márcus Aurélius Sacrificing

Encroachments upon the Frontiers.—During this reign the peace of the empire was first seriously threatened by invasions from without. The two great frontier enemies of Rome were the Párthians on the east and the Gérmans on the north. The Párthians were soon repelled. But the barbarians from the north, the Marcománni and Quádi, continued their attacks for fourteen years. Pressed by the Slavónians and the Turánians on the north and east, these tribes were the forerunners of that great migration of the northern nations which finally overran the empire. With courage and a high sense of his mission the emperor struggled against these hordes, and succeeded for the most part in maintaining the northern frontier. He died in his camp at Viénna, at his post of duty. However much we may condemn his policy with reference to the Christians, we must always admire him for the purity of his life and his nobility as a man.

Equestrian Statue of Márcus Aurélius, Musei Capitolini

Róman Philosophy.—Márcus Aurélius expressed in his life and writings the highest ideas of Róman philosophy. The Rómans cannot, however, be said to have shown any originality in their philosophical systems. These they derived almost entirely from the Greeks. The two systems which were most popular with them were Epicuréanism and Stóicism. The Epicuréans believed that happiness was the great end of life. But the high idea of happiness advocated by the Greek philosophers became degraded into the selfish idea of pleasure, which could easily excuse almost any form of indulgence. In Rome we see this idea of life exercising its influence especially upon the wealthy and indolent classes. The Stóics, on the other hand, believed that the end of life was to live according to the highest law of our nature. This doctrine tended to make strong and upright characters. It could not well have a degrading influence; so we find some of the noblest men of Rome adhering to its tenets, such men as Cáto, Cícero, Séneca, and Márcus Aurélius. The Stóic philosophy also exercised a great and beneficial influence upon the Róman jurists, who believed that the law of the state should be in harmony with the higher law of justice and equity.

CHAPTER XXVII

THE DECLINE OF THE EMPIRE

The Times of the Sevéri, I.—The Disintegration of the Empire, II.—The Illýrian Emperors, III.

I. THE TIMES OF THE SEVÉRI

Review of the Early Empire.—As we review the condition of the Róman world since the time of Augústus, we can see that the fall of the republic and the establishment of the empire were not an evil, but a great benefit to Rome. In place of a century of civil wars and discord which closed the republic, we see more than two centuries of internal peace and tranquility. Instead of an oppressive and avaricious treatment of the provincials, we see a treatment which is with few exceptions mild and generous. Instead of a government controlled by a proud and selfish oligarchy, we see a government controlled, generally speaking, by a wise and patriotic prince. From the accession of Augústus to the death of Márcus Aurélius (31 B.C. - A.D. 180), a period of two hundred and eleven years, only three emperors who held power for any length of time, Tibérius, Néro, and Domítian, are known as tyrants; and their cruelty was confined almost entirely to the city, and to their own personal enemies. The establishment of the empire, we must therefore believe, marked a stage of progress and not of decline in the history of the Róman people.

Symptoms of Decay.—But in spite of the fact that the empire met the needs of the people better than the old aristocratic republic, it yet contained many elements of weakness, The Róman people themselves possessed the frailties of human nature, and the imperial government was not without the imperfection of all human institutions. The decay of religion and morality among the people was a fundamental cause of their weakness and ruin. If we were asked what were the symptoms of this moral decay, we should answer: the selfishness of classes; the accumulation of wealth, not as the fruit of legitimate industry, but as the spoils of war and of cupidity; the love of gold and the passion for luxury; the misery of poverty and its attendant vices and crimes; the terrible evils of slave labor; the decrease of the population; and the decline of the patriotic spirit. These were moral diseases, which could hardly be cured by any government.

Military Despotism.—The great defect of the imperial government was the fact that its power rested upon a military basis, and not upon the rational will of the people. It is true that many of the emperors were popular and loved by their subjects. But behind their power was the army, which knew its strength, and which now more than ever before asserted its claims to the government. This period, extending from the death of Márcus Aurélius to the accession of Dioclétian (A.D. 180-284), has therefore been aptly called "the period of military despotism." It was a time when the emperors were set up by the soldiers, and generally cut down by their swords. During this period of one hundred and four years, the imperial title was held by twenty-nine different rulers, some few of whom were able and high-minded men, but a large number of them were weak and despicable. Some of them held their places for only a few months. The history of this time contains for the most part only the dreary records of a declining government. There are few events of importance, except those which illustrate the tyranny of the army and the general tendency toward decay and disintegration.

After the reign of Cómmodus, the unworthy son of Márcus, the soldiers became the real sovereigns of Rome. His successor Pértinax was dispatched by their swords; and the empire was offered to the one who would give them the largest donation. This proved to be a rich senator by the name of Dídius Juliánus. He held this place for about two months. In the meantime three different armies, in Brítain, in Pannónia, and in Sýria, each proclaimed its own leader as emperor.

Septímius Sevérus (A.D. 193-211).—The commander of the army in the neighboring province of Pannónia was the first to reach Rome; and was thus able to secure the throne against his rivals. The reign of Septímius is noted for the reforming of the prætórian guard, which Augústus had organized and Tibérius had encamped near the city. In place of the old body of nine thousand soldiers, Septímius organized a Róman garrison of forty thousand troops selected from the best soldiers of the légions. This was intended to give a stronger military support to the government; but in fact it gave to the army a more powerful influence in appointment of the emperors. Septímius destroyed his enemies in the senate, and took away from that body the last vestige of its authority. He was himself an able soldier and made several successful campaigns in the East.

Edict of Caracálla (A.D. 212).—The Róman franchise, which had been gradually extended by the previous emperors, was now conferred upon all the free inhabitants of the Róman world. This important act was done by Caracálla, the worthless son and tyrannical successor of Septímius Sevérus. The edict was issued to increase the revenue by extending the inheritance tax, which had heretofore rested only upon citizens. Notwithstanding the avaricious motive of the emperor this was in the line of earlier reforms and effaced the last distinction between Rómans and provincials. The name of Caracálla is infamous, not only for his cruel proscriptions, but especially for his murder of Papínian, the greatest of the Róman jurists, who refused to defend his crimes.

The Sevéran Tóndo: Emperor Septímius Sevérus with the Empress, Júlia Dómna, and their son, Caracálla. (The image of Géta, his brother, was defaced after his murder by Caracálla.)

Alexánder Sevérus (A.D. 222-235).—After the brief reign of Macrínus, and the longer reign of the monster Elagábalus, the most repulsive of all the emperors, the throne was occupied by a really excellent man, Alexánder Sevérus. In a corrupt age, he was a prince of pure and blameless life. He loved the true and the good of all times. It is said that he set up in his private chapel the images of those whom he regarded as the greatest teachers of mankind, including Ábraham and Jésus Christ. He tried as best he could to follow the example of the best of the emperors. He selected as his advisers the great jurists, Úlpian and Páullus. The most important event of his reign was his successful resistance to the Pérsians, who had just established a new monarchy on the ruins of the Párthian kingdom (A.D. 226).

II. THE DISINTEGRATION OF THE EMPIRE

Foreign Enemies of Rome.—Never before had the Róman Empire been beset by such an array of foreign enemies as it encountered during the third century. On the east was the new Pérsian monarchy established under a vigorous and ambitious line of kings, called the Sassánidæ. The founder of this line, Artáxares (Ardáshir), laid claim to all the Asiátic provinces of Rome as properly belonging to Pérsia. The refusal of this demand gave rise to the war with Alexánder Sevérus, just referred to, and to severe struggles with his successors.

But the most formidable enemies of Rome were the Gérman barbarians on the frontiers of the Rhine and the Dánube. On the lower Rhine near the North Sea were several tribes known as the Chátti, Cháuci, and the Cherúsci, who came to be united with other tribes under the common name of "Franks." On the upper Rhine in the vicinity of the Alps were various tribes gathered together under the name of Alemánni ("all men"). Across the Dánube and on the northern shores of the Black Sea was the great nation of the Goths, which came to be the terror of Rome. Under a succession of emperors whose names have little significance to us, the Rómans engaged in wars with these various peoples, not now wars for the sake of conquest and glory as in the time of the republic, but wars of defense and for the sake of existence.

Invasion of the Goths in the East.—The Goths made their first appearance upon the Róman territory in the middle of the third century (A.D. 250). At this time they invaded Dácia, crossed the Dánube, and overran the province of Mœsia. In a great battle in Mœsia perished the brave emperor Décius, descendant of the Décius Mus who devoted his life at Mt. Vesúvius in the heroic days of the republic. His successor, Gállus, purchased a peace of the Goths by the payment of an annual tribute. It was not many years after this that the same barbarians, during the reigns of Valérian and Galliénus (A.D. 253-268), made a more formidable invasion, this time by way of the Black Sea and the Bósphorus. With the aid of their ships they crossed the sea, besieged and plundered the cities of Ásia Minor. They destroyed the splendid temple of Diána at Éphesus; they crossed the Ægéan Sea into Greece, and threatened Ítaly; and finally retired with their spoils to their homes across the Dánube.

Invasion of the Franks and Alemánni in the West.—In the meantime the western provinces were invaded by the barbarians who lived across the Rhine. The Franks entered the western regions of Gaul, crossed the Pýrenees, and sacked the cities of Spain; while the Alemánni entered eastern Gaul and invaded Ítaly as far as the walls of Ravénna. It was then that the Róman garrison, which took the place of the old prætórian guard, rendered a real service to Rome by preventing the destruction of the city.

Attacks of the Pérsians in Ásia.—But all the disasters of Rome did not come from the north. The new Pérsian monarchy, under its second great king, Sápor, was attempting to carry out the policy of Artáxares and expel the Rómans from their Asiátic provinces. Sápor at first brought under his control Arménia, which had remained an independent kingdom since the time of Hádrian. He then overran the Róman provinces of Sýria, Cilícia, and Cappadócia; Ántioch and other cities of the coast were destroyed and pillaged; and the emperor Valérian was made a prisoner. The story of Sápor's pride and of Valérian's disgrace has passed into history; to humiliate his captive, it is said, whenever the Pérsian monarch mounted his horse, he placed his foot on the neck of the Róman emperor.

The Time of the "Thirty Tyrants."—In the midst of these external perils Rome beheld another danger which she had never seen before, at least to the same extent, and that was the appearance of usurpers in every part of the empire: in Ásia, in Égypt, in Greece, in Illýricum, and in Gaul. This is called the time of the "thirty tyrants"; although Gíbbon counts only nineteen of these so-called tyrants during the reign of Galliénus. If we should imagine another calamity in addition to those already mentioned, it would be famine and pestilence, and from these, too, Rome now suffered. From the reign of Décius to the reign of Galliénus, a period of about fifteen years, the empire was the victim of a furious plague, which is said to have raged in every province, in every city, and almost in every family. With invasions from without and revolts and pestilence within, Rome never before seemed so near to destruction.

III. THE ILLÝRIAN EMPERORS

Partial Recovery of the Empire.—For a period of eighty-eight years, from the death of Márcus Aurélius (A.D. 180) to the death of Galliénus (A.D. 268), the imperial government had gradually been growing weaker until it now seemed that the empire was going to pieces for the want of a leader. But we have before seen Rome on the verge of ruin in the early days of the Gauls, during the invasion of Hánnibal, and under the attacks of the Címbri. As in those more ancient times, so now the Rómans showed their remarkable fortitude and courage in the presence of danger. Under the leadership of five able rulers, Cláudius II., Aurélian, Tácitus, Próbus, and Cárus, they again recovered; and they maintained their existence for more than two hundred years in the West and for more than a thousand years in the East. Let us see how Rome recovered from her present disasters, and we may also understand how the early empire as established by Augústus was changed into the new empire established by Dioclétian and Cónstantine.

Cláudius II. and the Defeat of the Goths (A.D. 268-270).—One of the reasons of the recent revolts in the provinces had been general distrust of the central authority at Rome. If the Róman emperor could not protect the provinces, the provinces were determined to protect themselves under their own rulers. When a man should appear able to defend the frontiers the cause of these revolts would disappear. Such a man was Cláudius II., who came from Illýricum. He aroused the patriotism of his army and restored its discipline. Paying little attention to the independent governors, he pushed his army into Greece to meet the Goths, who had again crossed the Dánube and had advanced into Macedónia. By a series of victories he succeeded in delivering the empire from these barbarians, and for this reason he received the name of Cláudius Góthicus.

Coin Depicting Cláudius II. "Góthicus"

Aurélian and the Restored Empire (A.D. 270-275).—The fruits of the victories of Cláudius were reaped by his successor Aurélian, who became the real restorer of the empire. He first provided against a sudden descent upon the city by rebuilding the walls of Rome, which remain to this day and are known as the walls of Aurélian. He then followed the prudent policy of Augústus by withdrawing the Róman army from Dácia and making the Dánube the frontier of the empire. He then turned his attention to the rebellious provinces; and recovered Gaul, Spain, and Brítain from the hand of the usurper Tétricus. He finally restored the Róman authority in the East; and destroyed the city of Palmýra, which had been made the seat of an independent kingdom, where ruled the famous Queen Zenóbia.

The Emperor Aurélian (obverse)
"Concórdia Mílitum" – "Harmony of the Soldiers" (reverse)

The "Silent Invasions."—The successors of Aurélian, Tácitus, Próbus, and Cárus, preserved what he himself had achieved. The integrity of the empire was in general maintained against the enemies from without and the "tyrants" from within. It is worthy of notice that at this time a conciliatory policy toward the barbarians was adopted, by granting to them peaceful settlements in the frontier provinces. This step began what are known as the "silent invasions." Not only the Róman territory, but the army and the offices of the state, military and civil, were gradually opened to the Gérmans who were willing to become Róman subjects.

The New Class of "Colóni."—It became a serious question what to do with all the newcomers who were now admitted into the provinces. The most able of the barbarian chiefs were sometimes made Róman generals. Many persons were admitted to the ranks of the army. Sometimes whole tribes were allowed to settle upon lands assigned to them. But a great many persons, especially those who had been captured in war, were treated in a somewhat novel manner. Instead of being sold as slaves they were given over to the large landed proprietors, and attached to the estates as permanent tenants. They could not be sold off from these estates like slaves; but if the land was sold they were sold with it. This class of persons came to be called colóni. They were really serfs bound to the soil. The *colónus* had a little plot of ground which he could cultivate for himself, and for which he paid a rent to his landlord. But the class of colóni came to be made up not only of barbarian captives, but of manumitted slaves, and even of Róman freemen, who were not able to support themselves and who gave themselves up to become the serfs of some landlord. The *colóni* thus came to form a large part of the population in the provinces. This new class of persons, which held such a peculiar position in the Róman empire, has a special interest to the general historical student; because from them were descended, in great part, the class of serfs which formed a large element of Európéan society after the fall of Rome, during the middle ages.

Transition to the Later Empire.—The successful efforts of the last five rulers showed that the Róman Empire could still be preserved if properly organized and governed. In the hands of weak and vicious men, like Cómmodus and Elagábalus, the people were practically left without a government, and were exposed to the attacks of foreign enemies and to all the dangers of anarchy. But when ruled by such men as Cláudius II. and Aurélian they were still able to resist foreign invasions and to repress internal revolts. The events of the third century made it clear that if the empire was to continue and the provinces were to be held together there must be some change in the imperial government. The decline of the early empire thus paved the way for a new form of imperialism.

CHAPTER XXVIII

THE REORGANIZATION OF THE EMPIRE

The Reign of Dioclétian (A.D. 284-305), I.—The Reign of Cónstantine (A.D. 313-337), II.
The Successors of Cónstantine (337-395), III.

I. THE REIGN OF DIOCLÉTIAN (A.D. 284-305)

The New Imperialism.—The accession of Dioclétian brings us to a new era in the history of the Róman Empire. It has been said that the early empire of Augústus and his successors was an absolute monarchy *disguised* by republican forms. This is in general quite true. But the old republican forms had for a long time been losing their hold, and at the time of Dioclétian they were ready to be thrown away entirely. By the reforms of Dioclétian and Cónstantine there was established a new form of imperialism, an absolute monarchy *divested* of republican forms. Some of their ideas of reform no doubt came from the new Pérsian monarchy, which was now the greatest rival of Rome. In this powerful monarchy the Rómans saw certain elements of strength which they could use in giving new vigor to their own government. By adopting these Oriéntal ideas, the Róman Empire may be said to have become Oriéntalized.

The Policy of Diocletian.—Diocletian was in many respects a remarkable man. Born of an obscure family in Dalmátia (part of Illýricum), he had risen by his own efforts to the high position of commander of the Róman army in the East. It was here that he was proclaimed emperor by his soldiers. He overcame all opposition, assumed the imperial power, and made his residence not at Rome, but in Nicomédia, a town in Ásia Minor. His whole policy was to give dignity and strength to the imperial authority. He made of himself an Oriéntal monarch. He assumed the diadem of the East. He wore the gorgeous robes of silk and gold such a were worn by eastern rulers. He compelled his subjects to salute him with low prostrations, and to treat him not as a citizen, but as a superior being. In this way he hoped to make the imperial office respected by the people and the army. The emperor was to be the sole source of power, and as such was to be venerated and obeyed.

The "Augústi" and "Cǽsars."—Diocletian saw that it was difficult for one man alone to manage all the affairs of a great empire. It was sufficient for one man to rule over the East, and to repel the Pérsians. It needed another to take care of the West and to drive back the Gérman invaders. He therefore associated with him his trusted friend and companion in arms, Maxímian. But he was soon convinced that even this division of power was not sufficient. To each of the chief rulers, who received the title of *Augústus*, he assigned an assistant, who received the title of *Cǽsar*. The two Cǽsars were Galérius and Constántius; and they were to be regarded as the sons and successors of the chief rulers, the Augústi. Each Cǽsar was to recognize the authority of his chief; and all were to be subject to the supreme authority of Diocletian himself. The Róman world was divided among the four rulers.

Býzantine Sculpture Reputed to be the Tétrarchs, Venice

155

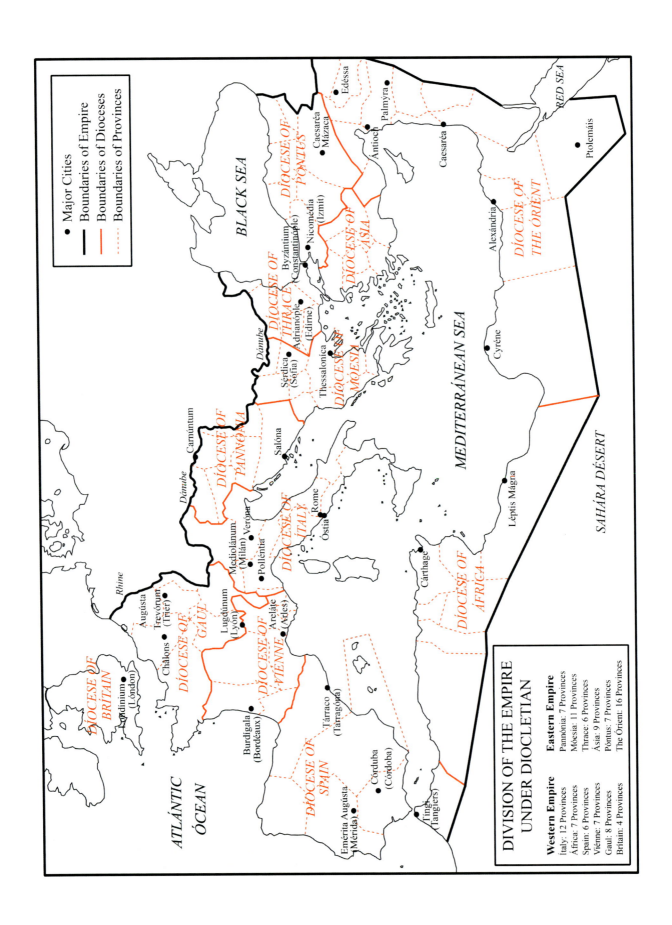

DIVISION OF THE EMPIRE
UNDER DIOCLETIAN

Western Empire

Italy: 12 Provinces
África: 7 Provinces
Spain: 6 Provinces
Viénne: 7 Provinces
Gaul: 8 Provinces
Britain: 4 Provinces

Eastern Empire

Pannónia: 7 Provinces
Móesia: 11 Provinces
Thrace: 6 Provinces
Ásia: 9 Provinces
Póntus: 7 Provinces
The Órient: 16 Provinces

Legend:
• Major Cities
Boundaries of Empire
Boundaries of Dioceses
Boundaries of Provinces

ATLÁNTIC ÓCEAN

BLACK SEA

MEDITERRÁNEAN SEA

RED SEA

SAHÁRA DÉSERT

DIOCESE OF BRÍTAIN
DIOCESE OF GAUL
DIOCESE OF VIÉNNE
DIOCESE OF SPAIN
DIOCESE OF PANNÓNIA
DIOCESE OF ITALY
DIOCESE OF AFRICA
DIOCESE OF THRACE
DIOCESE OF MOESIA
DIOCESE OF PONTUS
DIOCESE OF ASIA
DIOCESE OF THE ÓRIENT

Londinium (London)
Augústa Trevórum (Trier)
Chalons
Lugdúnum (Lyón)
Arelàte (Arles)
Burdígala (Bordéaux)
Tárraco (Tarragóna)
Córduba (Córdoba)
Emérita Augusta (Mérida)
Tíngis (Tangiers)
Mediolánum (Milán)
Veróna
Pollëntia
Rome
Óstia
Salóna
Carnúntum
Sérdica (Sófia)
Thessalónica
Adrianóple (Edírne)
Byzántium (Constantinóple)
Nicomédia (Izmit)
Caesaréa Mázaca
Edéssa
Palmýra
Antioch
Caesaréa
Ptolemáis
Alexándria
Cyréne
Cárthage
Léptis Mágna

Rhine
Dánube
Dánube

156

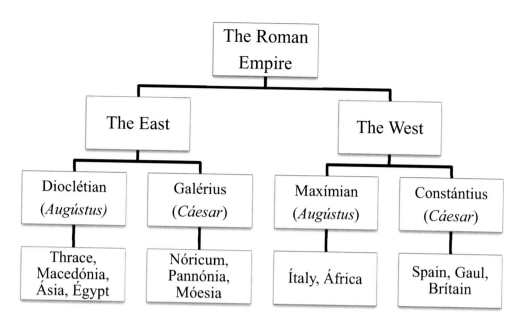

The Last Persecution of the Chrístians.—Dioclétian himself was not a cruel and vindictive man, and was at first favorably disposed toward the Chrístians. But in the latter part of his reign he was induced to issue an edict of persecution against them. It is said that he was led to perform this infamous act by his assistant Galérius, who had always been hostile to the new religion, and who filled the emperor's mind with stories of seditions and conspiracies. An order was issued that all churches should be demolished, that the sacred Scriptures should be burned, that all Chrístians should be dismissed from public office, and that those who secretly met for public worship should be punished with death. The persecution raged most fiercely in the provinces subject to Galérius; and it has been suggested that the persecution should be known by his name rather than by the name of Dioclétian.

Effects or Dioclétian's Policy.—The general result of the new policy of Dioclétian was to give to the empire a strong and efficient government. The dangers which threatened the state were met with firmness and vigor. A revolt in Égypt was quelled, and the frontiers were successfully defended against the Pérsians and the barbarians. Public works were constructed, among which were the great Baths of Dioclétian at Rome. At the close of his reign he celebrated a triumph in the old capital.

Abdication of Dioclétian.—After a successful reign of twenty-one years Dioclétian voluntarily gave up his power, either on account of ill health, or else to see how his new system would work without his own supervision. He retired to his native province of Dalmátia, and spent the rest of his days in his new palace at Salóna on the shores of the Adriátic. He loved his country home; and when he was asked by his old colleague Maxímian to resume the imperial power, he wrote to him, "Were you to come to Salóna and see the vegetables which I raise in my garden with my own hands, you would not talk to me of empire." But before he died (A.D. 313) Dioclétian saw the defects of the system which he had established. Rivalries sprang up among the different rulers, which led to civil war. At one time there were six emperors who were trying to adjust between themselves the government of the empire. Out of this conflict Cónstantine arose as the man destined to carry on and complete the work of Dioclétian.

II. THE REIGN OF CÓNSTANTINE (A.D. 313-337)

Accession and Policy of Cónstantine.—By a succession of victories over his different rivals, which it is not necessary for us to recount, Cónstantine became the sole ruler, and the whole empire was reunited under his authority. He was a man of wider views than Dioclétian, and had even a greater genius for organization. The work which Dioclétian began, Cónstantine completed. He in fact gave to Róman imperialism the final form which it preserved as long as the empire existed, and the form in which it exercised its great influence upon modern governments. We should remember that it was not so much the early imperialism of Augústus as the later imperialism of Cónstantine which reappeared in the empires of modern Éurope. This fact will enable us to understand the greatness of Cónstantine as a statesman and a political reformer. His policy was to centralize all power in the hands of the chief ruler; to surround his person with an elaborate court system and an imposing ceremonial; and to make all officers, civil and military, responsible to the supreme head of the empire.

Conversion of Cónstantine.—Cónstantine is generally known as the "first Christian emperor." The story of his miraculous conversion is told by his biographer, Eusébius. It is said that while marching against his rival Maxéntius, he beheld in the heavens the luminous sign of the cross, inscribed with the words, "By this sign conquer." As a result of this vision, he accepted

the Christian religion; he adopted the cross as his battle standard; and from this time he ascribed his victories to God, and not to himself. The truth of this story has been doubted by some historians; but that Constántine looked upon Christiánity in an entirely different light from his predecessors, and that he was an avowed friend of the Christian church, cannot be denied. His mother, Hélena, was a Christian, and his father, Constántius, had opposed the persecutions of Dioclétian and Galérius. He had himself, while he was ruler in only the West, issued an edict of toleration (A.D. 313) to the Christians in his own provinces.

The Vision of the Cross (1520-1524)
Fresco by Students of Raphaël

Adoption of Christiánity.—The attitude of the Róman government toward Christiánity varied at different times. At first indifferent to the new religion, it became hostile and often bitter during the "period of persecutions" from Néro to Dioclétian. But finally under Cónstantine Christiánity was accepted as the religion of the people and of the state. A large part of the empire was already Christian, and the recognition of the new religion gave stability to the new government. Cónstantine, however, in accepting Christiánity as the state religion, did not go to the extreme of trying to uproot paganism. The pagan worship was still tolerated, and it was not until many years after this time that it was proscribed by the Christian emperors. For the purpose of settling the disputes between the different Christian sects, Cónstantine called (A.D. 325) a large council of the clergy at Nicǽa, which defined what should be regarded as the orthodox belief.

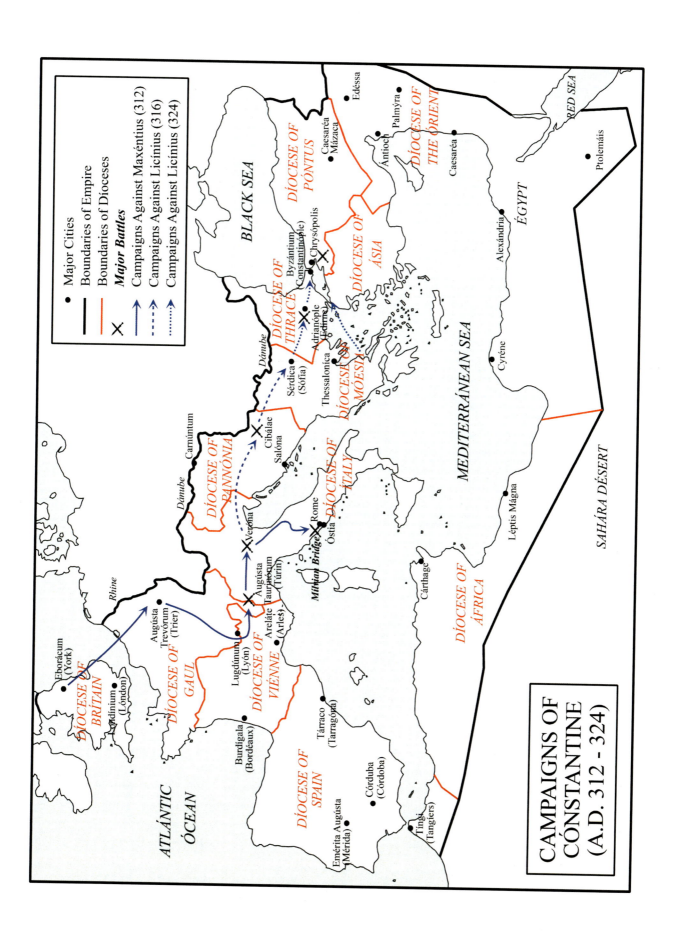

Major Cities
Boundaries of Empire
Boundaries of Dioceses

Major Battles

Campaigns Against Maxéntius (312)
Campaigns Against Licínius (316)
Campaigns Against Licínius (324)

RED SEA

DIOCESE OF THE ORIENT

Edéssa

Palmýra

Caesaréa
Mázaca

Antioch

Caesaréa

Ptolemáis

ÉGYPT

Alexándria

BLACK SEA

DIOCESE OF PÓNTUS

DIOCESE OF ASIA

Byzántium
Constantinóple
Chrysópolis

DIOCESE OF THRACE

Adrianóple
(Edírne)

Sérdica
(Sófia)

Thessalónica

DIOCESE OF MÓESIA

MEDITERRÁNEAN SEA

Cyréne

Dánube

Carnúntum

Cibálae
Salóna

DIOCESE OF PANNÓNIA

DIOCESE OF ITALY

Veróna

Rome

Milvian Bridge
Óstia

Léptis Mágna

SAHÁRA DÉSERT

Dánube

Rhine

Eborácum
(York)

Londínium
(Lóndon)

Augústa
Trevórum
(Trier)

DIOCESE OF BRÍTAIN

DIOCESE OF GAUL

Lugdúnum
(Lyón)

Arelátè
(Arles)

Augústa
Taurínorum
(Turín)

DIOCESE OF VIÉNNE

Burdigala
(Bordéaux)

Tárraco
(Tarragóna)

DIOCESE OF SPAIN

Córduba
(Córdoba)

Emérita Augústa
(Mérida)

Tíngi
(Tangiers)

Cárthage

DIOCESE OF ÁFRICA

*ATLÁNTIC
ÓCEAN*

CAMPAIGNS OF CÓNSTANTINE
(A.D. 312 – 324)

Removal of the Capital to Constantinóple (A.D. 328).—The next important act of Cónstantine was to break away from the traditions of the old empire by establishing a new capital. The old Róman city was filled with the memories of paganism and the relics of the republic. It was the desire of Cónstantine to give the empire a new center of power, which should be favorably situated for working out his new plans, and also for defending the Róman territory. He selected for this purpose the site of the old Greek colony, Byzántium, on the confines of Éurope and Ásia. This site was favorable alike for defense, for commerce, and for the establishment of an Oriéntal system of government. Cónstantine laid out the city on an extensive scale, and adorned it with new buildings and works of art. The new capital was called, after its founder, the city of Cónstantine, or Constantinóple.

Colossal Head of Cónstantine, Musei Capitolini

The New Court Organization.—Cónstantine believed with Dioclétian that one of the defects of the old empire was the fact that the person of the emperor was not sufficiently respected. He therefore not only adopted the diadem and the elaborate robes of the Asiátic monarchs, as Dioclétian had done, but reorganized the court on a thoroughly eastern model. An Oriéntal court consisted of a large retinue of officials, who surrounded the monarch, who paid obeisance to him and served him, and who were raised to the rank of nobles by this service. All the powers of the monarch were exercised through these court officials.

These Oriéntal features were now adopted by the Róman emperor. The chief officers of the court comprised the grand chamberlain, who had charge of the imperial palace; the chancellor, who had the supervision of the court officials and received foreign ambassadors; the quǽstor, who drew up and issued the imperial edicts; the treasurer-general, who had control of the public revenues; the master of the privy purse, who managed the emperor's private estate; and the two commanders of the bodyguard. The imperial court of Cónstantine furnished the model of the royal courts of modern times.

Lábarum (Chi-Rho)
Military Standard of Cónstantine

The New Provincial System.—Another important reform of Cónstantine was the reorganization of the Róman territory in a most systematic manner. This was based upon Dioclétian's division, but was much more complete and thorough. The whole empire was first divided into four great parts, called "préfectures," each under a prætórian prefect subject to the emperor. These great territorial divisions were (1) the Préfecture of the East; (2) the Préfecture of Illýricum; (3) the Préfecture of Ítaly; (4) the Préfecture of Gaul. Each préfecture was then subdivided into díoceses, each under a díocesan governor, called a vícar, subject to the prætórian préfect. Each díocese was further subdivided into provinces, each under a provincial governor called a cónsular, president, duke, or count. Each province was made up of cities and towns, under their own municipal governments. Each city was generally governed by a city council (*cúria*) presided over by two or four magistrates (*duúmviri, quattuórviri*). It had also in the later empire a defender of the people (*defénsor pópuli*), who, like the old republican tríbune, protected the people in their rights. The new divisions of the empire may be indicated as follows:

I
Préfecture of the East
(Five Díoceses)

(1) The East:	15 Provinces
(2) Égypt:	6 Provinces
(3) Ásia:	11 Provinces
(4) Póntus:	11 Provinces
(5) Thrace:	6 Provinces
	49 Provinces

II
Préfecture of Illýricum
(Two Díoceses)

(1) Dácia:	5 Provinces
(2) Macedónia:	6 Provinces
	11 Provinces

III
Préfecture of Ítaly
(Three Díoceses)

(1) Ítaly:	17 Provinces
(2) Illýricum:	7 Provinces
(3) África:	6 Provinces
	30 Provinces

IV
Préfecture of Gaul
(Three Díoceses)

(1) Spain:	7 Provinces
(2) Gaul:	17 Provinces
(3) Brítain:	5 Provinces
	29 Provinces

Total: 13 Díoceses and 119 Provinces

The New Military Organization.—Scarcely less important than the new provincial system was the new military organization. One of the chief defects of the early empire was the improper position which the army occupied in the state. This defect is seen in two ways. In the first place, the army was not subordinate to the civil authority. We have seen how the prætórian guards really became supreme, and brought about that wretched condition of things, a military despotism. In the next place, the military power was not separated from the civil power. In the early empire, every governor of a province had not only civil authority, but he also had command of an army, so that he could resist the central government if he were so disposed. But Cónstantine changed all this. He abolished the Róman garrison or prætórian guard. He gave to the territorial governors only a civil authority; and the whole army was organized under distinct officers, and made completely subject to the central power of the empire. This change tended to prevent, on the one hand, a military despotism; and, on the other hand, the revolt of local governors. The military ability of Cónstantine cannot be questioned. In commemoration of his early victories, the senate erected in the city of Rome a splendid triumphal arch, which stands today as one of the finest specimens of this kind of architecture.

Effect of Cónstantine's Reforms.—If we should take no account of the effects of Constantine's reforms upon the liberties of the Róman people, we might say that his government was a great improvement upon that of Augústus. It gave new strength to the empire, and enabled it to resist foreign invasions. The empire was preserved for several generations longer in the West, and for more than a thousand years longer in the East. But the expenses necessary to maintain such a system, with its elaborate court and its vast number of officials, were great. The taxes were oppressive. The members of every city council (*curiáles*) were held responsible for the raising of the revenues. The people were burdened, and lost their interest in the state. Constántine also, like Augústus, failed to make a proper provision for his successor. At his death (A.D. 337) his three sons divided the empire between them, and this division gave rise to another period of quarrels and civil strife.

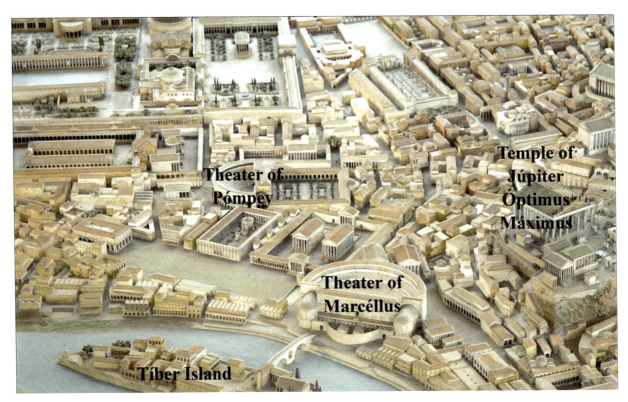

Temple of Júpiter Óptimus Máximus

Theater of Pómpey

Theater of Marcéllus

Tíber Island

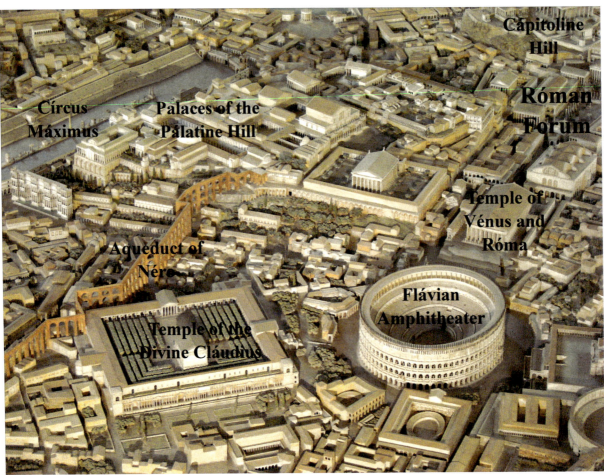

Cápitoline Hill

Róman Forum

Círcus Máximus

Palaces of the Pálatine Hill

Temple of Vénus and Róma

Aquéduct of Néro

Flávian Amphitheater

Temple of the Divine Cláudius

Above and Below: Views of a Model of Rome During the Age of Cónstantine (1930's), Italo Gismondi

162

III. THE SUCCESSORS OF CÓNSTANTINE (337-395)

Attempt to Restore Paganism.—The first event of grave importance after the reign of Cónstantine was the attempt of the Emperor Júlian (A.D. 360-363) to restore the old pagan religion, for which attempt he has been called "the Apóstate." Júlian was in many respects a man of ability and energy. He repelled the Alemánni who had crossed the Rhine, and made a vigorous campaign against the Pérsians. But he was by conviction a pagan, and in the struggle between Christiánity and paganism he took the part of the latter. He tried to undo the work of Cónstantine by bringing back paganism to its old position. He did not realize that Christiánity was the religion of the future, and was presumptuous in his belief that he could accomplish that in which Márcus Aurélius and Dioclétian had failed. He may not have expected to uproot the new religion entirely; but he hoped to deprive it of the important privileges which it had already acquired. The religious changes which he was able to effect in his brief reign were reversed by his successor Jóvian (A.D. 363-364), and Christiánity afterward remained undisturbed as the religion of the empire.

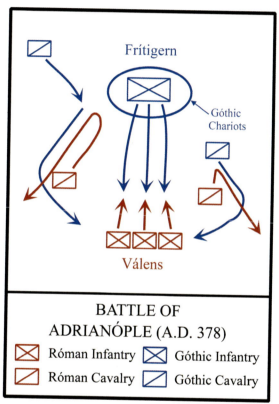

BATTLE OF ADRIANÓPLE (A.D. 378)

⊠ Róman Infantry ⊠ Góthic Infantry
⊠ Róman Cavalry ⊠ Góthic Cavalry

Revolt of the Goths.—After the death of Jóvian the empire was divided between Valentínian and his younger brother Válens, the former ruling in the West, and the latter in the East. Valentínian died (A.D. 375), leaving his sons in control of the West, while Válens continued to rule in the East. It was during this latter period that a great event occurred which forewarned the empire of its final doom. This event was the irruption of the Huns into Éurope. This savage race, emerging from the steppes of Ásia, pressed upon the Goths and drove them from their homes into the Róman territory. It was now necessary for the Rómans either to resist the whole Góthic nation, which numbered a million of people, or else to receive them as friends, and give them settlements within the empire. The latter course seemed the wiser, and they were admitted as allies, and given new homes south of the Dánube, in Mœsia and Thrace. But they were soon provoked by the ill-treatment of the Róman officials, and rose in revolt, defeating the Róman army in a battle at Adrianóple in which Válens himself was slain.

Reign of Theodósius and the Final Division of the Empire (379-395).—Theodósius I. succeeded Válens as emperor of the East. He was a man of great vigor and military ability, although his reign was stained with acts of violence and injustice. He continued the policy of admitting the barbarians into the empire, but converted them into useful and loyal subjects. From their number he reinforced the ranks of the imperial armies, and jealously guarded them from injustice. When a garrison of Góthic soldiers was once mobbed in Thessaloníca, he resorted to a punishment as revengeful as that of Márius and as cruel as that of Súlla. He gathered the people of this city into the circus to the number of seven thousand, and caused them to be massacred by a body of Góthic soldiers (A.D. 390). For this inhuman act he was compelled to do penance by St. Ámbrose, the bishop of Milán, which fact shows how powerful the Church had become at this time, to compel an emperor to obey its mandates. Theodósius was himself an ardent and orthodox Christian, and went so far as to be intolerant of the pagan religion, and even of the

worship of heretics. He was an able monarch, and has received the name of "Theodósius the Great." He conquered his rivals and reunited for a brief time the whole Róman world under a single ruler. But at his death (A.D. 395), he divided the empire between his two sons, Arcádius and Honórius, the former receiving the East, and the latter, the West.

Missórium of Theodósius I. (A.D. 388)
Theodósius Flanked by Valentínian II. and Arcádius,
Royal Academy of History, Madrid

St. Ámbrose Forbids Emperor Theodósius to Enter the Church (1615/1616)
Peter Paul Rubens (1577-1640), Kunsthistorisches Museum, Vienna

CHAPTER XXIX

THE EXTINCTION OF THE WESTERN EMPIRE

The Great Invasions, I.—The Fall of the Western Empire, II.

I. THE GREAT INVASIONS

The Divided Empire.—The death of Theodósius in A.D. 395 marks an important epoch, not only in the history of the later Róman Empire but in the history of Européan civilization. From this time the two parts of the empire—the East and the West—became more and more separated from each other, until they became at last two distinct worlds, having different destinies. The eastern part, the history of which does not belong to our present study, maintained itself for about a thousand years with its capital at Constantinóple, until it was finally conquered by the Turks (A.D. 1453). The western part was soon overrun and conquered by the Gérman invaders, who brought with them new blood and new ideas, and furnished the elements of a new civilization. We have now to see how the Western Empire was obliged finally to succumb to these barbarians, who had been for so many years pressing upon the frontiers, and who had already obtained some foothold in the provinces.

The General Stílicho.—When the youthful Honórius was made emperor in the West, he was placed under the guardianship of Stílicho, an able general who was a barbarian in the service of Rome. As long as Stílicho lived he was able to resist successfully the attacks upon Ítaly. The first of these attacks was due to jealousy and hatred on the part of the Eastern emperor. The Goths of Mœsia were in a state of discontent, and demanded more extensive lands. Under their great leader, Álaric, they entered Macedónia, invaded Greece, and threatened to devastate the whole

Ivory Díptych of Stílicho with his Wife Seréna and Child Euchérius

peninsula. The Eastern emperor, Arcádius, in order to relieve his own territory from their ravages, turned their faces toward Ítaly by giving them settlements in Illýricum, and making their chief, Álaric, master-general of that province. From this region they invaded Ítaly, and ravaged the plains of the Po. But they were defeated by Stílicho in the battle of Polléntia (A.D. 403), and forced to return again into Illýricum. The generalship of Stílicho was also shown in checking an invasion made by a host of Vándals, Burgúndians, Suévi, and Aláni under the lead of Radagaísus (A.D. 406). Ítaly seemed safe as long as Stílicho lived; but he was unfortunately put to death to satisfy the jealousy of his ungrateful master, Honórius (A.D. 408).

165

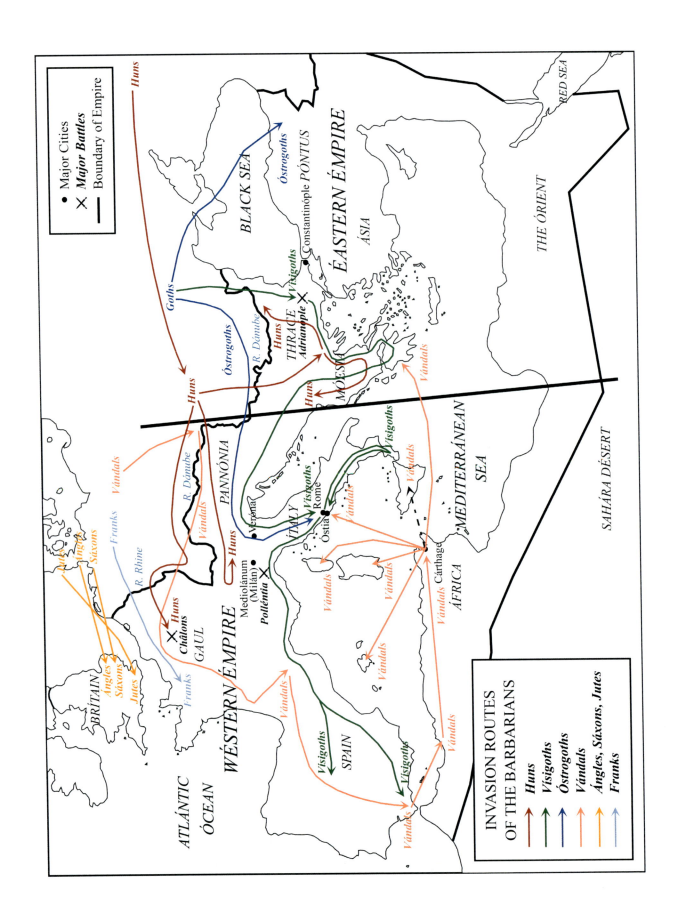

Major Cities
Major Battles
Boundary of Empire

INVASION ROUTES
OF THE BARBARIANS

Huns
Visigoths
Óstrogoths
Vándals
Ángles, Sáxons, Jutes
Franks

RED SEA

BLACK SEA

Óstrogoths

Constantinóple PÓNTUS

ÉASTERN ÉMPIRE

ÁSIA

THE ÓRIENT

Goths

Huns

Óstrogoths

R. Dánube

Visigoths

THRACE
Adriánople

Huns

MÓESIA

Huns

Vándals

SAHÁRA DÉSERT

Huns

R. Dánube

PANNÓNIA

Vándals

Visigoths

MEDITERRÁNEAN
SEA

Jutes
Ángles
Sáxons

Franks
Vándals

R. Rhine

Franks

Huns

Vándals

Mediolánum
(Milán)
Polléntia

Verona

ÍTALY
Visigoths
Rome

Óstia

Visigoths

Vándals

Vándals

Vándals

Huns
Châlons

GAUL

WÉSTERN ÉMPIRE

Cárthage

Vándals

ÁFRICA

BRÍTAIN

Ángles
Sáxons
Jutes

Franks

ATLÁNTIC
ÓCEAN

Vándals

Vándals

Vándals

Vándals

Visigoths
SPAIN

Visigoths

Vándals

Vándals

166

Invasion of Ítaly by the Goths.—With Stílicho dead, Ítaly was practically defenseless. Álaric at the head of the Vísigoths (Western Goths) immediately invaded the peninsula, and marched to Rome. He was induced to spare the city only by the payment of an enormous ransom. But the barbarian chief was not entirely satisfied with the payment of money. He was in search of lands upon which to settle his people. Honórius refused to grant this demand, and after fruitless negotiations with the emperor, Álaric determined to enforce it by the sword. He took the city of Rome and sacked it (A.D. 410). For three days the city was given up to plunder. He then overran southern Ítaly and made himself master of the peninsula. He soon died, and his successor, Adólphus (Átaulf), was induced to find in Gaul and Spain the lands which Álaric had sought in Ítaly.

The Rule of Placídia.—The great invasions which began during the reign of Honórius (A.D. 395-423) continued during the reign of Valentínian III. (A.D. 425-455). As Valentínian was only six years of age when he was proclaimed emperor, the government was carried on by his mother, Placídia, who was the sister of Honórius and daughter of Theodósius the Great. Placídia was in fact for many years during these eventful times the real ruler of Rome. Her armies were commanded by Aétius and Bóniface, who have been called the "last of the Rómans."

Invasion of the Huns under Áttila.—The next great invasion of the Western Empire was made by the Huns under Áttila. This savage people from Ásia had already gained a foothold in eastern Europe north of the Dánube. Under their great chieftain, Áttila, who has been called "the Scourge of God," they invaded Gaul, and devastated the provinces; they laid siege to the city of Orleans, but were finally defeated by the Róman general Aétius, with the aid of the Vísigoths. The battle was fought near Châlons (A.D. 451), and has been called one of the great decisive battles of the world, because it relieved Europe from the danger of Tártar domination. Áttila later invaded Ítaly, but retired without attacking Rome.

The Meeting between Pope Léo the Great and Áttila (1514), Raphaël (1483-1520), Vátican

167

Notwithstanding the brilliant service which Aétius had rendered, he was made the victim of court intrigue, and was murdered by his jealous prince Valentínian III. The fate of Aétius, like that of Stílicho before him, shows the wretched condition into which the imperial government had fallen.

Invasion of the Vándals under Génseric.—The Vándals who had fought under Radagaísus had, upon the death of that leader, retreated into Spain, and had finally crossed over into África, where they had erected a kingdom under their chief Génseric. They captured the Róman city of Cárthage and made it their capital; and they soon obtained control of the western Mediterránean. On the pretext of settling a quarrel at Rome, Génseric landed his army at the port of Óstia, took possession of the city of Rome, and for fourteen days made it the subject of pillage (A.D. 455). By this act of Génseric, the city lost its treasures and many of its works of art, and the word "vandalism" came to be a term of odious meaning.

Occupation of Brítain by the Sáxons.—While the continental provinces were thus overrun by the Goths, the Huns, and the Vándals, the Róman army was withdrawn from the island of Brítain. For many years it was left to govern itself. But the tribes of northern Gérmany, the Jutes and the Sáxons, saw in it a desirable place of settlement, and began their migration to the island (A.D. 449).

In the various ways which we have thus briefly described, the provinces of the Western Empire (Spain, África, Gaul, and Brítain) became for the most part occupied by Gérman barbarians, and practically independent of the imperial authority at Rome.

II. THE FALL OF THE WESTERN EMPIRE

Rícimer and the Last Days of the Empire.—The authority of the Western Róman emperors became limited to Ítaly, and even here it was reduced to a mere shadow. The barbarians were the real power behind the throne. The Róman armies were made up mostly of barbarians, under the control of barbarian generals; and even the direction of affairs at the capital was in the hands of barbarian chiefs. The place which Stílicho the Vándal had held under Honórius, was filled by Rícimer the Goth during the last years of the empire. This chieftain commanded the foreign troops in the pay of Rome. He received the Róman title of "patrician," which at this time was equivalent to regent of the empire. For seventeen years (455-472) Rícimer exercised absolute authority, setting up and deposing emperors at his will. The Róman Empire in the West had in fact already passed away, and nothing was now left but to extinguish its name.

Odoácer deposes Rómulus Augústulus (A.D. 476).—The part which Rícimer had played as "king-maker" was now assumed by Oréstes the Pannónian, who received the title of patrícian. Oréstes placed upon the throne his son, Rómulus Augústulus, a boy six years of age. The brief reign of this prince has no other significance than the fact that it was the last. The barbarian mercenaries demanded one third of the lands of Ítaly, and on the refusal of Oréstes, they placed their cause in the hands of Odoácer (a Herúlian, or a Rúgian chief). Rómulus was obliged to resign his title as emperor, and word was sent to the Eastern ruler that there was no need of another separate emperor in the West. Odoácer was given the title of patrícian, and ruled over Ítaly as the vicar of the Eastern emperor. The West was then deprived of the imperial title; and this event is called the "fall of the Western Róman Empire."

Relation of the West to the Eastern Empire.—If we were asked to define the relation between the East and the West after the deposition of Rómulus Augústulus, we might be in doubt how to answer the question. Since Odoácer was made a Róman ruler under the title of patrícian, and since he recognized the authority of the Eastern emperor, we might say that the Western Empire was not destroyed, but was simply reunited once more to the Eastern Empire. This would be true so far as it referred to a mere matter of legal form. But as a matter of historical fact this event does not mark a return to the old system of things which existed before the death of Theodósius, but marks a real separation between the history of the East and the history of the West.

Coin of Odoácer

Transition to a New Civilization in the West.—The West had gradually become peopled with various Gérman tribes. In África were the Vándals; in Spain and southern Gaul, the Vísigoths; in northwestern Spain, the Suévi; in southeastern Gaul, the Burgúndians; in Brítain, the Sáxons and the Jutes; in Ítaly, the Héruli. Only in the northern part of Gaul was the shadow of the Róman authority preserved by the governor, Syágrius, who still maintained himself for ten years longer against the invaders, but was at last conquered by the Franks under Clóvis (A.D. 486). The chiefs of the new Gérman kingdom had begun to exercise an independent authority and the Róman people had become subject to new rulers. The customs and manners of the Rómans, their laws and their language, were still preserved, but upon them became engrafted new customs, new ideas, and new institutions. As the fall of the old republic was a transition to the empire, and as the decline of the early empire was a transition to a new phase of imperialism; so now the fall of the Róman Empire in the West was in reality a transition to a new state of things out of which has grown our modern civilization.

GUIDE TO ROMAN NAMES AND PRONUNCIATION

Roman Names.—Róman men of the Republican and Imperial periods usually had three names. The given name, or *prænómen*, would be used only by family members or intimate acquaintances. By the late days of the republic, there were only a handful of common names. The following are the abbreviations of some names:

A.	Áulus	*Mam.*	Mamércus	*Q. or Qu.*	Quíntus
Ap.	Áppius	*M'.*	Mánius	*Sept.*	Séptimus
C.	Gáius or Cáius	*M.*	Márcus	*S. or Ser.*	Sérvius
Cn.	Gnǽus	*N.*	Numérius	*Sex.*	Séxtus
D.	Décimus	*O.*	Octaviánus	*Sp.*	Spúrius
K.	Kǽso or Cǽso	*Pro.*	Próculus	*Ti.*	Tibérius
L.	Lúcius	*P.*	Públius	*T.*	Títus

The *nómen* indicated the *gens*, or tribe, to which the individual belonged. A *cognómen* was added later, and was used to distinguish various individuals within a given *gens*. Eventually, these *cognómina* would also be inherited, so a man might have more than three names. This necessitated further distinctions based on an *agnómen*. This last name was not generally inherited. The suffix, *–iánus*, indicated the family from which a man was adopted. For example, *Cǽsar Augústus* was called *Octaviánus* ("Octávian") until he became emperor.

Roman women had only a single name, which derived from their father's *gens*. For example, the daughter of a man with *Cláudius* for *nómen* would be *Cláudia*. This was the case even if there were several daughters, so further distinctions would be made, *e.g. Cláudia Príma* (Cláudia the First), *Cláudia Secúnda* (Cláudia the Second). The distinction of *Máior* (elder) and *Mínor* (younger) could also be used to distinguish mothers and daughters of the same name.

Pronunciation.—There are three systems of pronunciation used in English-speaking countries. The first is the restored classical pronunciation, which approximates Látin pronunciation during the golden age of Róman literature. The second is the ecclesiastical pronunciation, which is used by the Róman Catholic Church in its liturgy and in official documents. The third is the English pronunciation. Choosing a consistently classical or ecclesiastical pronunciation is problematic, since many Látin names have passed over directly into English and have gained a familiarity that cannot be repressed. To use anything but their common pronunciation is jarring to the ear. Moreover, their names have been Englished in their spelling, making a proper Látin pronunciation truly impossible. The pronunciation index on the following pages therefore provides only the English pronunciation, with the understanding that instructors and students who wish to employ one of the others will know how to do so. To serve this end, names and other words capable of Látin pronunciation are bold-faced in the guide. Words found in the index have been given accents throughout the text which apply equally well to all three pronunciations. Groups of italicized letters in the index are to be pronounced together as a single vowel sound.

170

ábacus (AB-*uh*-k*uh*s)
Ábraham (AY-br*uh*-ham)
accénsi (ak-SEN-s*ahy*)
Achǽan (*uh*-K*EE*-*uh*n)
Acháia (*uh*-K*AY*-*uh*)
Áctium (AK-sh*ee*-*uh*m)
Adólphus (*uh*-DOL-f*uh*s)
Adrianóple (ay-dr*ee*-*uh*-N*OH*-p*uh*l)
Adriátic (*ay*-dr*ee*-AT-ik)
ǽdile (*EE*-d*ahy*l)
ǽdileship (*EE*-d*ahy*l-ship)
Ægátes (ih-G*AY*-teez)
Ægéan (ih-J*EE*-*uh*n)
Æmília (ih-MIL-*ee*-*uh*)
Æmílian (ih-MIL-ee-*uh*n)
Æmiliánus (ih-mil-ee-*AY*-n*uh*s)
Æmílius (ih-MIL-*ee*-*uh*s)
Ænéas (ih-N*EE*-*uh*s)
Ænéid (ih-N*EE*-id)
Æquian (*EE*-kw*ee*-*uh*n)
ærárii (ih-R*AI*R-*ee*-*ahy*)
ærárium (ih-R*AI*R-*ee*-*uh*m)
Aétius (*uh*-*EE*-sh*ee*-*uh*s)
Ætólian (ih-T*OH*-l*ee*-*uh*n)
África (AF-r*ih*-k*uh*)
Áfrican (AF-r*ih*-k*uh*n)
Africánus (af-r*ih*-K*AY*-n*uh*s)
áger (*AY*-jer)
Ágincourt (AJ-in-k*aw*rt)
Agrícola (*uh*-GR*IH*-k*uh*-l*uh*)
Agrigéntum (ag-r*ih*-JEN-t*uh*m)
Agríppa (*uh*-GR*IH*-p*uh*)
Agrippína (ag-r*ih*-P*AHY*-n*uh*)
Ahála (*uh*-H*AY*-l*uh*)
Aláni (*uh*-L*AY*-n*ahy*)
Álaric (AL-*uh*-rik)
Álba (*AHL*-b*uh*)
Álban (*AHL*-b*uh*n)
Alemánni (al-*eh*-MAN-*ahy*)
Alexánder (al-eg-ZAN-der)
Alexándria (al-eg-ZAN-dr*ee*-*uh*)
Álgidus (AL-j*ih*-d*uh*s)
Állia (AL-*ee*-*uh*)
Álpine (AL-p*ahy*n)
Alps (alps)
Ambrácia (am-BR*AY*-sh*ee*-*uh*)
Ámbrose (AM-br*oh*z)
Américan (*uh*-M*AI*R-*ih*-k*uh*n)
Amúlius (*uh*-MY*OO*-l*ee*-*uh*s)
Anchíses (an-K*AHY*-seez)
Ancóna (an-K*OH*-n*uh*)
Áncus (ANG-k*uh*s)
Andronícus (an-dr*uh*-N*AHY*-k*uh*s)
Ángelo (AN-j*eh*-l*oh*)
Ánio (AN-*ee*-*oh*)

Ánnius (AN-*ee*-*uh*s)
annónæ (*uh*-N*OH*-n*ee*)
Ántioch (AN-t*ee*-ok)
Antíochus (an-T*AHY*-*uh*-k*uh*s)
Ántium (AN-sh*ee*-*uh*m)
Ántonine (AN-t*uh*-n*ahy*n)
Antonínus (an-t*uh*-N*AHY*-n*uh*s)
Antónius (an-T*OH*-n*ee*-*uh*s)
Ántony (AN-t*uh*-n*ee*)
Ápennines (AP-*eh*-n*ahy*nz)
Apóllo (*uh*-POL-*oh*)
Apóstate (*uh*-POS-t*ay*t)
Áppia (AP-*ee*-*uh*)
Áppian (AP-*ee*-*uh*n)
Áppius (AP-*ee*-*uh*s)
Apúlia (*uh*-PY*OOL*-*ee*-*uh*)
Apúlian (*uh*-PY*OOL*-*ee*-*uh*n)
Áquæ (AK-w*ee*)
Aquitánia (ak-w*ih*-T*AY*-n*ee*-*uh*)
Arábia (*uh*-R*AY*-b*ee*-*uh*)
Aráusio (*uh*-R*AW*-sh*ee*-*oh*)
Arcádius (*ah*r-K*AY*-d*ee*-*uh*s)
Ardáshir (*ah*r-DASH-er)
Arícia (*uh*-R*IH*-sh*ee*-*uh*)
Aríminum (*uh*-RIM-*uh*-n*uh*m)
Ariovístus (*ah*r-ee-*uh*-VIS-t*uh*s)
Arménia (*ah*r-M*EE*-n*ee*-*uh*)
Armínius (*ah*r-MIN-*ee*-*uh*s)
Arrétium (*uh*-REE-sh*ee*-*uh*m)
Artáxares (*ah*r-TAK-s*uh*-reez)
ártes (*AHR*-teez)
Áryan (*AI*R-*ee*-*uh*n)
Ascánius (*uh*-SK*AY*-n*ee*-*uh*s)
Ásculum (AS-ky*uh*-l*uh*m)
Ásia (*AY*-zh*ee*-*uh*)
Asiátic (*ay*-zh*ee*-AT-ik)
assídui (*uh*-SID-y*oo*-*ahy*)
Assýria (*uh*-SEER-*ee*-*uh*)
Astýanax (*uh*-ST*AHY*-*uh*-naks)
Átaulf (AT-*aw*lf)
Athenǽum (ath-*eh*-N*EE*-*uh*m)
Athénian (*uh*-TH*EE*-n*ee*-*uh*n)
Áthens (ATH-enz)
átrium (*AY*-tree-*uh*m)
Áttalus (AT-*uh*-l*uh*s)
Áttila (AT-*ih*-l*uh*)
Áufidus (*AW*-f*ih*-d*uh*s)
Augústan (aw-GUHS-t*uh*n)
Augústi (aw-GUHS-t*ahy*)
Augústulus (aw-GUHS-t*uh*-l*uh*s)
Augústus (aw-GUHS-t*uh*s)
Áulus (*AW*-l*uh*s)
Aurélia (aw-R*EE*-lee-*uh*)
Aurélian (aw-R*EE*-lee-*uh*n)
Aurélius (aw-R*EE*-lee-*uh*s)

171

Áventine (AV-en-t*ahy*n)
Aventínus (av-en-T*AHY*-n*uh*s)
Bálbus (BAL-b*uh*s)
Baléaric (b*uh*-LEE-*uh*-rik)
bálneum (BAL-n*ee*-*uh*m)
Bárca (B*AH*R-k*uh*)
Bas (b*ah*)
basílica (b*uh*-S*IH*-lih-k*uh*)
Benevéntum (ben-*eh*-VEN-t*uh*m)
Béstia (BES-ch*ee*-*uh*)
bibliothéca (bib-l*ee*-*uh*-TEE-k*uh*)
Bíbulus (BIB-y*uh*-l*uh*s)
Bithýnia (b*ih*-THIN-*ee*-*uh*)
Blanc (bl*aw*ngk)
Bóniface (BON-*ih*-f*uh*s)
Bósphorus (BOS-per-*uh*s)
Boviánum (b*oh*-vee-*AY*-n*uh*m)
Brénnus (BREN-*uh*s)
Brítain (BR*IH*-t*uh*n)
Británnicus (br*ih*-TAN-*ih*-k*uh*s)
Brundísium (br*uh*n-D*IH*-zhee-*uh*m)
Brúttian (BR*UH*-tee-*uh*n)
Brúttium (BR*UH*-tee-*uh*m)
Brútus (BR*OO*-t*uh*s)
Burgúndian (ber-G*UH*N-dee-*uh*n)
Búrrhus (BER-*uh*s)
Býzantine (BIZ-*uh*n-t*ahy*n)
Byzántium (b*ih*-ZAN-shee-*uh*m)
Cæcílius (s*ih*-SIL-*ee*-*uh*s)
Cǽlian (SEE-lee-*uh*n)
Cǽlius (SEE-lee-*uh*s)
Cǽre (SEE-ree)
Cǽsar (SEE-zer)
Calábria (k*uh*-L*AY*-bree-*uh*)
cálculi (KAL-ky*uh*-l*ahy*)
Calígula (k*uh*-LIG-y*uh*-l*uh*)
Calpúrnius (kal-PER-n*ee*-*uh*s)
Camíllus (k*uh*-MIL-*uh*s)
Campánia (kam-P*AY*-nee-*uh*)
Campánian (kam-P*AY*-nee-*uh*n)
Cámpus (KAM-p*uh*s)
candélæ (kan-DEE-lee)
Cánnæ (KAN-*ee*)
Canuléia (kan-y*uh*-LEE-y*uh*)
Cápitol (KAP-*ih*-t*uh*l)
Cápitoline (KAP-*ih*-t*uh*-l*ahy*n)
Capitolínus (kap-*ih*-t*uh*-L*AHY*-n*uh*s)
Cappadócia (kap-*uh*-D*OH*-shee-*uh*)
Cápreæ (KAP-r*ee*-ee)
Cápua (KAP-*yoo*-*uh*)
Caracálla (k*air*-*uh*-KAL-*uh*)
Caráctacus (k*uh*-RAK-t*uh*-k*uh*s)
Cárbo (K*AH*R-b*oh*)
Cárthage (K*AH*R-thij)
Carthagínian (k*ahy*r-th*uh*-J*IH*-nee-*uh*n)

Cárus (K*AI*R-*uh*s)
Cássia (KASH-*ee*-*uh*)
Cássian (KASH-*ee*-*uh*n)
Cássius (KASH-*ee*-*uh*s)
Cástor (KAS-ter)
Cátiline (KAT-*ih*-l*ahy*n)
Catilínian (kat-*ih*-LIN-*ee*-*uh*n)
Cáto (K*AY*-toh)
Catúllus (k*uh*-T*UH*L-*uh*s)
Cátulus (KAT-*uh*-l*uh*s)
Cáudine (K*AW*-d*ahy*n)
Cáudium (K*AW*-dee-*uh*m)
Celtibérian (sel-t*ih*-B*EE*R-*ee*-*uh*n)
Céltic (SEL-tik)
céna (S*EE*-n*uh*)
cénsor (SEN-ser)
cénsorship (SEN-ser-ship)
cénsus (SEN-s*uh*s)
centuriáta (sen-ch*uh*-ree-*AY*-t*uh*)
cénturies (SEN-ch*uh*-reez)
Céres (S*EE*R-eez)
Chæronéa (k*ih*-r*uh*-NEE-*uh*)
Châlons (sh*uh*-L*AW*N)
chárta (K*AH*R-t*uh*)
Chátti (KAT-*ahy*)
Cháuci (K*AW*-k*ahy*)
Cherúsci (k*eh*-R*OO*-s*ahy*)
Chi-Rho (k*ahy*-roh)
Christ (kr*ahy*st)
Chrístian (KRIS-ch*uh*n)
Christiánity (kris-chee-AN-*ih*-tee)
Cícero (S*IH*-sih-roh)
Cilícia (s*ih*-LISH-*ee*-*uh*)
Címbri (SIM-br*ahy*)
Címbric (SIM-brik)
Cincinnátus (sin-s*ih*-N*AY*-t*uh*s)
Cíneas (SIN-*ee*-*uh*s)
Cínna (SIN-*uh*)
Circéii (ser-S*EE*-*ahy*)
Círcus (SER-k*uh*s)
Cisálpine (sis-AL-p*ahy*n)
Civílis (s*ih*-V*IH*-lis)
cívitas (S*IH*-v*ih*-tas)
civitátes (s*ih*-v*ih*-T*AY*-teez)
Civitátis (s*ih*-v*ih*-T*AY*-tis)
Cláudian (KL*AW*-dee-*uh*n)
Cláudius (KL*AW*-dee-*uh*s)
Cleopátra (klee-*uh*-PAT-r*uh*)
Cloáca (kl*oh*-*AY*-k*uh*)
Clódius (CL*OH*-dee-*uh*s)
Clóvis (KL*OH*-vis)
Clúsium (KL*OO*-zhee-*uh*m)
Cócles (K*OH*-kleez)
Cœle-Sýria (SEE-lee-S*IH*R-*ee*-*uh*)
coémptio (k*oh*-EM-sh*ee*-oh)

Collatínus (kol-*uh*-T*AHY*-n*uh*s)
collégia (k*uh*-LEE-jee-*uh*)
Cólline (KOL-*ahy*n)
colóni (k*uh*-LOH-n*ahy*)
colónus (k*uh*-LOH-n*uh*s)
Colosséum (kol-*uh*-SEE-*uh*m)
Colúmna (k*uh*-LUHM-n*uh*)
comítia (k*uh*-MISH-ee-*uh*)
comítium (k*uh*-MISH-ee-*uh*m)
commércium (k*uh*-MER-sh-ee-*uh*m)
Cómmodus (KOM-*uh*-d*uh*s)
concílium (k*uh*n-SIL-ee-*uh*m)
Concórdia (k*uh*n-K*AW*R-dee-*uh*)
confarreátio (k*uh*n-far-ee-*AY*-shee-*oh*)
conscrípti (k*uh*n-SCRIP-t*ahy*)
consílium (k*uh*n-SIL-ee-*uh*m)
Cónstantine (KON-st*uh*n-t*ahy*n)
Constantinóple (kon-stan-t*ih*-N*OH*-p*uh*l)
Constántius (kon-STAN-sh*ee*-*uh*s)
cónsul (KON-s*uh*l)
cónsular (KON-s*uh*-ler)
cónsulship (KON-s*uh*l-ship)
conúbium (k*uh*-NOO-bee-*uh*m)
Corfínium (k*aw*r-FIN-ee-*uh*m)
Córinth (K*AW*R-inth)
Coriolánus (k*aw*r-ee-uh-L*AY*-n*uh*s)
Cornélia (k*aw*r-N*EE*L-ee-*uh*)
Cornélii (k*aw*r-N*EE*L-ee-*ahy*)
Cornélius (k*aw*r-N*EE*L-ee-*uh*s)
Córsica (K*AW*R-s*ih*-k*uh*)
Crássus (KRAS-*uh*s)
Crete (kr*eet*)
Cróton (KR*OH*-t*uh*n)
culína (ky*oo*-L*AHY*-n*uh*)
Cúmæ (KY*OO*-mee)
Cunctátor (k*uh*ngk-T*AY*-ter)
curátor (ky*oor*-*AY*-ter)
cúria (KY*OOR*-ee-*uh*)
cúriæ (KY*OOR*-ee-ee)
curiáles (ky*oor*-ee-*AY*-leez)
curiáta (ky*oor*-ee-*AY*-t*uh*)
Curiátii (ky*oor*-ee-*AY*-shee-*ahy*)
cúries (KY*OOR*-eez)
cúrio (KY*OOR*-ee-*oh*)
Cúrius (KY*OOR*-ee-*uh*s)
Cúrsor (KER-ser)
cúrule (KY*OOR*-*ool*)
Cynoscéphalæ (sin-*uh*-SEF-*uh*-lee)
Cýprus (S*AHY*-pr*uh*s)
Cyrenáïca (s*ahy*-reh-N*AY*-ih-k*uh*)
Dácia (D*AY*-sh-ee-*uh*)
Dalmátia (dal-M*AY*-shee-*uh*)
Dánube (DAN-y*oo*b)
decémvir (d*eh*-SEM-ver)
Decémvirate (d*eh*-SEM-ver-it)

Décimus (DES-*ih*-m*uh*s)
Décius (D*EE*-shee-*uh*s)
decúrio (d*eh*-KY*OO*R-ee-*oh*)
delátion (d*eh*-L*AY*-shun)
delatóres (del-*uh*-T*AW*R-eez)
Denárius (d*eh*-N*AI*R-ee-*uh*s)
Dentátus (den-T*AY*-t*uh*s)
Diána (d*ahy*-AN-*uh*)
Dídius (DID-ee-*uh*s)
Dído (D*AHY*-d*oh*)
Dioclétian (d*ahy*-uh-KLEE-sh*uh*n)
Dionýsius (d*ahy*-uh-N*AHY*-shee-*uh*s)
Díptych (DIP-tik)
Dívi (D*ahy*-v*ahy*)
Domítian (d*uh*-MISH-*uh*n)
Dómna (DOM-n*uh*)
dómus (D*OH*-m*uh*s)
Drépanum (DREP-*uh*-n*uh*m)
Drúsus (DR*OO*-s*uh*s)
Duílius (d*oo*-IL-ee-*uh*s)
duúmvirate (d*oo*-UHM-ver-it)
duúmviri (d*oo*-UHM-ver-ee)
Dyrráchium (d*ih*-R*AY*-kee-*uh*m)
Ébro (*EE*-br*oh*)
Écnomus (EK-n*uh*-m*uh*s)
Edíctum (eh-DIK-t*uh*m)
Égypt (*EE*-jipt)
Elagábalus (el-*uh*-GAB-*uh*-l*uh*s)
Élba (EL-b*uh*)
Éngland (ING-gl*uh*nd)
Énnius (EN-ee-*uh*s)
Éphesus (EF-*eh*-s*uh*s)
Epicuréan (ep-*ih*-ky*oo*-R*EE*-*uh*n)
Epírus (*eh*-P*AHY*-r*uh*s)
équites (EK-w*ih*-teez)
Ésquiline (ES-kw*ih*-l*ahy*n)
Esquilínus (es-kw*ih*-L*AHY*-n*uh*s)
Etrúria (*eh*-TR*OO*R-ee-*uh*)
Etrúscan (*eh*-TR*UH*S-k*uh*n)
Euchérius (y*oo*-KEER-ee-*uh*s)
Eúnus (Y*OO*-n*uh*s)
Euphrátes (y*oo*-FR*AY*-teez)
Éurope (Y*OO*R-*uh*p)
Européan (y*oo*r-uh-PEE-*uh*n)
Eusébius (y*oo*-SEE-bee-*uh*s)
Fábian (F*AY*-bee-*uh*n)
Fábii (F*AY*-bee-*ahy*)
Fábius (F*AY*-bee-*uh*s)
far (f*ahr*)
farína (f*uh*-R*AHY*N-n*uh*)
fásces (FAS-*eez*)
Ferétrius (f*eh*-REE-tree-*uh*s)
fetiáles (f*eh*-shee-*AY*-leez)
Fidénæ (f*ih*-D*EE*-nee)
físcus (FIS-k*uh*s)

flámen (FL*AY*-men)
Flamínia (fl*uh*-MIN-*ee-uh*)
Flamínian (fl*uh*-MIN-*ee-uh*n)
Flaminínus (flam-*ih*-N*AHY*-n*uh*s)
Flamínius (fl*uh*-MIN-*ee-uh*s)
Flávian (FL*AY*-vee-*uh*n)
Flávius (FL*AY*-vee-*uh*s)
Flóra (FL*AWR-uh*)
florilégium (flawr-*ih*-LEJ-*ee-uh*m)
fóculi (FOK-y*uh*-lahy)
fœderátæ (f*ih*-deh-R*AY*-tee)
fórum (F*AW*R-*uh*m)
Fórum (F*AW*R-*uh*m)
France (frans)
Frank (frangk)
Fregéllæ (fr*eh*-JEL-*ee*)
Frentáni (fren-T*AY*-n*ahy*)
Frénto (FREN-t*oh*)
Fúcine (F*YOO*-sahyn)
Fúlvia (F*UHL*-vee-*uh*)
Fúrius (FY*OO*R-*ee-uh*s)
Gabínia (g*uh*-BIN-*ee-uh*)
Gádes (G*AY*-deez)
Gáius (G*AY-uh*s)
Galátia (g*uh*-L*AY*-shee-*uh*)
Gálba (GAL-b*uh*)
Galérius (g*uh*-LEER-*ee-uh*s)
Gállic (GAL-ik)
Galliénus (gal-ee-EE-n*uh*s)
Gállus (GAL-*uh*s)
Gaul (g*aw*l)
Gáurus (G*AW*R-*uh*s)
gens (jenz)
Génseric (JEN-ser-ik)
géntes (JEN-t*ee*z)
géntium (JEN-sh*ee-uh*m)
Gérman (JER-m*uh*n)
Germánicus (jer-M*AY*-n*ih*-k*uh*s)
Gérmany (JER-m*uh*-n*ee*)
Géstae (JES-t*ee*)
Géta (J*EE*T-*uh*)
gládii (GL*AY*-dee-*ahy*)
Gláucia (GL*AW*-shee-*uh*)
Gnæus (N*EE-uh*s)
Goth (goth)
Góthic (GOTH-ik)
Góthicus (GOTH-*ih*-k*uh*s)
Grácchi (GRAK-*ahy*)
Grácchus (GRAK-*uh*s)
Græcia (GR*EE*-shee-*uh*)
Greece (gr*ee*s)
Greek (gr*ee*k)
Hádrian (H*AY*-dr*ee-uh*n)
Halicarnássus (hal-*ih*-k*ah*r-NAS-*uh*s)
Hamílcar (h*uh*-MIL-k*ah*r)

Hánnibal (HAN-*ih*-b*uh*l)
Hánno (HAN-*oh*)
Hársa (H*AH*R-s*uh*)
harúspices (h*uh*-R*UH*S-p*ih*-seez)
Hásdrubal (HAZ-dr*oo*-b*uh*l)
hastáti (h*uh*-ST*AY*-t*ahy*)
Hébrew (H*EE*-br*oo*)
Hélena (HEL-*eh*-n*uh*)
Héllenism (HEL-*eh*-niz-*uh*m)
Héllespont (HEL-*eh*s-pont)
Helvétii (hel-V*EE*-shee-*ahy*)
Heracléa (h*air*-*uh*-KL*EE*-*uh*)
Herculáneum (her-ky*uh*-L*AY*-nee-*uh*m)
Hércules (HER-ky*uh*-leez)
Hérnican (HER-n*ih*-k*uh*n)
Hérod (H*AI*R-*uh*d)
Héruli (H*AI*R-y*uh*-l*ahy*)
Herúlian (h*eh*-R*OO*-lee-*uh*n)
Hómer (H*OH*-mer)
hómo (H*OH*-m*oh*)
honóres (h*uh*-N*AW*R-eez)
Honórius (h*uh*-N*AW*R-*ee-uh*s)
Horátian (hawr-*AY*-shee-*uh*n)
Horátii (hawr-*AY*-shee-*ahy*)
Horátius (hawr-*AY*-shee-*uh*s)
Hostílius (h*uh*-STIL-*ee-uh*s)
Hun (h*uh*n)
Iapýgia (y*uh*-PIJ-*ee-uh*)
Ibérus (*ih*-B*EE*R-*uh*s)
Icília (*ih*-SIL-*ee-uh*)
Ides (*ahy*dz)
ientáculum (yen-T*AY*-ky*uh*-l*uh*m)
ignóbiles (ig-N*OH*-b*ih*-leez)
Illýrian (*ih*-L*EE*R-*ee-uh*n)
Illýricum (*ih*-L*EE*R-*ih*-k*uh*m)
imáginis (*ih*-M*AY*-j*ih*-nis)
immúnes (*ih*-MY*OO*-neez)
imperátor (im-p*eh*-R*AY*-ter)
impérium (im-P*EE*R-*ee-uh*m)
Índo (IN-d*oh*)
Ísthmian (IS-mee-*uh*n)
Ísthmus (IS-m*uh*s)
Itálian (*ih*-TAL-*ee-uh*n)
Itálic (*ih*-TAL-ik)
Ítaly (IT-*uh*-lee)
iúdices (Y*OO*-d*ih*-seez)
iúgera (Y*OO*-jeh-r*uh*)
Iúlia (Y*OO*-lee-*uh*)
iunióres (yoon-Y*AW*R-eez)
iúra (Y*OO*R-*uh*)
ius (y*oo*s)
Janículum (j*uh*-NIK-y*uh*-l*uh*m)
Jánus (J*AY*-n*uh*s)
Jerúsalem (j*eh*-R*OO*-s*uh*-lem)
Jésus (J*EE*-z*uh*s)

174

Jew (joo)
Jéwish (JOO-ish)
Jove (johv)
Jóvian (JOH-vee-uhn)
Judéa (joo-DEE-uh)
Jugúrtha (juh-GER-thuh)
Jugúrthine (juh-GER-thahyn)
Júlia (JOO-lee-uh)
Júlian (JOO-lee-uhn)
Juliánus (joo-lee-AY-nuhs)
Júlii (JOO-lee-ahy)
Július (JOO-lee-uhs)
Június (JOO-nee-uhs)
Júno (JOO-noh)
Júpiter (JOO-pih-ter)
Jute (joot)
Júvenal (JOO-veh-nuhl)
Kaléndio (kuh-LEN-dee-oh)
Lábarum (LAB-er-uhm)
Lacínian (luh-SIN-ee-uhn)
Lævínus (lih-VAHY-nuhs)
Lanúvium (luh-NOO-vee-uhm)
Lars (lahrz)
Latiáris (lay-shee-AIR-is)
Látin (LAT-in)
Latína (luh-TAHY-nuh)
Látium (LAY-shee-uhm)
Lavínium (luh-VIN-ee-uhm)
legáti (leh-GAY-tahy)
légion (LEE-juhn)
légionary (LEE-juh-nair-ee)
Léo (LEE-oh)
Lépidus (LEP-ih-duhs)
Léptis (LEP-tis)
lex (leks)
líber (LAHY-ber)
Líber (LAHY-ber)
liberáles (lib-eh-RAY-leez)
Líbya (LIB-ee-uh)
Licínian (lih-SIN-ee-uhn)
Licínius (lih-SIN-ee-uhs)
líctor (LIK-ter)
Ligúria (lih-GYOOR-ee-uh)
Lilybǽum (lil-ih-BEE-uhm)
Líris (LIHR-is)
Lívia (LIV-ee-uh)
Lívius (LIV-ee-uhs)
Lívy (LIV-ee)
Lócri (LOH-krahy)
Lónga (LONG-guh)
Lúcan (LOO-kuhn)
Lucánia (loo-KAY-nee-uh)
Lucánian (loo-KAY-nee-uhn)
Lúcca (LOO-kuh)
Lúceres (LOO-seh-reez)

Lucéria (loo-SEER-ee-uh)
lucérnæ (loo-SER-nee)
Lúcius (LOO-shee-uhs)
Lucrétius (loo-KREE-shee-uhs)
Lucúllus (loo-KUHL-uhs)
Lusitánian (loo-sih-TAY-nee-uhn)
Lutátius (loo-TAY-shee-uhs)
Lýcia (LISH-ee-uh)
Lýdian (LID-ee-uhn)
Macedónia (mas-eh-DOH-nee-uh)
Macedónian (mas-eh-DOH-nee-uhn)
Machiavélli (mak-ee-uh-VEL-ee)
Mácra (MAK-ruh)
Macrínus (muh-KRAHY-nuhs)
Mæcénas (mih-SEE-nuhs)
Mǽlius (MEE-lee-uhs)
Mágna (MAG-nuh)
Magnésia (mag-NEE-zhee-uh)
Mágnus (MAG-nuhs)
maiestátis (mahy-uh-STAY-tis)
maióres (muh-YAWR-eez)
Mámertine (MAM-er-tahyn)
Manília (muh-NIL-ee-uh)
mániple (MAN-ih-puhl)
Mánlian (MAN-lee-uhn)
Mánlius (MAN-lee-uhs)
Marcéllus (mahr-SEL-uhs)
Március (MAHR-shee-uhs)
Marcománni (mahr-kuh-MAN-ahy)
Márcus (MAHR-kuhs)
Márian (MAIR-ee-uhn)
Márius (MAIR-ee-uhs)
Mars (mahrz)
Marseilles (mahr-SAY)
Mársian (MAHR-zhee-uhn)
Mártial (MAHR-shuhl)
Mártius (MAHR-shee-uhs)
Masáda (muh-SAH-duh)
Masiníssa (mas-ih-NIS-uh)
Massília (muh-SIL-ee-uh)
Mauretánia (mawr-eh-TAY-nee-uh)
Maxéntius (mak-SEN-shee-uhs)
Máxima (MAKS-ih-muh)
Maxímian (mak-SIM-ee-uhn)
Máximus (MAKS-ih-muhs)
Mediterránean (med-ih-teh-RAY-nee-uhn)
membrána (mem-BRAY-nuh)
Mesopotámia (mes-uh-puh-TAY-mee-uh)
Messalína (mes-uh-LAHY-nuh)
Messána (meh-SAY-nuh)
Metáurus (meh-TAWR-uhs)
Metéllus (meh-TEL-uhs)
Milán (mih-LAWN)
Mílitum (MIL-ih-tuhm)
Mílo (MAHY-loh)

Minérva (mih-NER-vuh)
Mínor (MAHY-ner)
minóres (mih-NAWR-eez)
Mintúrnæ (min-TER-nee)
Missórium (mih-SAWR-ee-uhm)
Mithridátes (mith-rih-DAY-teez)
Mœsia (MEE-shee-uh)
Móloch (MOL-uhk)
Mons (monz)
mórum (MAWR-uhm)
Múcius (MYOO-shee-uhs)
Múmmius (MUM-ee-uhs)
Múnda (MUHN-duh)
municípia (myoon-ih-SIP-ee-uh)
Mus (myoos)
Mútina (MYOO-tih-nuh)
Mýlæ (MAHY-lee)
Nǽvius (NEE-vee-uhs)
Náples (NAY-puhlz)
Narbonénsis (nahr-buh-NEN-sis)
Narcíssus (nahr-SIS-uhs)
Nasíca (nuh-SAHY-kuh)
Neápolis (nee-AP-uh-lis)
Néro (NEER-oh)
Nerónis (ner-OH-nis)
Nérva (NER-vuh)
Nérvii (NER-vee-ahy)
Nicǽa (nahy-SEE-uh)
Nicomédia (nik-uh-MEE-dee-uh)
Nile (nahyl)
Nimes (neem)
nóbiles (NOH-bih-leez)
Nóricum (NAWR-ih-kuhm)
nóvus (NOH-vuhs)
Núma (NOO-muh)
Numántia (noo-MAN-shee-uh)
Númantine (NOO-man-tahyn)
Numídia (noo-MID-ee-uh)
Numídian (noo-MID-ee-uhn)
Octaviánus (ok-tay-vee-AY-nuhs)
Octávius (ok-TAY-vee-uhs)
Odoácer (oh-doh-AY-ser)
Olýmpian (uh-LIM-pee-uhn)
Olýmpus (uh-LIM-puhs)
opíma (oh-PAHY-muh)
optimátes (op-tih-MAY-teez)
Óptimus (OP-tih-muhs)
Orchómenus (awr-KAW-muh-nuhs)
Oréstes (awr-ES-teez)
Oriéntal (awr-ee-EN-tuhl)
Oriéntalize (awr-ee-EN-tuh-lahyz)
Orleans (awr-lay-AWN)
Ósca (OS-kuh)
Óscan (OS-kuhn)
Óstia (OS-chee-uh)

Ótho (OT-oh)
Óvid (OV-id)
Pǽstum (PES-tuhm)
Palǽpolis (puh-LEE-puh-lis)
Pálatine (PAL-uh-tahyn)
Palatínus (pal-uh-TAHY-nuhs)
Pálestine (pal-eh-stahyn)
pálla (PAL-uh)
Pállas (PAL-uhs)
Palmýra (pal-MAHY-ruh)
Pamphýlia (pam-FIL-ee-uh)
Pannónia (puh-NOH-nee-uh)
Pannónian (puh-NOH-nee-uhn)
Panórmus (puh-NAWR-muhs)
Pánsa (PAN-zuh)
Pántheon (PAN-thee-on)
Papínian (puh-PIN-ee-uhn)
Papíria (puh-PEER-ee-uh)
Papírius (puh-PEER-ee-uhs)
papýrus (puh-PAHY-ruhs)
Párthia (PAHR-thee-uh)
Párthian (PAHR-thee-uhn)
Páter (PAY-ter)
paterfamílias (pay-ter-fuh-MIL-ee-uhs)
pátres (PAY-treez)
Pátriæ (PAY-tree-ee)
patrícian (puh-TRISH-uhn)
Páullus (PAW-luhs)
pédites (PED-ih-teez)
Pédum (PED-uhm)
Peloponnésus (pel-uh-puh-NEE-suhs)
peregrínus (pair-uh-GRAHY-nuhs)
Pérgamum (PER-guh-muhm)
Péricles (PAIR-ih-kleez)
peristýlum (pair-ih-STAHY-luhm)
perpétuæ (per-PET-choo-ee)
Perpétuum (per-PET-choo-uhm)
Pérseus (PER-see-uhs)
Pérsia (PER-zhuh)
Pérsian (PER-zhuhn)
Pértinax (PER-tih-naks)
Petrǽa (peh-TREE-uh)
phálanx (FAY-langks)
Phárnaces (FAHR-nuh-seez)
Pharsálus (fahr-SAY-luhs)
Phílip (FIL-ip)
Philíppi (fih-LIP-ahy)
Philíppics (fih-LIP-iks)
Phílo (FAHY-loh)
Phœnícia (fih-NEE-shee-uh)
Phœnícian (fih-NEE-shee-uhn)
Picénum (pih-SEE-nuhm)
Píctor (PIK-ter)
Pílate (PAHY-luht)
píleus (PIL-ee-uhs)

Píus (P*AHY-uh*s)
Placéntia (pl*uh*-SEN-sh*ee-uh*)
Placídia (pl*uh*-SID-*ee-uh*)
Pláto (PL*AY*-toh)
Pláutia (PL*AW*-sh*ee-uh*)
Pláutius (PL*AW*-sh*ee-uh*s)
Pláutus (PL*AW*-t*uh*s)
plebéian (pl*eh*-B*EE-uh*n)
plébis (PLEB-is)
plebiscíta (pleb-*ih*-S*AHY*-t*uh*)
plebs (plebz)
Plíny (PLIN-*ee*)
Plútarch (PL*OO*-t*ah*rk)
Po (p*oh*)
Polléntia (p*uh*-LEN-sh*ee-uh*)
Póllux (POL-*uh*ks)
Polýbius (p*uh*-LIB-*ee-uh*s)
Pompéian (pom-P*AY-uh*n)
Pompéii (pom-P*AY*-ee)
Pompéius (pom-P*AY-uh*s)
Pómpey (POM-p*ee*)
Pompílius (pom-PIL-*ee-uh*s)
Pons (ponz)
póntifex (PON-t*ih*-feks)
Póntine (PON-t*ahy*n)
Póntius (PON-sh*ee-uh*s)
Póntus (PON-t*uh*s)
Poplícola (p*uh*-PLIH-k*uh*-l*uh*)
Poppǽa (p*uh*-P*EE-uh*)
populáres (pop-y*uh*-L*AI*R-*ee*z)
Pórcius (P*AW*R-sh*ee-uh*s)
Porséna (p*aw*r-S*EE*-n*uh*)
Pórta (P*AW*R-t*uh*)
Pórtugal (P*AW*R-ch*uh*-g*uh*l)
Pórtus (P*AW*R-t*uh*s)
potéstas (p*uh*-TES-tas)
prædéctus (pr*ih*-FEK-t*uh*s)
Prænéste (pr*ih*-NES-t*ee*)
prætéxta (pr*ih*-TEKS-t*uh*)
prǽtor (PR*EE*-ter)
prætórian (pr*ih*-T*AW*R-*ee-uh*n)
prǽtorship (PR*EE*-ter-ship)
prándium (PRAN-d*ee-uh*m)
Préfecture (PR*EE*-fek-cher)
Príma (PR*AHY*-m*uh*)
prínceps (PRIN-seps)
príncipes (PRIN-s*ih*-p*ee*z)
príncipis (PRIN-s*ih*-pis)
Príscus (PRIS-k*uh*s)
priváta (pr*ih*-V*AY*-t*uh*)
Próbus (PR*OH*-b*uh*s)
procónsul (pr*oh*-KON-s*uh*l)
procónsular (pr*oh*-KON-sy*uh*-ler)
proconsuláre (pr*oh*-kon-sy*uh*-L*AI*R-*ee*)
professóres (pr*uh*-f*eh*-S*AW*R-*ee*z)

Propértius (pr*uh*-PER-sh*ee-uh*s)
proprǽtor (pr*oh*-PR*EE*-ter)
proscríptio (pr*oh*-SKRIP-sh*ee-oh*)
Ptólemy (TOL-*uh*-m*ee*)
pública (PUB-bl*ih*-k*uh*)
publicáni (pub-l*ih*-K*AY*-n*ahy*)
públicus (PUB-l*ih*-k*uh*s)
Publília (pub-L*IH*-lee-*uh*)
Publílius (pub-L*IH*-lee-*uh*s)
Públius (PUB-lee-*uh*s)
Púnic (PY*OO*-nik)
Putéoli (py*oo*-T*EE-uh*-l*ahy*)
Pýdna (PID-n*uh*)
Pýrenees (P*IH*R-*uh*-n*ee*z)
Pýrrhus (P*IH*R-*uh*s)
Quádi (KW*AY*-d*ahy*)
Quadráta (kw*ah*-DR*AY*-t*uh*)
quæstiónes (kw*ih*-st*ee*-*OH*-n*ee*z)
quǽstor (KW*EE*-ster)
Quínctius (KWINK-sh*ee-uh*s)
Quinquénnium (kwin-KWEN-*ee-uh*m)
quínquireme (KWIN-kw*ih*-reem)
Quintílian (kwin-TIL-*ee-uh*n)
Quíntus (KWIN-t*uh*s)
Quírinal (KW*IH*R-*ih*-n*uh*l)
Quirinális (kw*ih*r-*ih*-N*AY*-lis)
Quirínus (kw*ih*-R*AHY*-n*uh*s)
Radagaísus (rad-*uh*-g*uh*-*IH*-s*uh*s)
Rámnes (RAM-n*ee*z)
Ravénna (r*uh*-VEN-*uh*)
Regíllus (r*eh*-JIL-*uh*s)
Régulus (REG-y*uh*-l*uh*s)
Rémus (R*EE*-m*uh*s)
Res (r*ay*z)
Retiárius (r*ee*-sh*ee*-*AI*R-*ee-uh*s)
rex (reks)
Rhǽtia (R*EE*-sh*ee-uh*)
Rhéa (R*EE-uh*)
Rhégium (R*EE*-jee-*uh*m)
Rhodes (r*oh*dz)
Rhône (r*oh*n)
Rícimer (R*IH*-s*ih*-mer)
Róma (R*OH*-m*uh*)
Róman (R*OH*-m*uh*n)
Rómanize (R*OH*-m*uh*-n*ahy*z)
Románus (r*oh*-M*AY*-n*uh*s)
Rome (r*oh*m)
Rómulus (ROM-y*uh*-l*uh*s)
rorárii (r*aw*r-*AI*R-*ee*-*ahy*)
Rostráta (r*uh*-STR*AY*-t*uh*)
Rúbicon (R*OO*-b*ih*-kon)
Rúfus (R*OO*-f*uh*s)
Rúgian (R*OO*-jee-*uh*n)
Rulliánus (roo-lee-*AY*-n*uh*s)
rústicæ (R*OO*S-t*ih*-s*ee*)

177

Sabéllian (suh-BEL-ee-uhn)
Sabína (suh-BAHY-nuh)
Sábine (SAY-bahyn)
Sácer (SAY-ser)
sacrórum (suh-KRAWR-uhm)
Sagúntum (suh-GUHN-tuhm)
Salinátor (sal-ih-NAY-ter)
Sállust (SAL-uhst)
Salóna (suh-LOH-nuh)
Sálvius (SAL-vee-uhs)
Sámnite (SAM-nahyt)
Sámnium (SAM-nee-uhm)
Sápor (SAY-per)
Sardínia (sahr-DIN-ee-uh)
Sárdis (SAHR-dis)
Sassánidæ (suh-SAN-ih-dee)
Sáturn (SAT-ern)
Saturnínus (sat-er-NAHY-nuhs)
Sáxon (SAK-suhn)
Scǽvola (SEE-vuh-luh)
Scípio (SIP-ee-oh)
Secútor (seh-KYOO-ter)
Sejánus (seh-JAY-nuhs)
Seleúci (seh-LYOO-sahy)
Seleúcidæ (seh-LYOO-sid-ee)
Seleúcus (seh-LYOO-kuhs)
Semprónius (sem-PROH-nee-uhs)
senátus (sen-AY-tuhs)
Séneca (SEN-eh-kuh)
sénex (SEN-eks)
senióres (sen-YAWR-eez)
Sentínum (sen-TAHY-nuhm)
Septímius (sep-TIM-ee-uhs)
Seréna (seh-REE-nuh)
Sertórian (ser-TAWR-ee-uhn)
Sertórius (ser-TAWR-ee-uhs)
Sérvius (SER-vee-uhs)
Séxtiæ (SEKS-tee-ee)
Séxtius (SEKS-tee-uhs)
Séxtus (SEKS-tuhs)
Sevéran (seh-VEE-ruhn)
Sevéri (seh-VEE-rahy)
Sevérus (seh-VEE-ruhs)
Shákespeare (SHAYK-speer)
Síbylline (SIB-ih-lahyn)
Sicílian (sih-SIL-ee-uhn)
Sícily (SIS-ih-lee)
Sílarus (SIL-uh-ruhs)
Sílva (SIL-vuh)
Sílvia (SIL-vee-uh)
síne (SIN-eh)
Sinuéssa (sin-yoo-ES-uh)
sirócco (sih-ROK-oh)
Slavónian (sluh-VOH-nee-uhn)
sócii (SOH-see-ahy)

Sólon (SOH-luhn)
Spain (spayn)
Spániard (SPAN-yerd)
Spánish (SPAN-ish)
Spárta (SPAHR-tuh)
Spártacus (SPAHR-tuh-kuhs)
Spártan (SPAHR-tuhn)
spólia (SPOH-lee-uh)
sponsália (spon-SAY-lee-uh)
Spúrius (SPYOOR-ee-uhs)
Státor (STAY-ter)
Stéle (STEE-lee)
Stílicho (STIL-ih-koh)
stipendiáriæ (stih-pen-dee-AIR-ee-ee)
Stóic (STOH-ik)
stóla (STOH-luh)
Stólo (STOH-loh)
Strábo (STRAY-boh)
stýlus (STAHY-luhs)
Sublícius (suh-BLISH-ee-uhs)
Suéssula (SWES-yoo-luh)
Suetónius (swih-TOH-nee-uhs)
Suévi (SWEE-vahy)
suffétes (suh-FEE-teez)
suffrágio (suh-FRAY-jee-oh)
suffrágium (suh-FRAY-jee-uhm)
Súlla (SUHL-uh)
Súllan (SUHL-uhn)
Sulpícian (suhl-PISH-ee-uhn)
Sulpícius (suhl-PISH-ee-uhs)
Supérbus (soo-PER-buhs)
Sútrium (SOO-tree-uhm)
Syágrius (sahy-AY-gree-uhs)
Sylvánus (sil-VAY-nuhs)
Sýphax (SAHY-faks)
Sýracuse (SIHR-uh-kyooz)
Sýria (SIHR-ee-uh)
tablínum (tuh-BLAHY-nuhm)
tábula (TAB-yuh-luh)
Tácitus (TAS-ih-tuhs)
Tárentine (TAIR-en-tahyn)
Taréntum (tuh-REN-tuhm)
Tárquin (TAHR-kwin)
Tarquínii (tahr-KWIN-ee-ahy)
Tarquínius (tahr-KWIN-ee-uhs)
Tártar (TAHR-ter)
Tátius (TAY-shee-uhs)
Téllus (TEL-uhs)
Térence (TAIR-ens)
Terentílius (tair-en-TIL-ee-uhs)
Teréntius (teh-REN-shee-uhs)
Términus (TER-mih-nuhs)
Tétrarch (TEH-trahrk)
Tétricus (TEH-trih-kuhs)
Téutoberg (TOO-toh-berg)

178

Téutones (T*OO*-t*uh*-neez)
Thápsus (THAP-s*uh*s)
Theodósius (th*ee-uh*-D*OH*-sh*ee-uh*s)
Thermópylæ (ther-MOP-*ih*-lee)
Thessaloníca (thes-*uh*-l*uh*-N*AHY*-k*uh*)
Théssaly (THES-*uh*-lee)
Thória (TH*AW*R-*ee-uh*)
Thrace (thr*ay*s)
Thrácian (THR*AY*-sh*ee-uh*n)
Thucýdides (th*oo*-SID-*ih*-deez)
Thúrii (THUR-*ee-ahy*)
Tíber (T*AHY*-ber)
Tíberis (T*AHY*-ber-is)
Tibérius (t*ahy*-BEER-*ee-uh*s)
Tibúllus (t*ih*-B*UH*L-*uh*s)
Tíbur (T*AHY*-ber)
Ticínus (t*ih*-S*AHY*-n*uh*s)
Tigellínus (t*ih*-jeh-L*AHY*-n*uh*s)
Tígris (T*AHY*-gris)
Títies (TISH-*ee*-eez)
Títus (T*AHY*-t*uh*s)
tóga (T*OH*-g*uh*)
Tónans (T*OH*-n*uh*nz)
Tóndo (TON-d*oh*)
Torquátus (t*aw*r-KW*AY*-t*uh*s)
Trájan (TR*AY*-j*uh*n)
Transálpine (tranz-AL-p*ahy*n)
Trásimene (TRAZ-*ih*-meen)
Trasuménus (traz-y*uh*-M*EE*-n*uh*s)
Trébia (TREB-*ee-uh*)
tres (tr*ay*s)
triárii (tr*ee*-A*I*R-*ee-ahy*)
tríbunate (TRIB-y*uh*-nit)
tríbune (TRIB-y*oo*n)
tribúni (trib-Y*OO*-n*ahy*)
tribunícia (trib-y*oo*-NISH-*ee-uh*)
tríbus (TRIB-y*oo*s)
tribúta (trib-Y*OO*-t*uh*)
tribútum (trib-Y*OO*-t*uh*m)
triclínium (tr*ahy*-KLIN-*ee-uh*m)
tríreme (TR*AHY*-reem)
triúmvirate (tr*ahy*-U*H*M-ver-it)
Trójan (TR*OH*-j*uh*n)
Troy (tr*oi*)
Túllius (T*UH*L-*ee-uh*s)
Túllus (T*UH*L-*uh*s)
túnica (T*OO*-nih-k*uh*)
Turánian (ty*oo*-R*AY*-nee-*uh*n)
Turk (terk)
Túscus (T*UH*S-k*uh*s)
Tyre (t*ahy*r)
Tyrrhénian (t*ih*-R*EE*-nee-*uh*n)
Úlpian (*UH*L-p*ee-uh*n)
Últor (*UH*L-t*aw*r)
Úmbria (*UH*M-br*ee-uh*)

Úmbrian (*UH*M-br*ee-uh*n)
urbánæ (er-B*AY*-nee)
úrbi (ER-b*ahy*)
Útica (Y*OO*-t*ih*-k*uh*)
Vadimónis (vad-*ih*-M*OH*-nis)
Válens (V*AY*-lenz)
Valentínian (val-en-TIN-*ee-uh*n)
Valérian (v*uh*-LEER-*ee-uh*n)
Valério (v*uh*-LEER-*ee-oh*)
Valérius (v*uh*-LEER-*ee-uh*s)
Vándal (VAN-d*uh*l)
Várro (V*AH*R-*oh*)
Várus (V*AI*R-*uh*s)
Vátican (VAT-*ih*-k*uh*n)
Véientine (V*EE*-en-t*ayh*n)
Véii (V*EE*-y*ahy*)
Velítræ (veh-L*AHY*-tree)
Venétia (v*eh*-N*EE*-sh*ee-uh*)
Véneti (VEN-*eh*-t*ahy*)
Véni, vídi, víci (V*EH*-nee, V*EE*-dee, V*EE*-chee)
Vénice (VEN-is)
Vénus (V*EE*-n*uh*s)
Venúsia (v*eh*-N*OO*-zh*ee-uh*)
Vercéllæ (ver-SEL-*ee*)
Vercingétorix (ver-sin-JET-*uh*-riks)
Vérgil (VER-jil)
Vergínia (ver-JIN-*ee-uh*)
Vergínius (ver-JIN-*ee-uh*s)
Vérres (V*AI*R-*ee*z)
Vespásian (ves-P*AY*-zh*ee-uh*n)
Vésta (VES-t*uh*)
vestíbulum (v*eh*-STIB-y*uh*-l*uh*m)
Vesúvius (v*eh*-S*OO*-vee-*uh*s)
Véttii (VET-*ee-ahy*)
Vetúria (v*eh*-TY*OO*R-*ee-uh*)
vía (V*AHY-uh*)
viárum (v*ee*-A*H*R-*uh*m)
vícus (V*AHY*-c*uh*s)
Viénna (v*ee*-EN-*uh*)
vígilum (VIJ-*ih*-l*uh*m)
Víminal (VIM-*ih*-n*uh*l)
Viminális (vim-*ih*-N*AY*-lis)
Vindelícia (vin-d*eh*-LISH-*ee-uh*)
Viriáthus (v*ih*r-ee-*AY*-th*uh*s)
Vísigoth (V*IH*-zih-goth)
Vitéllius (v*ih*-TEL-*ee-uh*s)
Vólscian (VOL-sh*uh*n)
Volsínii (v*uh*l-SIN-*ee-ahy*)
Volúmnia (v*uh*-LUHM-nee-*uh*)
Vúlci (V*UH*L-s*ahy*)
Vúlso (V*UH*L-s*oh*)
Xanthíppus (zan-THIP-*uh*s)
Záma (ZAH-m*uh*)
Zéla (ZEE-l*uh*)
Zenóbia (z*eh*-N*OH*-bee-*uh*)

IMAGE CREDITS

Title Page: Príma Pórta Augústus (Author: Michal Osmenda, Wikimedia Commons; License: CC BY-SA 2.0)

Page 6: *Ænéas Bearing Anchíses from Troy* (Public Domain)

Page 6: Rómulus and Rémus Fed by She-Wolf (Public Domain)

Page 7: *The Abduction of the Sábine Women* (Public Domain)

Page 8: *The Oath of the Horátii* (Public Domain)

Page 8: Cápitoline She-Wolf (Public Domain)

Page 13: Bas Relief of Minérva (Public Domain)

Page 13: Statue of Mars (Public Domain)

Page 13: Colossal Statue of Céres (Public Domain)

Page 13: Flóra (Public Domain)

Page 13: Bronze Statue of Júpiter Státor (Public Domain)

Page 13: Flámen (Public Domain)

Page 14: Relief of Véstal Virgin (Public Domain)

Page 14: Priestess with Censer and Sacrificing Man (Public Domain)

Page 14: Preparation of a Sacrifice (Public Domain)

Page 14: Jánus (Public Domain)

Page 16: *Lúcius Június Brútus Kisses the Earth* (Public Domain)

Page 16: Relief of a Líctor Bearing the Fásces (Author: José Luiz Bernardes Ribeiro, Wikimedia Commons; License: CC BY-SA 4.0)

Page 17: Funerary Relief Depicting Cúrule Chair (Public Domain)

Page 17: Etrúscan Bridge at Vúlci (Public Domain)

Page 17: Modern Remains of the Sérvian Walls (Author: Salvatore Falco, Wikimedia Commons; License: CC BY-SA 1.0)

Page 18: *The Outlet of the Cloáca Máxima* (Public Domain)

Page 18: Modern Remains of the Círcus Máximus (Author: MM, Wikimedia Commons; License: CC BY-SA 3.0)

Page 22: Bronze Bust of Lúcius Június Brútus (Author: Ross Burgess, Wikimedia Commons; License: CC0.1.0)

Page 23: *The Líctors Bring to Brútus the Bodies of His Sons* (Public Domain)

Page 24: *Battle of Lake Regíllus* (Public Domain)

Page 24: *Múcius Scǽvola in the Presence of Lars Porséna* (Public Domain)

Page 27: *The Secession of the Plebéians to the Sacred Mount* (Public Domain)

Page 28: *The Family of Coriolánus* (Public Domain)

Page 29: *Cincinnátus Leaves the Plow for the Róman Dictatorship* (Public Domain)

Page 32: *The Death of Vergínia* (Public Domain)

Page 35: *Camíllus Rescuing Rome from Brénnus* (Public Domain)

Page 36: *The Triumph of Fúrius Camíllus* (Public Domain)

Page 41: *The Rómans Passing Under the Yoke* (Public Domain)

Page 43: Sámnite Soldiers from Frieze at Nóla (Public Domain)

Page 44: *The Consecration of Décius Mus* (Public Domain)

Page 45: Pýrrhus of Epírus (Public Domain)

Page 46: *Áppius Cláudius Entering the Senate* (Public Domain)

Page 47: Coin of Pýrrhus (Author: CNG, Wikimedia Commons; License: CC BY-SA 2.5)

Page 51: Róman Military Standards (Public Domain)

Page 51: Stéle of Róman Warrior (Public Domain)

Page 52: Áppian Way Near Quarto Miglio (Author: Kleuske, Wikimedia Commons; License: CC BY-SA 3.0)

Made in the USA
Las Vegas, NV
08 August 2023

75840287R00119